PRIVATE SCHOOLS AND PUBLIC POWER

a case for pluralism

PRIVATE SCHOOLS

AND PUBLIC POWER

a case for pluralism

E. Vance Randall

with a Foreword
by Bruce S. Cooper

DISCARD

TEACHERS
COLLEGE
PRESS

Teachers College, Columbia University
New York and London

Published by Teachers College Press, 1234 Amsterdam Avenue,
New York, N.Y. 10027

Library of Congress Cataloging-in-Publication Data

Randall, E. Vance.
    Private schools and public power : a case for pluralism / E. Vance Randall.
        p.   cm.
    Includes bibliographical references and index.
    ISBN 0-8077-3344-X (alk. paper)
    1. Private schools—United States—History.   2. Private schools—Law and legislation—
United States.   3. Education and state—United States.   4. Pluralism (Social sciences)—
United States.   I. Title.
    LC49.R36   1994
    371'.02'0973—dc20   94-1152

ISBN 0-8077-3344-X

Printed on acid-free paper
Manufactured in the United States of America
01 00 99 98 97 96 95 94   8 7 6 5 4 3 2 1

Dedicated to the Amish school boy whose fingers were pried loose from his school desk by the county superintendent as the tearful lad and his young school mates were forcibly removed from their unapproved Amish school to a public school. *Never again.*

CONTENTS

FOREWORD

This brilliant and essential book by E. Vance Randall on America's relationship with its private schools brought back memories of my first research, a dissertation on the 1960s style private "free schools," those romantic counter-cultural experiments in unstructured, progressive, libertarian, Rousseauian education. One afternoon at an urban free school in Chicago I had discovered, the police burst in and arrested the children and adults. They were accused of breaking the compulsory education mandates because, to quote one officer of the law, "Lady, this ain't a school!" Perhaps to him the school hardly resembled anything he had ever experienced. It was my first initiation into the capacity of the state to destroy at will a private school that was judged unacceptable by the police. This episode underlined just how delicate were the freedoms that most educators in the mainstream public system took for granted.

Randall opens his book with two similar accounts: the 1965 arrest of Old Order Amish families for attending "unapproved" Amish schools; and the jailing of Reverend Mr. Everett Sileven, a Baptist pastor who dared to open a Christian school in the Faith Baptist Church basement without the blessing of the state. It seems that the right in the United States to educate our children has become a frontier of religious and civil liberties, and thus deserves the attention that this powerful book bestows upon the topic.

In looking at private education, Randall addresses a difficult question: How can a society preserve its liberty, freedom of private schooling, and core values of society, and protect the right to believe, worship one's God, and bring up one's children without undue interference from the government? Randall treats the topic—private schools, pluralism, and the state—from three perspectives.

First, he examines the history of the private school in the United States from colonial times until the present, showing the complex love–hate relationship that Americans have with their private schools.

Second, he explores the important legal issues around the right of private schooling to exist, to hire teachers, and to teach its own curriculum, and the rights of parents.

And third, Randall treats the political philosophy of education, determining that individuals' rights and collective responsibility are best maintained by a pluralist policy that minimizes government interference while maximizing the role of parents, church, and community. If this sounds like a major undertaking, it was, as the author carefully combed the development of this nation educationally, historically, ethically, and politically to come up with a practical balance between the rights of the individual in education and the task of the government to protect its citizens and promote the common good.

While both state and parents lay claim to the best interests of students, these "agents for the child" see their task differently: Governments stress their role in preparing students for citizenship, participation, and the common good. Parents emphasize their need for authority, choice and options, and opportunities to seek the best educational experience available for their children. In a fundamental way, the issue boils down to the concept of who "owns" the child: the government or the family, the state or the community in which the child grows up.

Given these controversies, it is no wonder that Americans are somewhat ambivalent about private schools. Thus, the issues of private schooling provide fertile ground for some of the most profound arguments and important policies in national life.

Randall makes several concrete and useful conclusions in this book. First, government involvement in education should be minimal and focused only on clear problems. Any additional government control is wrong, unethical, and likely unconstitutional, according to Randall. And it is bad politics besides.

Second, Randall urges the ending of the government's role as "sovereign parent" and the reassertion of the "personhood of voluntary associations." Just as individuals have rights, according to Randall, so too do voluntary organizations such as churches, synagogues, mosques, private schools, clubs. While these suggestions sound complex, they are really quite practical and simple: Assert pluralism as the primary goal and use the standardizing fist of the state only to ensure families a healthy, safe, legal, and honest school.

Finally, this book makes the strongest case yet made for the primacy of the family over the state in the upbringing of children.

Hence, the issue of private education is bigger than schooling. It pertains to every important dimension of our society. It sets key precedents for the rights of religious education of children, the role of parents in making decisions for their children, and the nature of the school community itself.

This struggle over liberty and control, freedom and accountability, will never go away, nor should it. As Randall shows, we must cling tenaciously to both the characteristics of being a democratic, free, and moral society while at the same time guaranteeing every student an equal educational opportunity. We can thank E. Vance Randall for pointing these lessons out to us in this remarkable work.

Bruce S. Cooper
Fordham University

PREFACE

Both the state and private schools have legitimate interests and concerns in the provision of educational services. Some of these are held in common. Others are in direct opposition. To what degree should the state allow for educational diversity and what limits, if any, should the state set for pluralistic means and ends in education? How can the government protect its legitimate interests and yet leave the private education option with sufficient internal integrity to be a real choice for cultural, religious, and educational dissenters?

Fundamentally, this is a book about choice—individual and institutional. Its primary purpose is to explore the extent to which the state should intervene in the operations of a nonpublic school. The central thrust of this book is more normative and theoretical than descriptive and empirical. It is a philosophical inquiry into what should be the proper relationship between the state and private schools, between government and families.

This book argues that the indeterminate nature of education and the ambiguity of educational and social goals require that the state exercise a very conservative approach toward any kind of control over private schools. Extensive government regulation of private schools raises serious and deeply disturbing moral, constitutional, and educational questions. The only appropriate alternative, in terms of both efficiency considerations and moral-legal constraints, is to embrace a more structural and substantive pluralism in American education. This book suggests an outline of the basic pluralistic parameters that would satisfy the essential interests of the state and maximize choice for parents and private schools.

This book will be of great interest to those involved with the formulation and implementation of educational policy in both public and private education, especially issues touching on state control of education, parental rights, and matters of conscience. It will be useful to those involved with educational reform, particularly those reforms advocating some kind of restructuring of public education. In addition to the field of education, this book will have a broad appeal to scholars across a wide spectrum of academic disciplines such as history, law, sociology, political science, public policy, philosophy, and religion. A major contribution of this book is its holistic approach in developing a contextual and interpretive framework for understanding the dilemma of government intervention into private education and presenting a viable resolution.

Any work stands on the shoulders of previous scholarship and this one is no exception. I am deeply indebted to the authors cited in this book, especially the pioneering work done by Donald Erickson. Three colleagues and mentors at Cornell University, Emil J. Haller, Kenneth A. Strike, and E. Woody Kelley, made invaluable contributions to this book with their illuminating insights and generous guidance. In addition, this book has greatly benefited from the thoughtful critiques by Matthew Hilton and several anonymous reviewers.

With much appreciation, I recognize the wonderful assistance of Brian Ellerbeck and the staff at Teachers College Press. One could not ask for a more competent, professional editor or supportive staff.

In all of these grateful acknowledgments, however, I accept full responsibility for whatever errors may be found in the book.

PRIVATE SCHOOLS

AND PUBLIC POWER

a case for pluralism

1 ✛ INTRODUCTION

At present opinion is divided about the subjects of education. All do not take the same view about what should be learned by the young, either with a view to plain goodness or with a view to the best life possible.... Goodness itself, to begin with, has not the same meaning for all the different people who honour it ... it is hardly surprising there should also be difference about the right methods of practising goodness.

—Aristotle, *The Politics*

By the end of November 1965, all of Iowa and most of the nation had learned of the confrontation between the Amish or Plain People and the local officials in rural Buchanan County. Media accounts, complete with pictures and commentary, recounted the efforts of the school superintendent, the sheriff, and the county attorney to bring children attending unapproved Amish schools to the local public school. The scenes were pregnant with emotion. Some children ran for the cover of the cornfield at the approach of the local authorities, while others began sobbing as they huddled in the corner of the schoolhouse. Weeping mothers embraced their youngsters, and the superintendent kept trying to loosen the grip of a crying boy from his desk. Many of the Amish people were arrested and ordered to pay fines. When their personal funds were exhausted, much of their property was auctioned off by local officials to pay for the assessments levied against them (Erickson, 1969b).[1]

During the early morning hours of October 18, 1982, 15 carloads of deputies and state troopers under the direction of the sheriff arrived at the Faith Baptist Church in Louisville, Nebraska. They had a court order to secure the building with padlocks to prevent its continued use as the site of an unapproved school. The doors were to be opened only during worship hours. Inside were some 85 persons conducting a "prayer vigil" in behalf of their pastor, Reverend Mr. Everett Sileven, who had been jailed for operating an unapproved school. When the worshippers refused to leave, they were carried out by the law enforcement officials and the building was padlocked. Earlier, the pastor had asked God to convert or exterminate the civil authorities of Nebraska. A law enforcement officer had suggested the use of incendiary grenades as one way to compel compliance with the law. Numerous arrests were made and tensions were not reduced until the governor and state legislature intervened (Lines, 1986;

McCurry v. Tesch, 738 F.2d 271, 273 (8th Cir. 1984). To the credit of both sides, a compromise was eventually reached that allowed private schools sponsored by religious organizations to be approved by the state using less stringent criteria (Nebraska, *Revised Statutes* Sec. 79–1701, Supp. 1986).

While the two examples cited above are far more dramatic in nature than most confrontations between state[2] and private education officials over the control of nonpublic schools, they clearly demonstrate that the issue of government regulation of private schools is neither trivial nor transitory. It is a policy issue that profoundly touches the deepest convictions of many individuals and communities. Its complexity is heightened by the fact that both parties are well-intentioned and share the same general interest—the welfare of the child.

THE PROBLEM AND ITS SIGNIFICANCE

Although the importance of education is universally recognized and the strategic position it occupies in our republic is clear, the specific character it should assume has always been a matter of debate and controversy. The national polemic over the condition of education in America is current evidence of our continued commitment to education and our inability to reach an agreement as to its structure and substance. Not only does the present public controversy illustrate an indeterminacy in educational policy and practice but it also reflects a more fundamental problem. How does a democracy simultaneously promote two inherent principles—ideological pluralism and public values—that are antinomic (Levin, 1983)? Freedom of thought and conscience formation are central creeds in a democracy. On the other hand, it is essential that the rising generation be equipped with a shared set of values and a common core of skills in order to be competent and productive citizens. This dynamic tension clearly manifests itself in the often sharp public discussions about the proper role of private schools in a society with an extensive state-owned and -operated public school system.

The dilemma of determining what appropriate relationship ought to exist between private schools and the state is complicated further by the prominent position of private schools in American education since the colonial era. Until the creation of public or government schools during the middle of the nineteenth century, private sources—churches, communities, apprenticeships, tutors, independent schools, and families—performed the crucial task of passing on a way of life to the next generation. The establishment of state-supported schools signaled a fundamental and radical change in the relationship between the state and the individual, the family, the community, and the church (Tyack, 1976). The basic purpose of this public school system was fourfold: cultural and moral homogeneity, political competency, and economic sufficiency. Not only has public education made crucial contributions to the economic and industrial capacity of the United States, but it also has performed an important function in attempting to reduce social stratification and in-equality.

While the benefits bestowed by the formation of publicly controlled schools should not be depreciated by private school advocates, neither should the problems or dilemmas it has created for our democratic repub-lic be minimized by public school partisans. One of the key questions revolves around participation by private educational institutions in a soci-ety where a state sanctioned and supported school system is ideologically linked to the preservation and progress of the nation. One implication suggested by the establishment of a government school system and this linkage is the existence of some sort of majoritarian orthodoxy with re-spect to values, attitudes, and behavior. How do the various minority groups and subcultures in America, with their own sense of truth and reality, fit into American society? How can they transmit these particular world views to their children? These questions become especially trouble-some in light of our inability to arrive at a consensus on what constitutes a common curriculum, proper pedagogical procedures, and essential edu-cational goals. They touch the core of our society by asking which values should be embraced by all and who should select them (Damsen, 1986; Erickson, 1973; Ravitch, 1985; West, 1965). Furthermore, where is the line to be drawn between individual liberty and state interest; between pluralism and social unity; self-determination as opposed to government control; private purpose as opposed to public power?

The degree of state intervention in the educational processes of the public schools has always been problematic. It becomes even more so when the school is not an agency of the state but a private endeavor. "Few issues," notes Ravitch (1985), "have been as tortuous for our politi-cal system as trying to define the appropriate relation between the state and nonpublic schools" (p. 162). A high degree of state intervention that prescribes the scope and nature of private schools runs the risk of elimi-nating cultural diversity, innovative educational practices, and experi-mentation. Extensive and intrusive state regulation, albeit well-meaning, could severely damage the institutional integrity and mission of private schools by transforming them into privately financed public schools. Edu-cational pluralism, a hallmark of democracy, with its expansive allowance for different world views, values, beliefs, ideas, life styles, and practices could be significantly diminished by state regulations mandating a greater degree of homogeneity in education.

Attempts by the state to shape educational policy and practice in private schools carry the danger of running afoul of the rights of parents to direct the education of their children and of infringing on First Amendment rights protecting religious beliefs. On the other hand, lack of sufficient state oversight in the operation of private schools could allow unscrupulous directors and fly-by-night schools to exploit the innocent by compromising the physical safety and well-being of the students and failing to educate them (Sanders, 1969).

That the state has an important and legitimate interest in ensuring that all children receive an adequate education, whether in a state or nongovernment institution, is not in question. A fundamental issue to address, however, is the extent of that public interest and the best way to secure it in a public environment having other legitimate and competing interests. In the context of public policy concerns, to what degree should the state allow for social diversity, and just how different should private education be from public education? What limits should the state set for pluralistic means and ends in education? How much should government restrict the range of alternatives in education? The problem is succinctly summarized by Donald Erickson (1969a): "How can nonpublic education be both responsible and free? Responsible to serve the public interest; free to experiment and disagree. *Without* regulation, some schools may victimize patrons and endanger the general welfare. *With* regulation, dissent is jeopardized. Where should the balance be struck?" (p. 2).

Since the latter half of the nineteenth century, each state has produced its own response to the problem of regulating private schools. These regulations differ not just in amount or degree but also in kind. This great diversity in state regulations of private schools is symptomatic of the often ambiguous and vague nature of education. The wide variety of approaches in state supervision suggests that any number of regulatory arrangements are perceived to provide quality controls for private education. The question raised here is, how could such a diverse assortment of regulatory approaches produce similar results? Are there other factors beside state regulation that provide quality control for private education?

Efforts by the various states to ensure compliance frequently encounter determined resistance from private schools. Attempts to resolve the conflicts in a cooperative fashion often break down into bitter court battles (*Pierce v. Society of Sisters*, 268 U.S. 510 (1925); *State v. Faith Baptist Church*, 301 N.W. 2d 571 (1981)). Fifty-one court cases involving state regulations of private education were filed in state and federal courts between 1980 and 1983. This was nearly double the number of cases reported during the previous 80 years (Lines, 1986). The judicial decisions spawned by this increase in litigation have provided little in the way of consistent guidelines and principles to assist educational policy makers in fashioning appropriate regulations. The result has been continued conflict and confrontation between public and private school officials. Scarce resources that could have been spent on improving the quality of education in both sectors have been consumed in antagonistic and costly conflicts where no one is the winner—especially the children (Stone, 1982). Effective policy formation becomes stalemated in a struggle for control.

In one sense this should not be too surprising. Education is a process through which a person is created, a culture is reproduced, and a particular society is propagated. The type of education one receives influences how one perceives reality, what particular meanings one attaches to this knowledge, and which world views one considers legitimate. It is from these accepted world views that social arrangements and relationships are instituted and justified. Education, therefore, is a potential source of social conflict.

A major reason behind the increasing number of disputes, and their intensity, over state intervention in private schools seems to be a growing disagreement over what counts as a justifiable or legitimate regulation. The rationale supporting specific state intervention is sometimes not as clearly articulated as it could be. This is also true for the dissenting postures of the private schools. The search for common ground and for alternative means to the present regulatory approaches is often ignored. A dispassionate examination of the underlying assumptions and supporting data for both positions is sorely needed if a solution is to be found.

The necessity for such a conceptual analysis or framework of how the fundamental interests of each party can be preserved is accentuated by two additional factors. One is the rapidly growing number of private schools and enrollment in private education. In 1985–86 there were more than 27,000 private elementary and secondary schools in the United States. This represented an increase of 2,500 private schools during a 5-year period alone (National Center for Educational Statistics [NCES], 1991, p. 13). The number of students enrolled in these private schools increased from 5,331,000 in the fall of 1980 to 5,600,000 in the fall of 1985 (NCES, 1991, p. 31).[3]

The other factor is the possibility of government funding for nonpublic schools. If public funds in the form of tax credits, vouchers, and such do become a reality, additional public controls will almost inevitably follow (Encarnation, 1983). There has been very little public dialogue about what would constitute proper controls. The assumption seems to be that proper controls are whatever the state declares them to be. The onslaught of regulatory controls by the state that would follow could reduce educational diversity and genuine choice—the very thing the state was attempting to make more accessible to the public. At the very least these controls would cause private schools to change in ways that they would not voluntarily choose, and would most likely require private schools to be more like government schools. The provisions of public monies for private education would be self-defeating unless sound, cogent criteria were formulated that clearly marked the limits of state intervention in the operations of private schools.

The diversity of state regulations for private schools, the increase in the number and intensity of confrontations between state and private school officials, the rise in litigation, the expansive growth in private education, and the potential for public funding of private schools underscore the need to thoughtfully examine the fundamental questions raised by state intervention in private education. This step is an important prerequisite to the formulation of appropriate and necessary state controls. The relationship between private schools and the state in recent years, however, has been marked by "confused policy, schismatic philosophy, and stalemated politics" (Finn, 1982, p. 6). Understandably, it is considered by some as "one of the most serious issues" (Lines, 1983, p. 190) facing educational officials today.

REVIEW OF MAJOR RESEARCH

Studies of private schools can be divided into two general areas of focus—the nature of private education and the relationship of private schools to the state. Research investigating the nature of private education can be placed into three major categories. First, there are studies that look at the educational structures, practices, and problems of private schools. The studies by Abramowitz and Stackhouse (1980), Cibulka, O'Brien, and Zewe (1982), and Kraushaar (1972) are representative examples. An interesting variation of this approach has been a comparative study of private and public education. One of the earliest studies of this type was done by Koos (1931), who compared private and public high schools in Minnesota. A more recent and comprehensive longitudinal study of students in private and public high schools has been done by Coleman, Hoffer, and Kilgore (1982) and Coleman and Hoffer (1987).

A second type of inquiry into the nature of private education emphasizes a more sociological and anthropological approach. The ethnographic studies of fundamentalist schools by Peshkin (1986) and Rose (1985) have provided important insights into the milieu and operations of private religious schools.

The third way in which the nature of private education is studied is from a historical perspective (Jorgenson, 1987; Kraushaar, 1972). McGrew (1971) looks at private boarding schools, while Carper and Hunt (1984) sketch out the historical development and current status of various types of religious schools in America.

A few studies dealing with the relationship between the state and private schools have attempted a comprehensive examination of the relationship (Dixon, 1944; Scanlan, 1940; Smith, 1950). Most studies, however, usually pursue a more modest agenda, such as public aid for private schools (Cohen, 1985; Coons & Sugarman, 1972; James & Levin, 1983) or state intervention and regulation of private schools. These latter studies can be placed in two broad categories—those looking primarily at the dilemma of state regulation and control, and those examining the content of state regulations.

The most common approach taken to examine the relationship of the state and private schools in major studies has been to describe and categorize the plethora of state regulations. This is done on several levels. Carey (1949) and Snyder (1948) both give descriptive analyses of the legal relationship of private schools in a particular state as it evolved historically. (Also see Denver, 1953; Fowerbaugh, 1955; Gardner, 1954; Pelletier, 1950; Pickard, 1955; Shea, 1948; and Triesch, 1954.) Dixon (1944) expanded the scope of analysis to include five Middle Atlantic states, while Smith (1950) looked at the legal status of private schools in 11 Far Western states. Walther (1982) followed a similar approach with six states active in regulating private schools. In addition, Walther quantified the degree of regulatory burden in each of the six states and ranked them accordingly. Beach and Will (1958), Jellison (1975), Kephart (1933), Kinder (1982), and Lischka (1924) all compiled regulations in all 50 states, with a comparative analysis affecting such areas as accreditation, compulsory attendance, instructional programs, teacher certification, health and safety measures, and records and reports. Other studies covering all the states include McLaughlin's (1946) historical overview of private school legislation from 1870 to 1945, Stolee's (1963) review of controls governing instruction and curriculum, and Romans's (1981) focus on private religious schools and First Amendment considerations. (Also see Bainton, 1983; McCoy, 1983; and West, 1980.)

These status or statute snapshot studies furnish a brief overview of the issues raised by state regulation, a general summary of judicial principles guiding court decisions in approving or disapproving various regulations, and suggestions for modifying the present array of state regulations. Their value, however, in facilitating policy decisions rapidly decreases over time because of the changing content of state laws and regulations, and because of new precedents set in court decisions. Moreover, their heavy emphasis on descriptive analysis of the statutory structure results in a superficial treatment of the problematic issues raised by state intervention in private schools.[4] The usual solution offered by these studies is typified by Stolee's (1963) statement.

> The state and federal courts have held that the State did possess the right to regulate private schools, if reasonable regulations were made to achieve reasonable purposes and applied in a reasonable manner. (p. 110)

The term "reasonable" simply begs the question of proper state controls for private schools. Other equally enigmatic guidelines for appropriate areas of regulation by the state include a "basic education" with "certain minimum standards" (Walther, 1982, pp. 68, 103), which are "in the public interest" (Kinder, 1982, p. 109).

A second line of inquiry into the relationship of the state and private schools has been to carefully examine a specific court case. Johnson (1986), for example, gives a detailed account of the celebrated conflict between Nebraska officials and a fundamentalist Christian school that refused to comply with state regulations (*State v. Faith Baptist Church,* 1981). Johnson comes to an agnostic conclusion about whether the decision of the court against the private school was right or not. Other commentators, however, have come down on both sides of the question (Binder, 1982; Higgins, 1981–1982).

Theoretical work dealing with the issue of state regulation is normative in nature as opposed to the descriptive character of compiling and comparing regulations. These studies usually explore the rationale for state intervention and the dilemmas that ensue. They also give some suggestions as to what constitutes proper state controls. Kephart (1933) maintains that since private schools serve a public function in providing a basic education, they should be required to meet the same minimum standards as public schools. In doing so, however, he fails to adequately address the important issues of parents' rights in directing the education of their children, First Amendment difficulties, and extensive control of private schools by state officials, which would destroy the schools' unique character. R. O. Lyons (1983) concludes that regulations should be those that are "proper for the well-being of children" (p. 160). In addition, both he and Evenson (1980) see "deregulation" with only standardized tests to ensure an adequate education as a "model" for states to follow. (For similar views, see Toner, 1984–1985.) Bainton (1983) and West (1980), however, point out that standardized tests are not a panacea but could actually exert more control over private schools than traditional regulatory means because teachers would have to "teach the test." Lines (1983) maintains that the solution to the conflict over regulations lies with more carefully drafted legislation that touches only areas such as information required to verify attendance, health and safety standards, consumer protection, child abuse, and "minimum specifications of the course of study necessary to meet the compulsory requirements" (pp. 214–216. Also see Fletcher (1979) for additional discussion.). A problem that Lines does not address is what would keep legislators confined to this minimum area of regulation. Mandating basic curriculum, for instance, could easily expand to include an increasing number of courses of study. Would there be a limit and what would it be?

The signal work, however, in the difficult area of proper state regulations for private schools has been done by Donald Erickson (1969a, 1969b, 1973, 1982, 1984). He goes beyond the typical litany of the pros and cons of regulation, vague language, glossing over hard questions, and looking for quick fixes, by constructing a case built on the principle of educational pluralism. Government control of private schools should be minimal, he says, because of potential infringements on important liberties and the indeterminate nature of education. Programmatic controls, the traditional form of state regulations, should be eliminated and replaced with some kind of competency testing. Erickson's work has laid an important foundation for additional studies attempting to further define the exact nature of the proper relationship between the state and private schools.

Other studies (Magers, 1983) are far less ambitious in their scope and concentrate on more specific areas such as the problems confronting the state in its efforts to implement regulations.

Another important piece of work is Stephen Arons's (1986) provocative study of freedom of conscience in education. He calls for a separation of the state from public education and for the imposition of a "compelling interest" standard on most state regulations. (Also see Devins, 1983, and Romans, 1981.)

TEXTUAL ORGANIZATION

This book comprises six chapters. This chapter serves as an introduction to the issues and the dilemma expressed in our national motto, *e pluribus unum* (out of many, one) in the context of public and private education. How does a democracy strike a balance between pluralism and social solidarity, between diversity and commonality?

The current public stance and policy initiatives affecting private education were not created *ex nihilo* but were shaped and molded by historical events and legal precedents. Chapter 2 presents a historical overview of the evolving relationship between government and private schools from the colonial era to the present day. In revealing the historical progenitors of present policy, the rationale for current public policy becomes clearer and alternatives for future policy become more discernible. A historical framework will prove invaluable in avoiding the "fallacy of the present" with its myopic perspective of the present conditions and future possibilities. Colonial and state laws touching on private schools will provide an essential source of information in describing the relationship between the government and private schools. An important objective of Chapter 2 is to note the significant changes in that relationship and explore what some of the primary motivating factors behind that change might have been. The chapter is not intended, however, to present a comprehensive history of private education in America.

Working in tandem with statutory law, case law has also been a very influential tool in defining the relationship between the state and private schools. The focus of Chapter 3 will be on litigation arising from the efforts of the state to regulate nonpublic schools. The *American Digest System,* a compilation of state and federal appellate cases from 1658 to the present, and other legal case digests will be the primary source for compiling a list of private school cases. A summation and comparative analysis of court cases brought before the Supreme Court, along with other key federal, state, and circuit court cases, will outline the main parameters of state intervention in private schools. Of particular interest will be sources of disagreement between the state and private schools, the rationale for these differences, and the judicial principles guiding the various decisions.

Within the historical and legal context developed in the preceding chapters, Chapter 4 evaluates the state's justification for regulating private schools. As the costs and benefits of state regulation are assessed, is the current approach of state intervention the proper public policy? Chapter 5 suggests several viable recommendations for determining the extent to which the state should intervene in the operations of a private school. Chapter 6 offers a summary and conclusion.

This treatment of private schools and government regulation is limited in several ways. First, it is concerned only with state regulation of nonpublic elementary and secondary schools in the United States. Second, it is not intended to present an exhaustive analysis of state regulations of all nonpublic schools. It is an attempt to define the general contours of the public/private debate over state control of private educational institutions, to propose a conceptual framework for determining the proper limits of state intervention, and to outline specific areas needing intensive, in-depth study. Third, it will not specifically address the important issue of public support for private schools, except in the context of an environmental constraint that exacerbates the financial impact of certain types of regulations.

SUMMARY

This chapter has introduced the problems and dilemmas associated with the regulation of private schools by the state. The purpose of this book is a normative exploration of state intervention in private schools.

It is crucial not only that this introductory chapter communicate a clear understanding of the purpose of this study but also that it not create any misunderstandings or misconceptions. Despite the emphasis on the problems created by state intervention, this study should not be construed as an attack on public schools and an apology for private schools. It is neither anti-public education nor pro-private education, but an invitation to enhance rationality, mutual respect, and accommodation in American education.

Private schools have played a prominent part in American education and will continue to do so. The exact nature of that role will depend in large measure on determining the proper relationship between the state and private schools. A critical need exists for a careful examination of the assumptions underlying the current regulatory approach to private schools and for a discerning review of traditional conceptions of public and private education.

The value of this study, in its holistic approach, is found in the contextual and interpretive framework it provides to understand the present regulatory control of private schools. It proposes viable criteria for determining the appropriate extent of state intervention in nonpublic schools. If it is true, as Swiger (1983) claims, that the "most significant issues [in school law] in the coming decade will be presented in the legal battles concerning regulation and funding of nonpublic schools" (p. 917), then this study will make a valuable contribution, as it addresses these important educational issues involving pluralism and public policy.

2 ✛ LAWS AND LEGISLATURES

When the way is lost then come the laws.

—Lao Tse

Regulation or public law is an instrument of social control. It is often coercive in its intent to shape institutional and individual behavior into patterns that are deemed socially acceptable and necessary. It governs the relationship between the public and private spheres of society and between the state and the individual. It determines the extent and character of that relationship and the distribution of power in the public and private sectors (Nader & Nader, 1985). The degree of autonomy in decision making that individuals and private groups should have, as opposed to state action designed to ensure an "ordered liberty," has always been problematic and subject to dispute.

The controversies created by this dynamic tension between liberty and responsibility have social and historical components. It is important to our understanding of this complex problem that we do not neglect the historical and cultural context in which regulations are conceived and constructed. Regulations are but the visible tip of the social, legal, and political iceberg of a society. "We must not treat regulations," warns Friedman (1985), "as something that the stork brought suddenly one night" (p. 129). A crucial step in gaining a clearer understanding of the current dilemma of government regulation of private schools lies in uncovering its historical roots and subsequent development.

The primary objective of this chapter is to outline the legal relationship between the state and private schools as it has evolved from the colonial era to the present. The focus of this chapter is on the historical shift of power from the private realm to the public domain in private education in the United States. In addition to a descriptive narrative sketching the historical–legal link between the state and private elementary and secondary schools, critical turning points of that transfer are identified and analyzed.

It is far beyond the scope of this chapter to deal with all aspects of American educational law or even to present an exhaustive examination of law affecting private education. This chapter has a far more modest mission—to discover the major restrictions placed on private schools by the state and the significant social, ideological, political, and legal factors that contributed to this crucial shift of power in American education and society.

Following a brief introduction to educational history, Chapter 2 is subdivided into three major historical periods—the colonial and provincial era, the national period from 1776 to 1865, and the period from 1865 to 1990. These historical eras are pivotal epochs in their own right and serve as a backdrop for understanding the emerging and changing relationship between private schools and the state.

A principal premise of this chapter is based on two major points. One, education is by its very nature a value-laden enterprise. Education is not and cannot be neutral in content or pedagogy. Second, individuals possess values, opinions, preferences, viewpoints, and, in some cases, well articulated world views and ideologies. They often feel that their beliefs, values, perceptions, and ideas are "true" and correct and ought to be embraced by everyone. Many people will, therefore, seek various means such as political processes to have their private values and world views institutionalized through legislation and imposed on others. A very common approach has been to shape the educational experience of children through state laws and regulations along lines that are compatible with these personal beliefs, values, and world views.

INTRODUCTION

Traditional accounts of American education (Cubberly, 1919; Davidson, 1900; Monroe, 1905) often portray the "past [as] simply the present writ small" (Bailyn, 1960, p. 9), with the seeds of public schools planted in the Puritan soil of New England. The triumph of the common school over selfish sectarian and sectoral interests is presented as inevitable and part of the predestined development of the modern public school.[1] True Americans were for public schools only, and those who promoted private schools were suspect as to their loyalty and motives (Kephart, 1933).

While state-sponsored schools have played an important and significant role in the evolution of the American republic, "no one can deny, either, that the traditional chronicles of American education has been narrowly institutional, full of anachronism, painfully moralistic" (Cremin, 1970, p. x; see also Bailyn, 1960, pp. 5–15 for further discussion of topic). The customary account of American education has given a biased view of schooling in America. This distorted account has, in the minds of the Committee on the Role of Education in American History "'affected adversely the planning of curricula, the formation of policy, and the administration of educational agencies in the continuing crisis of American education'" (Tyack, 1967, p. xii). The traditional

> time-honored tale of the genesis, rise, and triumph of the public school has . . . failed to explain how Americans have gotten where they are in education and it has failed to stimulate fruitful debate over where they ought to go. It is coercive rather than liberating history, inspiring ideological commitment rather than informing public policymaking. (Cremin, 1970, p. ix)

A critical factor that has often been overlooked or marginalized in these traditional historical narratives has been the shift of power from the private to the public sector and the implications this has had for American society and education. Predominate in most public policy is the potent power of the state. Should the state intervene? How should this coercive force be used? By whom, and under what conditions? These are crucial questions that need to be explored before informed and effective public policy for private schools can be formulated and implemented.

Another important point to be aware of is the change in meaning of two common but fundamental words: *public* and *private*. We currently use the term *public* to describe something that is supported and/or controlled by the government. This somewhat narrow meaning, however, did not exist until the middle of the nineteenth century. The concept of "public" before that time designated

> anything that benefitted the community as a whole, and in reference to educational institutions, only to designate the lack of legal barriers to entrance. . . . Indeed, it is anachronistic even to say that private and public functions overlapped and merged before the nineteenth century: the distinctions by which to make such a statement were absent. (Bailyn, 1963, p. 133; see also Jorgenson, 1987, pp. 1–7 for additional discussion.)

With this perspective, a potential problem in understanding government regulation of private schools during the colonial and early national era can be avoided. It will also assist in understanding how the role of the state in education has changed as the meanings of these two concepts were modified.

THE COLONIAL AND PROVINCIAL ERA: TRANSIT AND TRANSFORMATION

When the first immigrants came to the New World, they brought their culture, their values, and their way of life. The American colonists set out to replicate, in varying degrees, English society in the New World.

The Puritans, for example, were determined to establish a Christian commonwealth in Massachusetts, a theocracy that would be a "home for the saints and a model for the regeneration of Christendom" (Tyack, 1967, p. 1). Since human nature was inherently evil and corrupt, it posed a constant threat to this idealized society and required the continual care and strict supervision of children. The primary goal of the Puritan society extended beyond vocational skills and socialization. It "sought nothing less than a radically transformed personality . . . a regenerate[d] man, a converted man, a person whose being had been transformed by the infusion of God's mercy and grace" (Hiner, 1973, pp. 5–6).

Being Anglicans, many colonists in the southern colonies, however, were more interested in reproducing the life of English gentry than a life of Puritan piety. The Renaissance Man, well-educated for public service as a civic or religious leader, with the accompanying social status, was the objective of the aristocratic landowners in the South. They were not in the business of establishing a new social order but of replicating existing class structures as defined in English culture.

The Middle Colonies were a mixture of the New England and Southern Colonies. Settled by socially, religiously and ethnically diverse groups of immigrants, each with its own world view and belief systems, they coexisted under an uneasy truce. Power was not concentrated in the hands of an aristocratic class nor was there a strong bond between the state and any particular religious group. This fragmentation of power also reflected their systems of educational governance and structure. Each religious or cultural group decided for itself the substance and process of its educational endeavors (Cremin, 1970; Curti, 1974; Meyer, 1957).

But what the colonists all had in common was a desire to survive the harshness of the New World and the "barbarism" of the wilderness, with their culture, religion, and ethnic identity intact, and to preserve and replicate what they had brought with them. Education was used as an instrument of control and social order. The initial forms that this educational process took were, as in England, "largely instinctive and traditional, little articulated and little formalized" (Bailyn, 1960, p. 15).

The primary agency used by the colonists to preserve and transmit their civilization—knowledge, skills, culture, and values—was the family (S. S. Cohen, 1974; Cremin, 1970; Hiner, 1973). The reasons are fivefold. One, the fundamental source of education and socialization in England was the extended, patrilineal family, and this heritage the colonists brought with them. Second, the passage of the Statute of Artificers and the Poor Laws in England gave legal recognition to the traditional idea that parents had the primary responsibility to provide for and educate their children. Third, because of great distances between farms, geographic realities required that many families be self-sustaining and sufficient. This included the education of their children. Fourth, the ideology of the Puritans taught that parents had a divine obligation to teach their children and that the family was "the basic unit of church and commonwealth and, ultimately, the nursery of sainthood" (Cremin, 1970, p. 135). And fifth, many of the supporting social institutions that were available in England, such as schools, colleges, universities, and churches, were nonexistent, or present only to a limited extent, in the colonies (Cremin, 1970, p. 124).

Seen from this perspective, the educational laws of 1642, 1647, and 1648 in Massachusetts were not the forerunners of public schools as Cubberley (1934) and others (Kephart, 1933) would have us believe, but were the concerned response of the Puritan theocracy to address the growing departure of the rising generation from the norms of society and the apparent failure of many parents to fulfill their educational and parental obligations (Bailyn, 1960; Meyer, 1957; Tyack, 1967). Bailyn (1960) points out that these laws

> expressed more than a traditional concern for schooling, and more even than a Puritan need for literacy. It flowed from the fear of the imminent loss of cultural standards. . . . The Puritans quite deliberately transferred the maimed functions of the family to formal instructional institutions, and in so doing not only endowed schools with a new importance but expanded their purpose beyond pragmatic vocationalism toward vaguer but more basic cultural goals. (p. 27)

Other colonies soon followed suit with similar laws (Connecticut in 1650, New Haven in 1655, New York in 1665, Plymouth in 1672, Pennsylvania in 1683.) These laws could also be considered as the first attempts to regulate private education in America. The 1642, 1647, and 1648 laws lament the "great neglect" of parents and masters in providing their children "training . . . in learning, and labor, and other implyments," in securing for their charges a "good education," and the impending loss of the "learning . . . of our fathers in the church and commonwealth." The General Court condemned this negligence as "evill" and subject to a fine of "twenty schillings." Civic officials, the "prudentials of the towne" or "selectmen," were charged with the responsibility to see that parents and masters fulfilled their obligations. The state mandated curricular subjects and standards. Each child, male and female, was to be able to read "perfectly . . . the english tongue," write, and have a knowledge of the "capitall lawes of this country" and the "grounds and principles of Religion," which meant Puritan religion. The selectmen were instructed to occasionally check the competency of their young charges. Those parents and masters who continued to be derelict in their duties would have their children or apprentices taken from them and given to more responsible adults for their education.[2]

The remainder of the seventeenth century was marked by a continued effort to supplement and provide institutional assistance to bolster and support familial education. The lines delineating family, church, and state, as well as formal and informal schooling, were often obscure and indistinct (Gaustad, 1984).

The forms that education took and the means by which it was supervised are evidence of the bewildering variety of schooling in early America. In the New Netherlands, the Dutch West India Company established a school in New Amsterdam in 1638 and paid the teacher's salary, while the Classis of Amsterdam licensed the schoolmaster. Control of schools was soon shared with the local civic officials and local church council.

In New England, schools were initiated by the individual towns themselves. They were far from uniform, as each settlement explored ways to set up schools that would best meet their needs and preferences. In addition to these village-initiated schools, there were individuals— ministers, women, town schoolmasters—who set up their own independent educational enterprises.

It is important to note that while the "state" was directly involved in starting up schools, the "state" consisted primarily of local officials who often were also the religious leaders. In the New England towns, with their theocratic bent, state and church were often indistinguishable (McMillan, 1984; Meyer, 1957; Updegraff, 1907). Citizenship requirements included church membership as well as property holdings (Butts & Cremin, 1953). In addition, the smallness of the towns allowed families to have a far greater say in educational matters.

Religious bodies were also sponsors of schools. One of the first schools in Maryland was established by the Jesuits. Nearly all schools in the middle colonies were products of various denominations.

In the southern colonies, the family and the church were the primary sponsors of formal education. Except for rudimentary education for the poor and orphans, the posture of the state was one of "official disinterest" and allowed education to be fashioned and controlled by those who provided it (S. S. Cohen, 1974, pp. 126–127).

Indeed, state involvement in the educational affairs of the American colonies was limited primarily to the granting of charters or acts of incorporation, setting governing boards, and approving teachers. There were few regulations to oversee education. The primary requirement was that the teacher had to be of the right religious persuasion and of good character (Cremin, 1970; Seybolt, 1935).

As the seventeenth century drew to a close, it was becoming obvious that the efforts of the original colonists to transplant European society into colonial soil was not succeeding. To meet these circumstances, new educational arrangements were required; with these new configurations would come a transfer of power. The earlier trend of relying more on formal than informal or familial education was magnified and intensified. Education began to take on a more "entrepreneurial" character as innovative individuals and institutions attempted to meet the educational needs of the people. The opening up of educational alternatives in the eighteenth century produced an independence and scattering of authority unparalleled in the colonial period. "It led in education," notes Cremin (1970), "to a popularizing of conduct and control as well as of access and substance" (p. 556; see also Axtell, 1974, pp. 132, 282, 286 for additional comments.).

One of the reasons for this was the passage in England of the Act of Toleration in 1689. This act put an end to official state coercion in forcing uniformity of doctrinal views and religious practice. It was a large step away from establishment of the state church and put other Protestant religions on equal footing with the Anglican church, thereby loosening the notions of religious orthodoxy and promoting denominationalism. In terms of education, the specific religious criteria previously necessary to teach became of little or no concern to the state. In addition, the religious requirement for voting was deleted and suffrage was granted to non-church members (Curti, 1974).

The subsequent rise of denominationalism in education added to the variety of educational institutions and helped to accommodate the educational aspirations of a large segment of the population. The importance of education was given further impetus by the evangelical character of the Great Awakening, which was a "large-scale educational movement" in itself (Cremin, 1970, p. 316).

Concurrent with this increase in schools sponsored by various denominations was the proliferation of a variety of secular educational alternatives, such as the academy, that were responding to the practical needs of the colonists for a more utilitarian education. In describing the academy, which replaced the old Latin schools, Benjamin Franklin declared "Youth will come out of this school fitted for learning any business, calling, or profession" (Tyack, 1967, p. 51).

Another change dramatically affecting the homogeneous colonial landscape was the rapid influx of immigrants with a variety of ethnic and cultural values. They were non-English immigrants from Scotland,

Ireland, France, Germany, and Africa. These groups (except the blacks) settled as ethnic or religious communities and organized schools around their religion to help them preserve what they had brought with them and protect them from the English hegemony. For the English colonists, this presented an additional threat to their way of life and produced reactionary measures to Anglicize the new immigrants (Bailyn, 1960).[3] Although these formal efforts to assimilate such varied cultures into the English way of life failed, they foreshadowed one of the challenges that would confront the nineteenth-century common school movement and that still eludes a satisfactory solution today.

Another factor that would have an indelible impact on the political and educational life of the colonies was the intellectual revolution on the Continent. The "new empirical science" of Newton and the "new empirical politics" of Locke, with its radical notions of rationality, rights, and liberty, would provide much of the philosophical underpinnings for the new American republic (Cremin, 1970, p. 255). These doctrines of the Enlightenment would dramatically alter the way in which the basic ontological and teleological questions of humankind and society would be answered.[4]

All of these factors—the decline of the theocratic state in New England and the rise of denominationalism from the Act of Toleration, the increasing heterogeneity in colonial culture, the dispersion of the population, the rise of the middle class, the increasingly secular nature of colonial life, the educational and religious fervor of the Great Awakening, the creation of new institutions of formal education—produced a shift in power from the state church to various denominational and secular educational institutions (S. S. Cohen, 1974; Jernegan, 1919a; Mehl, 1963; Updegraff, 1907). The openness of the eighteenth century produced an educational pluralism unparalleled in American history.

> Inevitably, the openness of the environment and the competition for clients made institutions themselves responsive, in that they displayed a characteristic readiness to introduce what the populace seemed to demand. . . . In the last analysis, it seemed less important to maintain traditional definitions of education than it did to accommodate those who desired it. Virtually anyone could teach and virtually anyone could learn, at least among whites, and the market rather than the church or the legislature governed through multifarious contractual relationships. (Cremin, 1970, p. 559; see also Butts & Cremin, 1953; Jernegan, 1919b; Middlekauff, 1963; Miller, 1969 for supplementary information.)

The basic societal elements—the family, community, church, and schools—remained but they were recast with substantially different social roles. Many of the responsibilities of education and culture transfer were passed to formal institutions. With that reassignment of cultural custody to formal institutions, went an automatic, corresponding transfer of authority to these institutions. In the absence of state-sponsored schools and a diminished capacity of the family and community to transmit culture, the individual churches and educational institutions assumed a more prominent role in the transfer of a particular culture and ethnic identity. By the end of the colonial period,

> education no longer was a cohesive force serving one master but was used freely to further the ends of separate ideological entities, both religious and secular. . . . Wishing to preserve their own religious views, individual communities undertook to block any effort that would infringe on their rights to establish school policies. Diversity of belief was protected by law and custom. (Mehl, 1963, pp. 13–14)

THE NATIONAL ERA, PART I: CIVIL RELIGION, COMPETITION, AND THE COMMON SCHOOL

Aside from the disruption of formal education for several years and the destruction of educational facilities, the Revolutionary War did not have an immediate and direct impact on the nature of education in the colonies. Education proceeded on as before with its diversity in configuration, content, and control (Kaestle, 1972). Federal and state constitutions and legislation, for the most part, merely confirmed or legalized the current state of educational affairs (Bailyn, 1960; Cremin, 1980; Curti, 1974).

There were, however, several pieces of legislation that would have a profound impact on education. First, on the federal level, Article I, Section 10 of the United States Constitution (1787) prohibited states from interfering with contracts between private parties.[5] Since the provision of education was contractual in nature until the entrance of government-sponsored schools, this was of great importance and protection to providers of educational services. Second, the First Amendment (1791) gave constitutional protection to religious belief and mandated a legal separation of church and state.[6] Butts and Cremin (1953) correctly point out that

> when church was separated from state, the state retained its legal rights to control education and to authorize private and religious education under a grant of power from the state by charter and legislative enactment. This is of

paramount importance in the history of American education. (p. 29; see also Karier, 1986, p. 35 for additional discussion.)

This also established religious pluralism as a public policy and removed the possible legal threat of religious orthodoxy as a requirement for teachers. The problem this presented, however, was who would be the social integrator, the articulator and guardian of the culture and its norms. Who would replace the church in the performance of these crucial functions and how would that be decided? For Thomas Jefferson the answer would be found in the state, that bastion of rationality and objectivity.

Third, since education is not mentioned in the Constitution, the Tenth Amendment (1791), by implication, gave to the various states the power to govern educational matters.[7] This arrangement simply reflected the long-standing practice of independence between colonies and policies of local control in educational governance and educational pluralism. Finally, the Northwest Ordinance of 1785 and 1787 set aside huge tracts of public lands for schools. These provisions would become a major factor in the shift of control over education from the private to the public sector and the establishment of state school systems (Atkinson & Maleska, 1965). Control is a corollary to funding. The full significance and impact, however, of these government initiatives were not felt initially or even envisioned.

There was, however, a concern about the accumulation of power in the hands of a few, government or private. On a national level, the division of powers between the three branches of government—the executive, judiciary, and legislative—was a practical attempt to fragment and disperse the powers of the state. The prevailing political philosophy was that liberties could best be preserved where power was decentralized and dispersed (Tribe, 1978; Tyack & James, 1986). The involvement of state governments with education was quite modest and was usually limited to the granting of acts of incorporation to private schools, continuing the colonial practice of providing some form of rudimentary education for the poor, and assisting and encouraging various educational institutions in their efforts to provide opportunities for education.[8]

Some states did attempt to bring some sort of state system and organization to the various types of schools. Virginia made three attempts between 1816 and the outbreak of the Civil War to establish a state system of primary schools and a state-subsidized system of academies but succeeded only in setting up a system of schools for the poor (Cremin, 1980). Michigan set up a "centralized comprehensive scheme" with a university attached to primary and secondary feeder schools (Cremin, 1980, p. 162).

New York established a Board of Regents in 1784 to supervise Columbia College and any other schools the state might create. Legislation contained the additional proviso that allowed anyone to establish an educational institution independent of the Regents (Miller, 1969). These unincorporated schools were not subject to any of the Regents' regulations but were "regulated only by the law of supply and demand and were far greater in number and enrollment until after the end of the nineteenth-century than the incorporated academies" (Miller, 1969, p. 32). The Act of 1787 stipulated the requirements for the incorporation of academies under the auspices of the Board of Regents. Regents were also charged to

> visit and inspect all the Colleges, Academies and Schools, which are or may be established in this State; examine into the State and System of Education and Discipline therein, and make a yearly Report thereof to the Legislature; . . . and to make such Bye-Laws and Ordinances . . . as they may judge most expedient for the Accomplishment of the Trust hereby reposed in them. (Session Acts, chap. 82, art. 3, passed April 13, 1787; as quoted in Miller, 1969, p. 22)[9]

The New York legislature also granted acts of incorporation to schools and in some instances indicated that the particular school was exempt from the visitation requirements by the Regents. In 1795 an act was passed to encourage schools and provided some state funds for them. In 1813 legislation was passed that provided for a state superintendent of schools and plans for a system of schools. The legislature dealt directly with town schools. As Cremin (1980) notes, "For all the power of the drive toward systematization, then, the results in New York were several systems and subsystems, each comprising institutions of varying degrees of publicness" (p. 152). Samuel Adams, Governor of Massachusetts (1793–1797), however, did block the incorporation of academies during his administration. Besides giving the educational enterprise legal entity, these acts of incorporation often included a government subsidy. The attempts to create state systems of schooling before the common school movement in the 1830s and 1840s were "at best uneven and fluctuant" and even within the "systems" themselves "there was considerable variation from community to community and from school to school" (Cremin, 1980, pp. 171–172).

Voluntarism, where public responsibilities were delegated to private groups, in the provision of social goods and services, often aided by government subsidies, was deemed as the best way of providing them. "Belief in the release of private individual and group energies," notes Hurst (1956), "thus furnished one of the working principles which gave coherence of character to our early nineteenth-century public policy" (p. 32; see also Cremin, 1980, p. 63 and Meyer, 1957, p. 96 for additional discussions on this topic).

The rise of the denominational groups, along with other private organizations, and the state in the new republic presented two major institutional forces and potential adversaries. One of the primary concerns of these private organizations was whether they would have control over what they had organized and established. The seizure of the College of Philadelphia in 1776 and the Bank of North America later on by the state provoked a debate that "was one of the most significant of the entire Revolutionary period" (Bailyn, 1960, p. 47). The issue was finally resolved in the Supreme Court in the Dartmouth College case that protected private groups and institutions from being taken over by governmental bodies (*Dartmouth College v. Woodward*, 17 U.S. (4 Wheat.) 518 (1819)).

On the other hand, the prominence of private organizations that dominated the political and social life in early America caused some uneasiness within the comparatively weak state governments. Massachusetts, New Hampshire, and Connecticut restricted the amount of income-producing property that an incorporated body could possess for educational purposes. "Such provisions," notes Middlekauff (1963), "implied no distrust of education; they reflected the common concern that no corporation grow so large as to challenge the state" (p. 141).

Two of the most pressing problems facing the nascent nation were survival and identity. There was no "American" ethos or tradition and culture that people could turn to for guidance and direction. Noah Webster lamented that "our national character is not yet formed" (Tyack, 1967, p. 93). The creation of the new American republic accentuated the need for the early Americans to define who they were and to develop the mechanism to preserve and perpetuate the new American culture. The recent and violent demise of the French republic was striking evidence of the potential for national suicide. It was ample proof "that a republic must be sustained by a public virtue" and of the urgent need to keep "political democracy from spilling over into cultural or moral democracy" (Meyer, 1976, pp. 211, 183).

What was needed was an American culture, a basic set of values, principles, and way of life that would eclipse sectarian, sectoral, ethnic, and class factions and provide a common meeting ground for the heterogeneous American populace. Benjamin Franklin, in his "Proposals Relating to the Education of Youth in Pennsylvania" in 1749, mentioned the need for a *"Publick Religion"* in America as early as 1749 (Tyack, 1967, p. 75). But what would be the source of this "public religion" or, to use

Rousseau's term, "civil religion" that would allow political democracy to function and the American state to survive?[10] Meyer (1976) contends that the principal sources of this civil religion or public morality were the Enlightenment philosophy and Protestant Christianity.

> From where were the elements of America's public commitment to come? Here is where the Enlightenment, joined with the principles of Protestant Christianity, comes into the picture. The ideals of the Enlightenment, modified to conform to the Christian faith and the dictates of common sense, provided the Americans with a national credo that was up-to-date, rational, and universal in its appeal. Commitment to human rights—including the rights of life, liberty, and property (as set forth in the Whig tradition)—renunciation of all "superstition," trust in the natural sciences, confidence in rational morality, belief in individual freedom balanced by a concern for public welfare, an empirical attitude toward politics that was not burdened by undue respect for custom and authority: These ingredients went into the formation of an American faith. Combined with this, always, was that unshakable American belief . . . in a broad cultural commitment to basic religious truths that presumably all sects share in common and that stand as the basis of public virtue. (pp. 213–214)

With the democratization of political participation, the separation of church and state, the need to define and create the American character, and the necessity of inculcating public virtue for national survival, came calls for state systems of education.[11] The preservation of the nation could not be left to chance. Something had to be purposely set in place as an "integrative mechanism" for the new republic. "A good system of Education," wrote Noah Webster, "should be the first article in the code of political regulations. . . . [It] gives every citizen an opportunity of acquiring knowledge and fitting himself for places of trust . . . [and is] the *sine qua non* of the existence of the American republics" (Tyack, 1967, pp. 97–98).

Benjamin Rush, writing to the Englishman Richard Price, observed that

> we changed our forms of government, but it remains yet to effect a revolution in our principles, opinions, and manners, so as to accommodate them to the forms of government we have adapted. This is the most difficult part of the business of the patriots and legislators of our country. It requires more wisdom and fortitude than to expel or reduce armies into captivity. (Cremin, 1980, p. 1)

Rush proposed that this "revolution," this transformation of character or conversion to American nationalism, should be accomplished by the establishment of a single system of education.

> Our schools of learning, by producing one general, and uniform system of education, will render of the mass of the people more homogeneous, and thereby fit them more easily for uniform and peaceable government. (Tyack, 1967, p. 103)

Not only did Rush think it possible to "convert men into republican machines," but he believed that it "must be done, if we expect them to perform their parts properly, in the great machine of the government of the state" (Cremin, 1980, p. 118).

Thomas Jefferson called attention to the need for educated people to prevent tyranny and serve as government leaders in his "Bill for the More Diffusion of Knowledge" introduced to the Virginia legislature in 1779 and 1817. In a letter written to George Washington, Jefferson held that "it is an axiom in my mind that our liberty can never be safe but in the hands of the people themselves, and that, too, of the people with a certain degree of instruction. This is the business of the state to effect, and on a general plan" (Karier, 1986, p. 30).

While Thomas Jefferson advocated a "liberal education" for those who would be public servants, Rush and Webster had a somewhat narrower view of what constituted the essential curriculum, more like indoctrination than education. "The *virtues* of men are of more consequence to society," Webster maintained, "than their *abilities;* and for this reason, the *heart* should be cultivated with more assiduity than the *head*" (Tyack, 1967, p. 99). Rush held that "the only foundation for a useful education in a republic is to be laid in Religion. Without this there can be no virtue, and without virtue there can be no liberty" (Tyack, 1967, p. 103). Rush, in the heat nationalistic fervor, wanted to see young people have a

> "SUPREME REGARD TO THEIR COUNTRY, inculcated upon them. . . . Our country includes family, friends and property, and should be preferred to them all. Let our pupil be taught that he does not belong to himself, but that he is public property . . . [furthermore] he must be taught to amass wealth, but it must be only to increase his power of contributing to the wants and demands of the state." (Tyack, 1967, 105, 106)[12]

A further indication of the linkage between education and national survival and how it was to be accomplished can be found in an essay contest sponsored by the American Philosophical Society in 1795. The topic of this particular essay contest was what would be the best educational system for Americans. Of the seven entries, Samuel Knox and Samuel Harrison Smith were selected as co-winners. Both of their essays proposed some sort of national system of education. In comparing these proposals with other contemporaneous educational plans of the day,

Cremin (1980) observes that the essence of this emerging republican educational thought held that the

> success—nay, the salvation—of the Republic lay in education; that education consisted of the diffusion of knowledge, the nurturance of virtue including patriotic civility, and the cultivation of learning; that the best means of providing education on the massive scale required were schools and colleges; and that the most effective way of obtaining the number and kind of schools and colleges needed was via some *system* ultimately tied to the polity. . . . What was essentially new in the republican style was the dual emphasis on system and on relationship to the polity. (pp. 124–125)

Despite the rhetorical outpouring of plans and formulations for various types of educational systems, the astonishing aspect is not in what was said but that for the first 50 or 60 years of America's history, none of these grandiose schemes were implemented in full or in part. They would eventually, however, find partial fulfillment in the establishment of the "common school," but that would be more the result of new social pressures and would be on a state rather than national level. The initial value of the plans was in cultivating and preparing the conceptual and ideological landscape of American culture for a radical departure from traditional educational patterns.

Some of the salient points of this new educational trend seemed to be: the idea of a system that brought uniformity and standardization to the educational process; the need for this system and its operation to be directly tied to the state to ensure this uniformity; accessibility to education for all (excepting blacks and Native Americans); educational objectives such as instilling a public morality, patriotism, and the subjugation of individual desires and interests in behalf of the public welfare; and the principle that the child belonged to the state, that an individual was a "tabula rasa" that could be molded by the environment, and that people and society could be perfected.

Piety, civility, and learning—the colonial goals of education—were Protestantized, republicanized, and secularized as they were transformed into patriotism and citizenship as well as personal and national economic self-sufficiency (Cremin, 1980). The emphasis of education became "this world" instead of "other worldly." Instead of a Puritan commonwealth, it was a Protestant commonwealth built on an amalgamation of two powerful ideologies—"American nationalism and American Protestantism" (Higham, 1974, p. 15). Schools, agencies of the state, became the keepers and integrators of society and replaced churches as the cultural custodians of social values and practices.

At the bottom of all these opinions, plans, and campaigns was a vision of human beings as perfectible through education, of social institutions capable of perfecting them, and of a society dedicated to the enhancement of their dignity. It was, in effect, the vision of the millennium. (Cremin, 1980, p. 121)

Common School Movement

The America of the 1830s and 1840s was quite different from the America of Thomas Jefferson, Benjamin Rush, and Noah Webster. New social forces and pressures were causing many to re-evaluate just how well traditional answers were solving current challenges, much in the same way the colonists had done at the turn of the seventeenth century. In addition to sectarian strife and the traditional regional conflicts of North versus South and Eastern establishment versus the West, came new elements that were potentially divisive and threatening. Not only did these elements of cultural conflict add to the social disharmony, but they also stimulated responses that attempted to ameliorate resulting social evils.

For instance, when the potato famine in Ireland and social unrest in Germany pushed large numbers of immigrants to America, nativist movements were organized to protect economic and cultural dominance and to ensure the proper Americanization of the foreigners. In response to the exploitation of women and children, which resulted from the Industrial Revolution, Sunday schools were instituted and child labor laws were passed to provide some modicum of rudimentary education and protection to children. Labor parties were organized to protect the interests of the workers and reduce the growing chasm in wealth and power between the industrial rich and the laboring poor. The need for a concentrated work force led to a faster rate of urbanization and its accompanying social ills (Schultz, 1973).

In an ethos of voluntarism, a variety of humanitarian groups, social reformers, and philanthropists responded in an effort to reduce ignorance, crime, injustice, poverty, disease, immorality, slavery, and the use of alcohol. Suffrage granted to all white males added a new and potentially threatening dimension to political affairs. The election of Andrew Jackson, a westerner, ended the domination of American politics by eastern landowners and wealthy businessmen who had controlled the political process since the Revolution. It was a time of much social upheaval and unrest, which called for new solutions and a significant restructuring of current public policy to address the growing social instability (Karier, 1986; Ravitch, 1974; Tyack, 1967).

It is here that the dominant groups in America turned again to education, as they had done in the colonial era, as a primary means of adapting, with their influence intact, to new social conditions (Karier, 1986). Led by crusading social reformers and humanitarians, many believed that education provided by a government-sponsored system of "common schools" was the sure foundation of any meaningful social reform.[13] The purpose of the common school was to bring cultural harmony, economic prosperity, and social justice to the American nation. It would perform this role of a social panacea by educating the young in a socially shared core of practical and cultural knowledge in a common school house that was sponsored, supported, and controlled by the state. The primary mission of the common school was not literacy, although cognitive skills and learning to read, write, and perform basic computations were part of the schooling process. The main emphasis was moral, that is, character education (Curti, 1974). Without the proper training in public morality, the common schools would produce, in Horace Mann's opinion, only "grander savages . . . a more dangerous barbarian" (Cremin, 1980, p. 141). "It is by general instruction," stated Daniel Webster, "[that] we seek, as far as possible, to purify the whole moral atmosphere" (Tyack, 1967, p. 126).

The principal population targeted to receive this state-sponsored moral education were those who, in the minds of the reformers, had demonstrated the most serious character defects and thus posed the greatest social threat—the children of the working poor. In a secular reworking of the Calvinistic notion of evidences of God's grace and salvation, the poor were considered morally deficient. Their poverty was ample proof of their degraded state and of negligence on the part of their parents. "It was presumed—and without need of proof or opportunity for rebuttal—that those who had not the 'moral character' to raise themselves out of poverty similarly lacked the qualities to rear their children" (Nasaw, 1979, p. 10).

The obvious solution for many was to remove these children from their bad home environment to a place where they could be taught the requisite character traits needed for economic success and the rules of social and political discourse. Social problems such as poverty, crime, disease, and unrest would simply disappear, since social problems had their origin in the individual, particularly the poor, and not with the basic economic or societal structure.[14] The state and its variety of institutions would become the new parents. The common school would be the central institution in this effort to restructure society. "Education, then, beyond all other devices of human origin," wrote Horace Mann in the *Twelfth Annual Report*, "is the great equalizer of the conditions of men—the balance-wheel of the social machinery. . . . It does better than to disarm the poor of their hostility towards the rich; it prevents being poor" (Karier, 1986, pp. 60–61).

Joel Spring (1986, pp. 71–72) observes that the common school differed from past educational practices in three significant ways: (1) It was a "school that was attended in common by all children and where a common political and social ideology was taught."[15] (2) It included the "idea of a direct linkage between government educational policies and the solving and control of social, economic, and political problems." (3) And growing out of (1) and (2) was the "creation of state agencies to control local schools." The state was the only social agency, in the eyes of the reformers, that could create and sustain the type of universal community they envisioned in an efficient manner. Universality, equality, and efficiency were the rhetorical watchwords (Cremin, 1951).

The direct and deliberate participation of the state in the provision of educational services on such a wholesale level as in the establishment of common schools constituted the beginnings of a radical restructuring of the roles the individual, the family, the church, and the community would fulfill in relation to each other and especially in relation to the state. It also stands as an anomaly in nineteenth-century public policy infused with voluntarism (Tyack & James, 1986). In terms of control over education, this development marked the inauguration of a profound shift in power and direction away from the family and traditional private agencies such as the church and other community institutions to the state.[16] This shift, however, has occurred over time. Horace Mann and his associates never envisioned the centralization of educational decision making in the offices of today's government.

An important reason behind the acceptance of the common school concept was the idea of local control, a concept advocated by Thomas Jefferson. The community would decide what version of the American ideology it believed in and how it would be taught in the local school (Katz, 1975). Initially, the state government played a very small supervisory role in education. Bernard Mehl (1963) notes that

> the local community, on their own terms, hire teachers and select textbooks to flavor the school with the particular religious leanings of the local group. As long as a community was united more or less in religious persuasion, it had nothing to fear from the common school because, in fact, it controlled the school's curriculum. (p. 21)

An important question to consider at this point is why a system of schools directly tied to the state was finally realized during the 1830s and 1840s and not before. In Joel Spring's (1986) useful summary of a variety of historical explanations (pp. 72–80), Ellwood Cubberley (1934) and Merle Curti (1974) see the common school movement as the victorious culmination of the liberal forces of democracy fighting for social justice and equality over the aristocratic, conservative elements that had dominated American politics since the Revolution. On the other end of the spectrum, Michael B. Katz's (1968) revisionist account portrays the common school movement as a means by which those in control of the political and economic affairs in America *retained* their control to protect their interests (Tyack & Hansot, 1982).[17] Others, for example, Rush Welter (1963), have pointed to the importance of various social groups such as the labor parties that supported the common school movement. Carl Kaestle's thesis (1983) is that the primary moving force behind the movement was a desire by nativists to ensure the continued hegemony of a white, native-born, middle class, Protestant, Anglo-American culture. Spring (1986) concludes that

> no single interpretation provides an adequate explanation. Rather, the common school appears to have been a result of a complicated set of often-conflicting social and economic factors that included a humanitarian impulse to create the good society; a desire by the working class to enhance its political and economic position in society; a desire by manufacturers to have a disciplined and well-trained work force; a desire of the upper classes to protect their economic and social privileges; and a desire to maintain an American Protestant culture. (p. 80)[18]

The assessment that the establishment of common schools was formed in the crucible of "often-conflicting social and economic factors" is probably correct but still does not penetrate the "black box" of how it happened. One common thread that weaves itself through the various historical explanations and that might tie them together in a more coherent whole is the existence of various groups with particular interests. But how could one interest group—common school advocates such as Horace Mann and Henry Bernard—gather sufficient support for a common cause from other interest groups that often were fighting each other?

Mancur Olson (1971) in his insightful work on the theory of groups, *The Logic of Collective Action*, asserts that large groups will not advance their common cause without some form of coercion and/or the inducement of some incentive that is separate from the common cause and is distributed on an individual basis. Small, organized groups are much more likely to be successful in advancing their common interests than large, unorganized groups. The reasons for this are threefold. First, size is inversely related to the amount of reward or benefit that any one member would receive. Second, with the shrinkage in the size of the benefit or collective good, there is a corresponding increase in the likelihood that the costs involved will not make the venture a profitable one. Third, with an increase in size comes a parallel increase in the start up and maintenance costs of an organization. Olson concludes that "however immense the benefits of a collective good, the higher the absolute total costs of getting any amount of that good, the less likely it is that even a minimal amount of that good could be obtained without coercion or separate, outside incentives" (pp. 47–48).

Since the common school interest group had no means at their disposal to coerce acceptance of the idea of state schools, they were left with providing individual incentives that would outweigh the costs of supporting the movement. Olson (1971) describes leaders of small groups as "political entrepreneurs" (p. 177) who are creative in finding the right incentive for other individuals/groups to induce their support. The success of such reformers as James Carter, Horace Mann, Henry Bernard, Caleb Mills, and many others in reorienting and restructuring public policy in education was due, in part, to their ability to "articulate and focus the generalized American belief in education and to make it relevant to the aspirations and anxieties of the age" (Tyack, 1967, p. 124; see also Tyack, 1986, p. 215 for additional discussion on this topic).

But the genius of Horace Mann and his associates, many of whom were Protestant ministers, prominent citizens, and the social elite, was to build a sufficiently large coalition of various interest groups to support a common cause by offering selective and individual incentives to each group that was separate and apart from the common school movement (Jorgenson, 1968; Smith, 1966–1967; Tyack, 1966b).

> To the individual who feared the effect of universal suffrage on the politics of the new republic, the common school was a useful vehicle for educating the new masters. To the property owner, the school was a protective insurance policy against the threat of mob violence. To the entrepreneur, the school was a means of producing more effective workers as well as a greater number of customers. To the laborer, the school was a device for social mobility; and to the egalitarian social reformer, the school was a means to equalize knowledge, which in turn would presumably have the effect of equalizing wealth and power. To the nativist, the school provided a way to Americanize the immigrant; and to the extreme anti-Catholic, the school was a vehicle to Protestantize the Catholic immigrant's children. (Karier, 1986, p. 45)

The cost side of the equation had also been lowered for each of the groups mentioned above. The common schools would be supported by a property tax and land grants from the federal government. The common school reformers had been astute enough to emphasize localized benefits to individuals, while distributing the costs in a general manner.

The start-up and maintenance costs for the common school interest group had also been reduced to such an extent that it became a "profitable" venture. Many of the advocates were members of a variety of religious, humanitarian, and social reform groups. Organizational structure was already in place. Common schools were simply added to the group's action agenda, placed on the lecture circuit, and integrated into the Sunday sermon.

Another very significant factor in reducing the cost of organizing was the creation of government positions for education. New York created the office of state superintendent of education in 1812. Other states soon followed with positions of a similar nature or delegated the responsibility to the secretary of state. By 1861 28 of the 34 states had a state officer of education (Cubberley, 1934). Many of the leading lights of the common school movement, such as Horace Mann in Massachusetts, Henry Bernard in Connecticut, Calvin Wiley in North Carolina, Samuel Lewis in Ohio, and Caleb Mills in Indiana, were appointed to these paid positions and even received additional money from private sources (Nasaw, 1979).

The significance of this development should not be underestimated. It provided an opportunity for a particular and private educational view to be articulated and promulgated with the trappings of state endorsement with state monies. Other points of view were placed at a decidedly distinct disadvantage. The common school movement was the imposition of a particular educational ideology, with significant political and social implications, by a small group of astute and articulate advocates with their own vision of humankind and the good society (Cremin, 1980; Curti, 1974).

That the common school movement appealed to many should not be mistaken as a consensus on American education. It involved a bitter contest over whose private values and ideologies would be elevated to the status of public beliefs. In addition, each interest group supported the common school movement for different and sometimes conflicting reasons. In their efforts to build a majority through a federation of interest groups, the common school advocates had created an unrealistic set of expectations and had made extravagant claims for this new state school that would provide continual fodder for the ubiquitous debate over the end and means of education and the role of schools in our society. A major cost inherent in the establishment of state-sponsored schools in America was an educational program with conflict built into the system. The government school would always be a center of controversy because it had been touted as the universal elixir for individual and social ills and embodied the legitimization of particular values and beliefs. It could not be all things to all people, especially when some of the services demanded of it were conflicting and contradictory in nature and touched on fundamental beliefs about humankind and society (Besag & Nelson, 1984; Karier, 1986).

Opposition to the common school movement was widespread and came from many quarters. State referendums on the establishment of state schools passed with bare majorities in several states. While Horace Mann scarcely survived an attempt in 1840 to abolish his position, Henry Bernard in Connecticut was not so lucky, as his position was abrogated 4 years after its establishment. Although clearly in favor of universal education, but without government control, Orestes Brownson was a sharp critic of the common school movement and of the infatuation Mann and other reformers had with the highly centralized, systematized, and tightly state-controlled Prussian school system. Brownson voiced the fears and concerns of many when he observed that

> a government system of education in Prussia is not inconsistent with the theory of Prussian society, for there all wisdom is supposed to be lodged in the government. But the thing is wholly inadmissable here . . . because, according to our theory, the people are supposed to be wiser than the government. Here, the people do not look to the government for light, for instruction, but the government looks to the people. The people give the law to the government. To entrust, then, the government with the power of determining the education which our children shall receive is entrusting our servant with the power to be our master. This fundamental difference between the two countries, we apprehend, has been overlooked by the board of education and its supporters. (Nasaw, 1979, p. 64)

Private Schools and State Schools

The effect of the common school movement on private schools was felt in a number of ways. Numerous private schools were forced to close their doors as many parents could no longer afford to pay both tuition and taxes for the state schools. Many others, especially those sponsored by various Protestant denominations, were simply absorbed into the public school system. By 1850 only 138 private schools remained in New York City from the 430 in 1829. In Massachusetts, private academies declined from 1,308 in 1840 to 350 some 40 years later (Nasaw, 1979). Several Protestant denominations, such as the Calvinists, Lutherans, Episcopalians, Quakers, and Dutch Reformed, strengthened or established their own school systems in response to the diluted Protestantism and the perceived "godlessness" in the state school, or in an effort to preserve their culture and language (Jorgenson, 1968; Kraushaar, 1972).

> Many immigrant groups supported, often at great sacrifice, their own private schools designed to perpetuate their religion and ethnic heritage. Norwegian Lutherans in Minnesota, Polish Catholics in Chicago, Russian Jews in Boston created their own educational systems, sometimes to supplement the public schools and sometimes to compete with them, but always to preserve their own culture. They juxtaposed their own enthnocentrisms against American ethnocentrism. (Tyack, 1967, p. 231)

In the political arena, a major confrontation between private schools and the government was over the disbursement of state monies. It had been customary in many states to subsidize religious and nonreligious educational institutions (Jorgenson, 1987; Spring, 1990). With the entrance of the state as a participant and competitor, the reformers argued that the compulsory property tax should be reserved for the common schools. A sharing of tax monies among all interested parties would simply dilute any concentrated efforts of educational reform and would violate the First Amendment in the case of schools sponsored by religious bodies (Cremin, 1980; Nasaw, 1979).[19]

The great "school war" in New York between common school advocates and the Catholics provides a good example of how a cultural and religious minority group fought the assimilation process of the state school. The Catholics viewed the new common schools as anti-Catholic, generic Protestant schools that had an innate bias against everything that was not Protestant and Anglo-American.[20] They posed both a religious and an ethnic threat since most Catholics were recent immigrants from Ireland and Germany (Lines, 1984). The outcome of the political and legislative battles left tax monies firmly in place for state schools (Cubberley, 1934). With the loss of state subsidies for their schools, the only alternative in the eyes of many was cultural and religious capitulation or the establishment of a separate but costly private school system.[21]

It was at this time that determining whether state subsidies should continue to flow to private schools forced a more precise definition of "public" and "private." "Public" was given a more narrow definition, as that which receives state monies and is controlled by the state (Cremin, 1980; Jorgenson, 1987).

Clearly, the continued presence of private schools alongside state schools was a source a genuine irritation and concern for common school advocates and social reformers. These private schools represented a threat to their efforts at restructuring society because of the differing visions of humankind and society that were taught. They were potential, if not actual, sources of educational, ideological, and social heresy. They distracted from the "common" efforts to establish the political and social millennium envisioned by Mann and his colleagues. Private schools were ideological and educational competitors.

The private schools allegedly did this in three ways: (1) they diminished the ability of the state school as a social "leveler" to reduce class stratification, (2) money that could have been spent by those attending state schools and paying rate bills was spent elsewhere, and (3) attention and effort in making state schools a success were diverted in other directions (Cremin, 1951, 1980; Miller, 1969; Tyack, 1967). While James Carter and Henry Bernard wanted to abolish private schools, Horace Mann felt they would die a natural death as people forsook them for superior state schools (Curti, 1974; Karier, 1986; Nasaw, 1979; Tyack, 1967).[22] Although no state passed any legislation regulating or attempting to ban private schools before 1870, some states, such as Michigan, took a less than friendly attitude toward private schools (Cremin, 1980; McLaughlin, 1946).

> It is clear that to a certain extent the idea of a common school receiving all classes and groups in the community in the role of "common mother" was incompatible with the existence of private schools. And although the reformers maintained that they could not possibly deny the rights of private schools without doing violence to the legal and moral principles of an individualist-capitalist economy, the incompatibility of the two commitments are evident. The resolution, perhaps, rested in the argument that if the common schools were good enough, there would be no reason for people to send their children to private ones. . . . Thus, although nothing could be done to restrain the operation of private institutions while remaining loyal to the commitment of private enterprise, the mores of competition dictated that if the common school was made good enough, few would forsake it for private institutions. (Cremin, 1951, pp. 61–62)

The establishment of government-sponsored schools during the common school crusade was a dramatic departure from the previous practice of voluntarism and inaugurated a massive shift of decision-making power away from individuals, families, communities, and private organizations to the state. It was an excellent example of the "new politics" in America—of ideologues cloaking their personal interests in the garb of public policy to enthrone their personal and particular values as public and universal values. In the process, it was the reformers' version of America, their version of Protestantism and republicanism, that was established as the public view. The common schools were a reflection of their values and beliefs and the means to homogenize and assimilate ethnic, religious, and cultural outsiders into what was now defined as mainstream America (Cremin, 1980; Nasaw, 1979).

In institutionalizing much of the nationalistic and Protestant ideology and rhetoric of the preceding 60 years, the common school movement had established, in one sense, a state church. The civil religion of nationalism, Whiggish republicanism, Enlightenment doctrines, capitalism, and generic Protestantism was just as "sectarian" as the beliefs of the traditional religious denominations. The state school assumed more and more functions traditionally performed by the church and "is probably the closest Americans have come toward creating an established church" (Tyack & Hansot, 1982, p. 249; also see McCarthy, Skillen, & Harper, 1982; Rushdoony, 1978). It became the source, the guardian, and the articulator of social values. Not unlike the Puritans, the common school advocates used education and government schools to advance and perpetuate their own view of humankind and vision of society. For the Puritans it was the advancement of the kingdom of God. For Mann and his associates it was also the advancement of the kingdom of God, namely, their particular version of America (Higham, 1974; Tyack & Hansot, 1982). The primary objective was to mold and shape the social misfits, those who were different and did not meet the cultural, religious, and social standards, into acceptable and proper members of society. Those who most often felt the brunt of this forced assimilation and socialization were also those least able to resist—the poor, immigrants, members of an ethnic or religious minority.

What had once been the quintessential American institutions—the private school, the church, and the family—were now becoming institutional outsiders in American society. The politicalization and socialization of education through the creation of state schools had placed public schools in the center of efforts to restructure society and engage in social engineering. Although the conceptual patterns, educational themes, and institutional foundations for the modern state in education formed during this era would be expanded and refined, one pivotal piece of the structure was missing—the coercive power of the state. This essential element was quick in coming, however, in the form of compulsory schooling laws.

THE NATIONAL ERA, PART II: COMPULSION, CONFORMITY, AND CONFLICT

The Civil War in the United States beginning in 1861 was for many a national nightmare come true, an effort to commit national suicide. It was the American equivalent of the French Revolution some 60 years earlier, and it produced a profound effect on the role of government and the formulation of public policy.

The former ways of engendering a loyalty beyond self and parochial interests, of creating a national identity and social stability through voluntarism, were rejected. Liberty had to be an ordered liberty. Individual interests had to be channeled in proper directions. Unity and conformity in matters designated as issues of public concern and welfare took precedence over private ventures and social diversity. Social solidarity and homogeneity assumed a greater social value than pluralism and variety. The Reconstructionist governments of the post-Civil War era turned to social compulsion through legislation in an effort to forge a new and stronger national identity and loyalty. The dominant cultural group in America— white, middle class, Protestant, Anglo-American—turned to the police powers of the state to have personal values legitimated as public values and imposed on the minority. Acceptance and compliance were compelled through revisions in state constitutions, legislative enactments, administrative regulations, and judicial pronouncements (Burgess, 1976; Jorgenson, 1987; Tyack, James, & Benavot, 1987).[23]

The "search for order," the "lure of instant stability-by-statute," thrust the state into areas of personal, family, and community life that had traditionally been untouched or very narrowly restricted (Burgess, 1976, p. 205; see also Wiebe, 1967 for further discussion). A particular focus of the legislative and regulatory efforts was the child. Through the legal doctrines of *parens patriae* and *in loco parentis,* the state dramatically increased its intervention in family life and education. The rights of the natural parents or guardians to raise their children and direct their education were diminished and circumscribed. No longer did the state have to prove parental incompetence *before* it could intervene into familial affairs. The government had, by legislative fiat, declared itself as an additional parent with equal if not superior right to care for the child. "The state could do what it judged reasonable and proper in order to perpetuate itself" (Burgess, 1976, p. 214; Jorgenson, 1987, pp. 150–154 for additional discussion). As a result, a variety of state-sponsored custodial institutions such as public education, orphanages and foster homes, reform schools, and special institutions for the physically and mentally handicapped were created and expanded to correct youthful offenders and to ensure that children were properly socialized and educated in the right way (Burgess, 1976). In its effort to restructure post-Civil War society, the controlling majority began the transformation of the state from that of a social referee to that of a parent—a "Super Parent."[24]

David Tyack (1986) sees antebellum educational legislation oriented toward "enticement" as a means of persuading the public to embrace various public policy initiatives such as public schools. After the Civil War there was a distinct change in the nature of education legislation from that of coaxing to coercing. Tyack labels this type of educational legislation as "normative dominance." In harmony with the temper of the times, the cultural majority sought to impose its particular values in education through statutory law.

> Toward the end of the century and during the Progressive era . . . certain ethnocultural groups decided that they should enforce their values on others in public education through legislation. Americans who believed that the United States was not only God's country but also *their* nation—mostly native-born Anglo-Saxon citizens of pietist Protestant persuasion and respectable station—decided that their preferred future required the force of state sanction and that they could no longer rely on voluntary action or an unconscious consensus. (Tyack, 1986, p. 221; see also Brown, 1912, p. 56; Hurst, 1956, p. 86 for concurring views.)

Compulsory Education Laws

In the area of education, the coercive impulses in this "Age of Compulsion" were manifested primarily in the passage of compulsory education and attendance laws.[25] These laws had a profound effect on American education and represented a significant reordering of the relationship between the family and the state. They became a legislative mechanism through which state intervention in education was realized. While recognizing the right of parents to educate their children, the state posited its right, *parens patriae* and *in loco parentis,* to see that the child was educated to ensure the perpetuation of the state. These laws were "nothing less than a debate over who owned the child" (Schultz, 1973, p. 302). Charles Burgess (1976) holds that

> [of] all the changes in American education [during the last quarter of the nineteenth century] . . . none was more momentous than the state-by-state endorsement of the arguments that the state could compel children to attend schools, could punish parents and guardians who did not abide by the attendance laws, and, as a final measure, could confine truants along with other delinquent children in appropriate boarding institutions. (p. 212)

Compulsory education laws were not entirely new. The Puritan commonwealth had enacted such measures in 1642 and 1647. These colonial laws had emphasized achievement, however, whereas the new compulsory education laws emphasized attendance. Education was no longer in the familial stage, where parents decided the best means of educating their children. Education had now taken on an "institutional" character, where attendance became the operational definition of becoming educated. Compulsory education became synonymous with compulsory schooling (Katz, 1974).

In 1852 Massachusetts became the first state to pass a compulsory education law. It is curious that neither Mann nor his successor nor the board of education advocated such a measure. The initial support came from labor parties and philanthropic groups in an effort to protect children in the factories, minimize their exploitation by factory owners, and reduce youthful vagrancy (Cremin, 1980). By 1918 all of the states had passed compulsory attendance laws.[26]

Compulsory attendance laws, like the establishment of common schools, did not really have much of an initial effect on school attendance. The statutory wording was often vague, enforcement provisions were missing or inadequate, and officials were initially reluctant to demand compliance. The net effect of the common schools and compulsory education laws was to enroll and educate those who had previously been enrolled in private schools.[27] The target population of the common school reformers, the children of the poor, were not attending school. The reason was obvious. The child was an important economic factor in the survival of the family. The family could not afford to have children attend school and to forego the wages they had been earning. It was only with the passage of child labor laws along with school attendance laws that a significant increase in enrollment in public schools resulted (Ensign, 1921).

The passage of compulsory attendance laws encountered stiff opposition. As with the common school movement, the rhetoric from both sides came fast and furious. Advocates considered compulsory education laws as not only imminently rational and necessary in providing universal education but essential for the survival of the American nation. Those in disagreement included people who felt the reach of the state had gone too far into matters of private concern—rights of parents to educate their children and intervention into the operations of private schools. Each position accused the other of being disloyal Americans.[28]

Private Schools and State Regulations

For private schools, the passage of compulsory education laws was of immense importance. Although the government recognized attendance at private schools as fulfilling compulsory attendance laws, these laws became the legislative justification and legal mechanism through which the state could intervene and regulate the activities of private schools.[29] With attendance at school required by state law, private schools performed a function mandated by the state. They performed a public function, public in the new sense of the term as representing something that the state was personally involved with. In order to ensure that the intent of the legislature was being fulfilled, the state would have to investigate and intervene to some degree in the operations of private schools. Intervention was necessary to ensure compliance with state law (McLaughlin, 1946).

Early efforts by the state to regulate and control private schools were nonexistent or modest by present standards and were a subset of public school regulations. Compulsory education statutes generally allowed students to attend state schools or private schools with, few, if any, requirements. The restrictions placed on private schools ranged from none to a variety of items such as the need to have state approval, to have competent teachers, the keeping and submission of attendance records and reports, teaching subjects in the English language, and teaching the same subjects with the same quality of instruction as found in the public schools (McLaughlin, 1946).

In addition, a few states were beginning to require private schools to comply with basic health and safety standards such as fire drills (New York, Indiana, Montana, Washington), health certificates certifying freedom from tuberculosis (New Mexico), and medical examinations of students (Indiana). Other miscellaneous regulations held that private schools could not instruct blacks and whites together (Kentucky) and that students transferring from private schools to public schools had to pass an entrance examination (Kansas). However, by 1918 only about one-half of the states had enacted any form of government control over private schools (McLaughlin, 1946).

There were, however, several strict measures passed or proposed before the turn of the century that would have severely restricted or abolished private schools (Kraushaar, 1972). In 1874 the California compulsory education statute contained a proposed provision making enrollment in a private school a criminal offense unless the local board of education gave specific approval for the child in question. Massachusetts passed a comprehensive provision for the approval of private schools in 1888 (Jorgenson, 1987; McLaughlin, 1946). This legislation required that

> "school committees shall approve such instruction only when it is given by the use of the English language, and when they are satisfied that it is equal in thoroughness and efficiency to the instruction given in the public schools." (quoted in McLaughlin, 1946, p. 71)

Although it did not pass, a bill was submitted to the New York legislature in 1889 that would have required teachers in private schools to take the same qualifying exams as public school teachers (Ensign, 1921). The Bennett Law in Wisconsin and Edwards Law in Illinois passed in 1889 required that certain subjects be taught in English.[30] And finally, many states in the South and for a limited period of time in Ohio and Rhode Island denied private schools a tax-exempt status (McLaughlin, 1946).

The first quarter of the twentieth century found America embroiled in war on two fronts that would have a great impact on both public and private education. The first "war" had been in the making for some time as shocking exposés by muckraking journalists and investigative reporters brought to public attention the extent of political corruption, the capture of government by big business, and the decadence and poverty in America. Whether it was Upton Sinclair's *The Jungle* (1906) revealing the contamination of meat and food, Demarest Lloyd's *Wealth Against the Commonwealth* (1894) exposing the Standard Oil Trust, Joseph M. Rice's *The Public School System of the United States* (1893) revealing the public schools as the "most dehumanizing institution" he had seen, or Jacob Riis's telling portrayal of poverty in *How the Other Half Lives* (1902), it was clear to many that society was in trouble. All of this, combined with the social crisis of the 1890s caused by the depression in 1893, the massive influx of immigrants from southern Europe, the continuing problems of urbanization and industrialization, and the political corruption of the Boss Tweeds and the Tammany Halls, was striking evidence that traditional social and political arrangements were not successful in dealing with current social problems. There was a fear that society was slipping into chaos. Things needed to be changed.

From these turbulent conditions emerged the Progressive Era bent on reforming society and restoring calm and stability. The major premise of Progressive reformers, most of whom were white, middle to upper class, well-educated, and Protestant, was that the individualism and *laissez faire* attitude of the state had to be changed. The state had to be purified of special interest groups, that is, big business, and its police powers and resources expanded and brought to bear directly on the ills of society. State intervention was the answer. What these Progressive reformers, a collage of a variety of reform groups, envisioned was the modern welfare state. The state would take an aggressive stance in a planned, systematic, bureaucratic restructuring of American society. In contradistinction to the eighteenth- and nineteenth-century political philosophy, liberty would be preserved best where power was centralized and concentrated. The state would assume an even greater responsibility for the care and socialization of the young. Rather than supplement what the family, church, and community had previously done, it would in large measure supplant them (Graham, 1971; Link, Link, & Catton, 1986; McConnell, 1970).

The Progressive attack had two major thrusts in reforming political institutions in order to bring political control closer to the people. Reforms such as direct primaries, referendums and recalls, and a commission-type arrangement for city government were widely adopted. The second major thrust in the efforts to depoliticize government was to turn much of the work of government over to managerial science and the experts. Administrative science and scientific expertise would remove the corroding effects of personal prejudice and bias from governmental operations and make government more efficient. The usurpation of public power by private interests would be eliminated for good. Ironically, what the Progressives did not realize was that their reform program merely substituted one form of private power and interest for another. Nor did they realize that they themselves constituted a "special interest" group attempting to use public power to advance their own private interests and ideology (McConnell, 1970).[31]

In the midst of this political and social upheaval, the United States found itself a participant in a world war. The addition of an outside threat to the social order only sharpened the sense of uncertainty and fear.

The Progressive Era had a very significant impact on American education that is still with us today. "The most quickened profession, the most altered social institution outside of politics," notes Graham (1971), "was surely education" (p. 26). A new educational philosophy championed by John Dewey emphasized the importance of preparing students to be successful and productive members of society.[32] This call for a more practical emphasis in education was reinforced by the startling discovery that 25% of World War I draftees were illiterate (Ensign, 1921, p. 1). This more pragmatic orientation for education would also prepare students "hygienically, morally, and politically for what reformers considered responsible behavior in a modern, industrial society" (Link, Link, & Catton, 1986, p. 61). Even though there were important curricular changes, the intent, as usual, was control rather than liberty. Link, Link, and Catton (1986) state that

> it is clear, from hindsight, that the changes which they brought about put less emphasis on social justice than on social control and the overall efficiency of an industrial society. Social-policy reformers were determined to use schools to shape and form the future. If children could be molded into responsible, productive citizens through curricular changes, then the progressive school would become an essential instrumentality to insure stability in a modern society. (pp. 61–62)

Reformers turned once again to education as a major means of addressing social instability. Because of the demand for a major revamping of the school curriculum, all of the states not only passed compulsory education laws but were, for the first time, aggressively enforcing them. These laws were no longer "dead letters" but became powerful instruments in the hands of reformers (especially when coupled with child labor laws) to get every youngster into an approved school—public or private (Kotin & Aikman, 1980; Tyack, James, & Benavot, 1987).

In keeping with a basic tenet of Progressivism, public education was turned over to the educational expert.

> Society would control its own evolution through schooling; professional management would replace politics; science would replace religion and custom as sources of authority, and experts would adapt education to the transformed conditions of modern life. (Tyack & Hansot, 1982, p. 107)

Through legislation and administrative regulations, often pushed by state education associations, which were powerful lobbies for teachers and administrators, authority and decision making for educational matters were being taken away at an alarming rate from the local level and transferred to the state level (Tyack, James, & Benavot, 1987). Consolidation of schools and districts into larger and more efficient administrative units reduced local control even more. The school year was lengthened and requirements for teaching licenses and administrative credentials became more rigorous as professional educators sought to control the entrance of others into their profession. Reformers

> joined with professional administrators in the school systems to push for less popular involvement and greater central, bureaucratic control through supervision of the schools. By 1920, urban educational reformers had largely succeeded in converting a decentralized system into a rationalized bureaucracy. (Link, Link, & Catton, 1986, p. 61)[33]

Power in educational matters largely had been transferred to an "interlocking directorate of urban elites," a growing cadre of educational experts and an expanding educational bureaucracy with their own vested interests and their view of the "one best system" of education based on their concepts of humankind and the good society (Tyack, 1974). The earlier ideology of common values or beliefs was exchanged for an ideology of technology and expertise. The "certainties grounded in . . . God's will" were replaced with the "assurance of expert knowledge" (Tyack & Hansot, 1982, p. 4). Hansot and Tyack conclude that

> much of the awesome power to define what was normal and desirable in schooling—the creation of a template of approved practice—fell to non-

elected private individuals and groups claiming special competence to judge what is in the public good. (p. 7)

The initial effects of the reforms of the Progressive Era on private elementary and secondary schools were stricter compliance with the provisions of compulsory attendance laws that applied to private schools. Furthermore, there was the spillover effect from increased regulations of public schools for certain required courses. By the middle of the 1920s, the legislative foundation for regulating private schools had been set in place and would receive incremental additions during the succeeding decades.

The most significant effect, however, came in the form of legislation stipulating that only attendance at public schools would satisfy compulsory education laws and prohibiting the teaching of certain subjects. The motivation for such legislation, which essentially outlawed private schools or seriously intervened in their operations, was not the tenets of technological ideology of the educational expert. This would occur later. Instead, it was the result of conservative groups reacting to the xenophobia engendered during the war, religious and racial bigotry, and an attempt to force some sense of moral and cultural stability on a rapidly changing, increasingly secular society.[34]

Michigan was one of the first states to try to legally prohibit the existence of private schools.[35] Its first attempt in 1920 to amend the state constitution was unsuccessful by a two to one margin. Attempts to place the amendment on the ballot in 1922 failed for want of sufficient signatures (Reeder, 1923). The amendment proposal was placed on the ballot a second time, in 1924, and again it was defeated (760,571 to 421,472). The fanatical nationalistic fervor of its advocates, mixed with the usual doses of nativistic racial, religious, and cultural bigotry, fanned the flames of intolerance and called for the police powers of the state to impose their world view on others (McLaughlin, 1946).[36]

The next state to legislate against the right of private schools to exist was Oregon in 1922. Unlike efforts in Michigan, the proposed initiative took the form of a change in the state compulsory education law rather than an amendment to the state constitution. The proposed change in this case was ratified by Oregon voters by a nearly 12,000 vote margin. As in the Michigan case, supporters wrapped themselves in the American flag and equated public schools with true patriotism. Conservative and even fascist groups gave their hearty endorsement and support to the measure (Jorgenson, 1987).

A Catholic parochial school and a military academy filed suit in federal court that the measure was unconstitutional. Their claim of unconstitutionality was upheld by the federal district court in March 1924 and a restraining order was issued against the state of Oregon. The state governor, Walter M. Pierce, then appealed the decision to the United States Supreme Court. In its landmark decision rendered in 1925, the United States Supreme Court sustained the lower court ruling and declared the Oregon Compulsory Education Law unconstitutional (*Pierce v. Society of Sisters*, 268 U.S. 510 (1925); *Pierce v. Hill Military Academy*, 268 U.S. 510 (1925)). While the Supreme Court's decision firmly established the right of private schools to exist, it also confirmed the right of states to issue reasonable regulations governing the operations of private schools (McLaughlin, 1946; *Wisconsin v. Yoder*, 406 U.S. 205 (1972)).

Other states attempting to outlaw private schools with referendums were California and Washington, but they were also unsuccessful (Belleau, 1931; McLaughlin, 1946; Tyack, James, & Benavot, 1987).

In addition to legislation that, in effect, prohibited private schools, other statutes were passed regulating the curriculum. In 1919, three states, Nebraska, Iowa, and Ohio, passed analogous acts requiring that instruction in all schools, public and private alike, must be given in the English language (Ensign, 1921; McLaughlin, 1946; Tyack, 1976).

Ostensibly, these 1919 enactments were designed to assist in the Americanization of immigrants to ensure public safety. Their real focus, however, was directed toward the large German-speaking communities in these three states and were a manifestation of postwar xenophobia. All three legislative acts were challenged in state courts as unconstitutional, and all three state courts ruled in favor of the state (*Nebraska District of Evangelical Lutheran Synod of Missouri et al. v. McKelvie*, 175 N.W. 531 (1921); *Bohning v. State of Ohio*, 132 N.E. 20 (1921); *Pohl v. State of Ohio*, 132 N.E. 20 (1921); *Bartels v. Iowa*, 181 N.W. 508 (1921)). These state court rulings were appealed in 1923 to the United States Supreme Court, where they were overturned (262 U.S. 404 (1923)) on the grounds of violation of liberties protected under the Fourteenth Amendment (*Meyer v. Nebraska*, 262 U.S. 390 (1923)).

In 1921, the New York legislature, reacting to the fear of communism and radical political doctrine, required state approval of the curriculum in all private schools not sponsored by a religious group. State action to close a private school sponsored by the Socialist party was sustained when the school refused to follow the approval process (*People v. American Socialist Society*, 202 A.D. 640 (N.Y. 1922)).

The increasing regulatory role of the state in private schools was a cause of great concern to many. In the Preface to his 1924 study of the legal status of private schools, Charles N. Lischka concludes that there can no longer be any doubt that many legislators consider private schools not merely a part of the educational resources of the state, but practically a part of its educational system, subject to indefinite regulation and restriction. If the present tendency to make laws affecting the private school persists, a situation will gradually but inevitably arise, where private elementary schools will be purely private only in the sense that they will be allowed to teach religion, to be supported privately, and to retain direct administration. (p. 5)

Lischka's concern that private schools would be regulated to such an extent that they would be private in name only was realized sooner than he thought. The territory of Hawaii, out of a misplaced fear of foreigners, passed a series of acts and administrative regulations that resulted in near total control of foreign language schools. Suit was filed by the private schools to enjoin the territorial government from enforcing the legislation. In *Farrington v. Tokushige,* 273 U.S. 284 (1927), the Supreme Court declared the statutes unconstitutional.

With the U.S. Supreme Court rulings in *Meyer, Pierce,* and *Farrington* setting the broad parameters of state intervention in private schools, the subsiding of extreme nativism, the national preoccupation with the Depression and another world war, regulation of private schools slipped into the background of the public arena for the next 40 years. Additional regulatory efforts by the states were mostly modest, incremental, and sporadic.

By the 1980s, however, the social, religious, and educational landscape of America had changed dramatically. Not only had a Catholic been elected president, but racial segregation, prayer, and bible reading had been outlawed by the Supreme Court in public schools (*Brown v. Board of Education,* 347 U.S. 483 (1954); *Engel v. Vitale,* 370 U.S. 421 (1962); *Abington School District v. Schempp,* 374 U.S. 203 (1963)). The social upheaval of the 1960s had caused many to question traditional institutions and sources of authority. At the same time education was tied even more closely to the socialization and political goals of government, especially on the federal level, "as schools were asked to win the cold war in the 1950's, end poverty in the 1960's, . . . solve problems of unemployment in the 1970's" and re-establish the nation as the economic and technological leader of the world in the 1980s (Spring, 1986, p. 336).

The public schools saw waves of innovations and reform, with open classrooms, accountability, competency testing, and back-to-basics movements. The "interlocking directorate" of professional educators, state and federal education officials, and education departments at universities, with their version of the "one best system" and their vision of America, continued to control education with an avalanche of new programs and legislation. This was matched only by a burgeoning bureaucracy to administer and implement these new programs. Such action was often justified by the "ideology of professionalism"—the political and educational experts know best (Tyack & Hansot, 1982, p. 226). Free schools or "alternative" schools were established as educational options to the public school system. Catholic enrollment at parochial schools declined dramatically as Catholics found the public schools "de-Protestantized" by the increased secularity in society and, thus, far more palatable. The Protestant ideology, so ubiquitous in nineteenth-century public policy, had been subsumed in the twentieth century by the full flowering of Enlightenment ideology, with its secularism (indifference to religious truths), naturalism (denial of the supernatural), and positivism (limitation of inquiry only to those areas that can be investigated empirically) (Meyer, 1976; see also Whitehead & Conlan, 1978 for further discussion of this topic).

In a reactionary response to the "godlessness" of the public schools with the growing problems of discipline, drugs, sex, poor educational programs, and crime, all concurrent with instruction in sex education and evolution, many fundamentalist Protestants, other conservative groups, and concerned parents abandoned the public school system and established their own schools (Schaller, 1979, Skerry, 1980). Many no longer felt a sense of loyalty to an institution involved in practices and beliefs so offensive and alien to their own. Efforts to initiate reforms or to have a meaningful voice in determining the educational environment of children were unsuccessful. Exit was the only acceptable option left (Erickson, 1986; Hirschman, 1970).[37]

In 1961–62 there were only between 250 and 300 private Protestant schools in the entire nation. By 1984 this figure was over 6,000. Between 1971 and 1981 there was a 47% increase in the number of Protestant private schools, a 91% increase in enrollment, and a 116% increase in the number of teachers (Erickson, 1986, pp. 88–89). The explosive growth of these new, often independent and unaffiliated schools thrust the issue of private school regulation back into the forefront of the public arena.

Many of these new private schools have adamantly refused to comply with the few, if any, state regulations on the basis of First Amendment violations (see Chapter 4). These regulations are a subset of public school regulations and expand as public school regulation increases.[38] State and local education officials, firmly convinced of their expertise, often have been equally determined to enforce these regulations, with the outcome frequently determined in the courts. This has turned the issue of appropriate regulations into a policy dilemma. In the context of an increasingly pluralistic society, this social controversy has raised anew all of the old but fundamental questions about the nature of humankind and the good society, who controls the child, the power of the state, and whose values and beliefs will ultimately prevail.

Summary and Conclusion

The social, legal, and cultural context of state intervention into the operation of private elementary and secondary schools is basically the same as that for public education. Although the extent of state control in private schools is less, often far less, than that in public schools, the rationale, justifications, and legal mechanisms are identical. The state and society have the right to preserve and perpetuate themselves. The transfer of ideology and the socialization of the young into proper citizens are accomplished primarily through compulsory schooling. Compulsory schooling laws are the legal means by which this is accomplished. The justification of state control in education, or the lack of it, has ranged from the ideology of pluralism before 1830, to the ideology of common values and beliefs with the founding of the state school systems, to the ideology of technology and professionalism that took over during the first quarter of this century and still prevails today. These ideological shifts were brought about by a crisis perceived to be threatening to social stability and order.

Initial efforts to regulate private schools through compulsory schooling laws in the nineteenth century were quite modest by today's standards. Extensive regulation did not begin until the first quarter of the twentieth century and was part of the extensive intervention by the state into society as a whole. The bureaucratization of government and education, with its emphasis on uniformity and standardization, paved the way for increased regulation of private schools.

American education has borrowed much from its English heritage, transformed it, and added its own unique flavor of American Protestantism, American Enlightenment, and American nationalism, which have formed the basis of an American civil religion. A central theme in American education has been popularization of form, content, access, and control. This epitomized American education from the colonial days until the common school movement in the 1830s and 1840s.

Juxtaposed to this theme has been the drive for systemization, uniformity, standardization, and government control—in essence, the "one best system." What is disturbing about the historical record of American education is the frequent use of this system to impose cultural, ethnic, religious, and moral norms of the majority on various minority groups without allowing adequate recourse for members of these groups to choose their own best way. Private values and ideologies have been transformed into public values through codification and legislation. It has been the use of education and the law in a systematic and coercing manner to impose a majoritarian world view—with its view of humankind and society, and millennial vision—that should be unsettling not only to those associated with private schools but also to those involved with public education.

Private schools have functioned as a social safety valve, a way in which those with views and values different from the majoritarian ideology can find legitimate expression in the education of their children. Their ability to do so, however, is determined by the extent of state intervention and regulation. The centralization of decision making and socialization in the hands of the state has been a gradual process in which the spheres of influence and control have been wrested away from families, churches, communities, and other nongovernment organizations. These other sources of ideological pluralism have been severely restricted. Parents have been declared incompetent and negligent. Churches have been labeled as sectarian, narrow, and provincial. Private schools have been painted as unpatriotic and undemocratic, the bastions of aristocracy and privilege. Communities no longer have the expertise or are too small to offer the kind of education deemed adequate by the expert. The transfer of power from the private to the government sector has been massive.

The courts have frequently been the only source of protection for the rights of minorities and the preservation of pluralism in America. The courts saved private schools from legal extinction in the 1920s but left the door open for state regulation. A central concern for private schools is whether the right to exist as an educational and ideological alternative will continue to be realized in actuality or whether the encroachment by the state will be sufficient to destroy the qualities that make private education a true alternative in American education. Chapter 3 examines the constitutional protections afforded private schools as defined by the courts in their effort to retain institutional autonomy and integrity.

3 ✝ THE COURTS AND CONSTITUTIONAL CONSTRAINTS

> As governmental pressure toward unity becomes greater, so strife becomes
> more bitter as to whose unity it shall be. Probably no deeper division of our
> people could proceed from any provocation than from finding it necessary to
> choose what doctrine and whose program public education officials shall com-
> pel youth to unite in embracing.
>
> —*West Virginia Board of Education v. Barnette* (1943)

Education is an inherently value-laden enterprise. American education
has never been neutral nor has it been static. The changes in education
during the last three hundred years have been changes not only of size
but of substance as well. Education has been used to perpetuate or modify
particular ways of looking at humankind, society, and the social relationships that ought to exist in American society. Education operates in a
paradoxical fashion as it simultaneously emancipates and captivates the
student. It brings enlightenment as well as defines what is orthodox and
proper in society. The specific character of education to be selected, therefore, becomes as much a political, ideological, and moral issue as it is a
pedagogical question.

The configuration and content of American education have been
largely determined by legal devices such as constitutions, statutes, and
administrative regulations. The substance of these legal instruments has
been greatly influenced by a variety of interest groups in American politics. These interest groups and interested individuals attempt to have their
own particular values and world views legitimated and enforced as public
values and universal world views through legal codification and the police power of the state.

Nonpublic education has not escaped the pruning arm of the state
either. Through a variety of regulations and controls, private education,
like public education, has been required to conform, to a greater or lesser
degree, to the sort of educational experience deemed proper by those
social and political forces governing public education at any particular
point in time. Generally speaking, these constraining actions have gradually increased both in breadth and depth over the years since the establishment of government schools during the nineteenth century. As the

state has pursued an ever-enlarging circle of greater government control over private education, the protective response from many private schools has increasingly been litigation, a typically American form of redress.

In addition to legislative action, the courts have assumed a very prominent and important role in refining and redefining the specific contours that American education may take and the nature of the relationship between private education and the government.[1] The heightened significance of this role is due to at least two factors—a more active judiciary and an increasing number of cases being brought to trial (Glazer, 1975; Neely, 1981; Rebell & Block, 1982).

The primary purpose of this chapter is to present an overview of published opinions arising from litigation involving the state and private elementary and secondary schools in the United States. It is to discover what major issues have been brought to the courts involving the supervision and regulation of private schools by the government, the rationale behind the competing positions, the final outcome of the litigation, and the reasons supporting the various court decisions. A key objective of this chapter is to distill from the descriptive analysis of various court cases a set of directing principles delineating the current connection between the state and private education. From these basic principles the legal parameters marking the extent of public power over private education, as interpreted in court opinions, are outlined and analyzed.

This chapter contains an introductory section on the litigation involving private schools and examines the types and number of private school cases brought before state and federal appellate courts. All United States Supreme Court cases dealing with attempts by the government to supervise and regulate educational activities in private schools are summarized and analyzed. From this analysis, a set of primary legal principles is derived and explored. A sketch of the legal boundaries determining the present link between the state and private schools is made.

The brief survey of court cases in this chapter focuses on decisions of the United States Supreme Court. The reasons for using Supreme Court cases to stake out the judicial perimeters of the legal relationship between private schools and state government are threefold. One, to the Supreme Court is delegated the power to declare with finality the constitutionality of federal and state laws and the minimum level of protection of basic rights that must be given to all citizens. It sets the limits of permissibility on legislation and the police power of the state (*Marbury v. Madison*, 5 U.S. (1 Cranch) 137 (1803)). Second, the Supreme Court deals with fundamental issues of common concern and general application. And third, the magnitude and complexity of issues discussed in a single chapter preclude an extensive review of all or even a majority of court cases between private schools and the state. A few rulings from lower courts will be included, however, to supplement areas that the Supreme Court has not fully addressed or has declined to address.

INTRODUCTION

The eclipse of private elementary and secondary education by state-sponsored schools during the last quarter of the nineteenth century cast the perspectives of private school partisans into the category of minority viewpoints. This was a significant social and political phenomenon in education. The tie between nationalism and state education became formalized. Education became systematized, centralized, and bureaucratized. The power to make educational decisions shifted significantly from the private sector to the government sector. Education became politicized. What had once been the dominant and distinguishing feature of American education was now relegated to a minor role. Instead of exemplifying and defining the essence of American education, private schools became educational and social outsiders. They did not fit neatly into the emerging orthodoxy that defined what it meant to be an American—white, Protestant, Anglo-Saxon, and middle class. For a few public school zealots such as James Carter and Henry Bernard, extinction of the private school alternative would have been preferable.

Like many groups with nonmajoritarian status, the capacity of private school groups, such as the Germans in Nebraska and the Catholics in Oregon, to exercise any substantive influence on public policy decisions that affected them in a negative way was minimal (Tyack, James, & Benavot, 1987). Lacking the political clout of the majority, unaware of or unable to access administrative hearings, and often facing an unsympathetic government bureaucracy, minority groups, individuals, and private schools turned increasingly to the courts for redress of perceived wrongs. Although the results, as found in published court opinions, have been uneven, litigation in the twentieth century has become an important avenue for balancing the interests of the majority against the rights of individuals or groups holding different opinions of proper public policy (Tyack, James, & Benavot, 1987). Litigation also serves as one measure of social consensus on public policy, of social conflict, and of the degree of toleration and pluralism in American society.

Table 3.1 shows the number of private school cases by category that have been brought before the state and federal appellate courts from 1658 to 1986.[2] Of the 639 appellate cases recorded since the first private school

TABLE 3.1 Number of state and federal appellate cases dealing with private schools, 1817–1986.

	1817–1907	1907–1916	1916–1926	1926–1936	1936–1946	1946–1956	1956–1966	1966–1976	1976–1986	Case totals	% of total
1. Establishment and status in general	3	0	0	0	3	8	7	4	9	34	5%
2. Incorporation and organization	3	2	2	0	4	2	0	3	1	17	3%
3. Public aid	8	1	1	3	8	7	11	44	36	119	19%
4. Regulation and supervision	4	1	4	0	2	11	13	12	39	86	13%
5. Property, funds, contracts, and liabilities	21	1	7	4	4	16	21	17	10	101	16%
6. Governing board and officers	4	1	0	2	0	3	0	2	1	13	2%
7. Teachers and other instructors	4	3	1	2	2	3	4	11	16	46	7%
8. Pupils, tuition, and discipline	9	9	12	21	8	12	8	57	87	223	35%
Totals	56(6.22)*	18	27	32	31	62	64	150	199	639	100%
Percent for each decade	1.0**	2.8	4.2	5.0	4.9	9.7	10.0	23.5	31.1	100%	
Population in millions	35.9**	92.0	105.7	122.8	131.7	150.7	178.5	203.3	226.5		
Number of cases/million of population	0.17**	0.20	0.26	0.26	0.24	0.41	0.36	0.74	0.88		

*Average total cases per decade for time period 1817–1907
**Average for time period 1817–1907

case in 1822, over 91% (583) occurred in the past 80 years and nearly 55% (349) in the past 20 years.[3] This parallels the increasing tendency in American society of resorting to litigation to resolve social conflict.

The breakdown of appellate cases into the eight categories shows a rough grouping into three sets. The "Pupils, Tuition and Discipline" category not only contains the highest number of cases (35%) but is nearly double the amount of "Public Aid," the second highest category.[4] The second cluster contains three categories that are approximate in size, "Public Aid" (19%), "Property, Funds, Contracts and Liabilities" (16%) and "Regulation and Supervision" (13%). "Teachers and Other Instructors" (7%), "Establishment and Status in General" (5%), "Incorporation and Organization" (3%), and "Governing Board and Officers" (2%) complete the third set.

Within this general setting of appellate cases dealing with private schools, cases concerning regulation and supervision of private schools have also increased dramatically. Fifty-nine percent of these cases occurred from 1966 to 1986, with 45% of the cases appearing in the past 10 years. The category of "Regulation and Supervision" ranks fourth overall but was the second highest category, behind "Pupils, Tuition and Discipline" during the latest decennial period of 1976–1986.

One possible source of the increase in litigation may be due to a simple increase in the population. The data in Table 3.1, however, still show an increase in court cases when the population is held constant over each of the 10-year periods. The average number of cases for each decade in the nineteenth century per million population was 0.17. The number of cases per million population increased over 500% to 0.88 cases by the latest decennial period of 1976–1986. As shown in Figure 3.1, which graphically illustrates the data from Table 3.1, the number of private school cases being appealed has simply multiplied at a much faster rate than the increase in the population, especially in the past 20 years.[5]

This striking increase in litigation suggests an escalating level of educational conflict between private schools and the state. The forces behind such increase could be any number or combination of factors. Former methods of resolving differences and reaching compromises at a local level or in an informal manner may not be working any longer. There may be a more determined effort by the state to enforce existing statutes and regulations, or the state may be creating new or additional legislation aimed at a greater regulatory role over private schools. Whatever the exact cause(s) may be, the dramatic rise in court cases involving private schools suggests that state regulation of private schools is a significant and rapidly growing problem. It is an important matter that needs to be thoughtfully and carefully addressed.

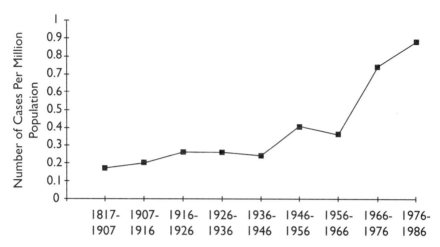

FIGURE 3.1 Number of State and Federal Appellate Cases Dealing With Private Schools Per Million Population

THE SUPREME COURT AND THE REGULATION OF PRIVATE SCHOOLS

The American judicial system is based on a case law approach where court decisions decide what is the law. Precedence becomes critical in any decision. Present decisions are guided by past decisions and become the foundation for future decisions. The approach, therefore, used in examining the relevant Supreme Court cases will be chronological.

Decisions of the United States Supreme Court determine the legality of government action on a federal, state, and local level. These decisions cannot be appealed and have the force of law. They cannot be overturned except by a subsequent ruling by the Supreme Court or by a constitutional amendment and thus become the standard that all other courts use in arriving at their decisions. The rulings by the Supreme Court establish a minimum level of protection for rights and liberties guaranteed under the United States Constitution. Federal, state, and local governments may grant new rights or expand existing ones, but they cannot reduce or eliminate the basic rights enunciated by the Constitution and interpreted by the Supreme Court. It is essential, therefore, that any study of legal parameters begin with rulings by the United States Supreme Court. This provides the foundation upon which an understanding of the legal issues is built.

Dartmouth College v. Woodward, 17 U.S. (4 Wheat.) 518 (1819)

In 1816 the New Hampshire legislature passed two acts that altered significantly the structure of the board of trustees of Dartmouth College, a private college established by a charter from George III in 1769. The changes would have allowed the state government to gain control of the operations and property of the college through the appointment of trustees by the governor. The board of trustees filed suit against the state of New Hampshire. The superior court of New Hampshire upheld the legality of the legislative action, whereupon the trustees appealed to the Supreme Court. In a landmark decision, the Supreme Court overturned the lower court ruling and declared the legislative acts in violation of Article I, Section 10 of the United States Constitution, which forbids any state to "pass any bill . . . impairing the obligation of contracts." In validating the original charter, the Supreme Court affirmed the right of all private bodies or institutions to be free from arbitrary interference from the state and to control and direct what they had established. In other words, a private institution is a "person," and as such has a right to exist and pursue its own interests just as an individual does and to enjoy the same constitutional protections from unwarranted intrusions by the state.

Berea College v. Commonwealth of Kentucky, 211 U.S. 45 (1908)

While private institutions are given constitutional protection, the scope of the protection may be less than that afforded to individuals and may be circumscribed by legislation.

In 1904 the Kentucky legislature passed an act forbidding the simultaneous instruction of white and black children in the same school. Berea College, a private nonsectarian school, was indicted for violating the act. The college filed suit against the state of Kentucky contending that the act was unconstitutional in light of liberties guaranteed in the Fourteenth Amendment[6] and that the word "person" in the Amendment is applicable to corporations as well (211 U.S. at 50). An appeal of lower court rulings in favor of the state was made to the Supreme Court (Circuit Court, Madison County, 94 S.W. 623 (Ky. 1906)).

In a split decision, Mr. Justice Brewer, speaking for the Court, affirmed the lower court rulings. Berea College had been incorporated under the statutes of the state of Kentucky in 1854 and reincorporated in 1899. These statutes contained a provision that allowed the state the right to revoke, alter, or amend "'every grant of a franchise, privilege or exemption'" (211 U.S. at 57). This power to change the conditions of incorporation is not absolute and cannot "'defeat or substantially impair the

object of the grant'" (211 U.S. at 57). Although the act of 1904 prohibiting the instruction of black and white children together did indeed
amend the original charter calling for the "'education of all persons who
may attend,'" it did not completely inhibit the school from doing so (211
U.S. at 65). It simply could not teach black and white children at the same
place at the same time.[7]

It must be noted that there are several substantive differences between the *Dartmouth* and *Berea* cases. Dartmouth College, unlike Berea
College, had been created by charter from George III in 1769 before the
New Hampshire legislature existed. The state of New Hampshire was unable to justify its actions on the basis of pre-existing provisions. In contrast, Berea College was incorporated under the general statutes of Kentucky, which also granted the legislature the "full power of amendment"
(211 U.S. at 57). Furthermore, the state of Kentucky was not attempting
to gain full control of Berea College, as was the case with Dartmouth
College.

The *Berea* decision modified the extent to which private schools were
considered as "persons" in the Fourteenth Amendment. The Court maintained that "in creating a corporation a State may withhold powers which
may be exercised by and cannot be denied to an individual. It is under
no obligation to treat both alike (211 U.S. at 54). All of this may be true;
however, a corporation is but a group of individuals so the distinction
seems to be more self-serving than real.

If private body or school is incorporated under state law, the state
may, at any time and for almost any reason, significantly change or alter
the conditions of the charter. The Court quoted approvingly the assertion
made by the Kentucky Court of Appeals that the college "as a corporation
created by this state, has no natural right to teach at all. Its right to teach
is such as the state sees fit to give to it. The state may withhold it altogether, or qualify it" (*Berea College v. Commonwealth*, 94 S.W. 623, 629 (Ky.
1906); 211 U.S. at 53). Of crucial importance was the assertion of the
lower court that the "state may withhold it [the right to teach] altogether,
or qualify it." The court seems to be suggesting that the nature of the
educational experience and even the right of private schools to exist, as
such, is entirely up to the state.

Meyer v. Nebraska, 262 U.S. 390 (1923)[8]

The right of the state to "qualify" what a private school may teach
was brought before the Court for the first time in 1923.

Mr. Meyer, a teacher in Zion Parochial School, was convicted of violating a 1919 Nebraska statute prohibiting the teaching of any modern

language, except English, to any child who had not yet successfully completed the eighth grade.[9] Specifically, Mr. Meyer had taught reading in German, using a collection of Bible stories, to Raymond Parpart, a student who had not completed the eighth grade and was enrolled in a parochial school sponsored by the Zion Evangelical Lutheran Congregation. The district court conviction was appealed to the Nebraska Supreme Court where it was upheld. An appeal was subsequently made to the Supreme Court. Counsel for the plaintiff argued that the Nebraska statute was unconstitutional because it violated liberty rights guaranteed by the Fourteenth Amendment in the following ways: individuals had the right to pursue a legitimate vocation in which the rights of others were not infringed; teaching a foreign language was not "inherently immoral or inimical to the public welfare"; the statute created an unjustified contraction of knowledge; the statute did not "allow each person to live his own life in his own way, unhampered by unreasonable and arbitrary restrictions;" and equal protection was denied since the law prohibited the teaching of modern languages only in schools and not by private teachers or tutors (262 U.S. at 391–393). The state of Nebraska contended that a "danger exists" where children of foreign immigrants would not be sufficiently Americanized if they learned a foreign language in their "tender years." The key elements of Americanization included English as the mother tongue and "sympathy with the principles and ideals of this country." There was an implied assumption that the learning of a foreign language indoctrinated one with a particular set of national, cultural, ethical, and civic values (262 U.S. at 393–395).

The Court's split decision delivered by Justice McReynolds struck down the Nebraska statute as unconstitutional and reversed the decisions of the lower courts. The decision of the Court proceeded first to lay the constitutional groundwork in explaining the general nature and application of the Fourteenth Amendment. The Court specified some of the liberties guaranteed by the Amendment. These included

> freedom from bodily restraint . . . right of the individual to contract, to engage in any of the common occupations of life, to acquire useful knowledge, to marry, to establish a home and bring up children, to worship God . . . and generally enjoy those privileges long recognized at common law as essential to the orderly pursuit of happiness by free men. (262 U.S. at 399)

The Court further stated that the

> established doctrine is that this liberty may not be interfered with, under the guise of protecting the public interest, by legislative action which is arbitrary

or without reasonable relation to some purpose within the competency of the State to effect. (262 U.S. at 399–400)

In addressing the particular case at hand, the Court made four major points in support of its decision that the state action was arbitrary and unreasonable (262 U.S. at 400–403). First, the statute clearly infringed on the rights of modern language teachers to pursue their vocation. Second, it limited the rights of children to learn. Third, it encroached on the duty and right of parents to direct the education of their children. Fourth, the means used by the state to "foster a homogeneous people" exceeded its authority in violating the right of the individual to be left alone. This was especially true in view of the fact that the nation was basking in a season "of peace and domestic tranquility." There did not exist any threatening conditions that would justify such a long reach by the arm of the state to Americanize immigrant children.

The issues of compulsory education and "reasonable regulations for all schools [public or private]" were not matters in dispute and thus were not addressed by the Court (262 U.S. at 402). The Court simply ruled that the Nebraska statute forbidding the teaching of modern languages to children before the completion of eighth grade was "arbitrary and without reasonable relation to any end within the competency of the state" (262 U.S. at 403). Thus it "unreasonably infringe[d] the liberty guaranteed . . . by the Fourteenth Amendment" (262 U.S. at 399).

Pierce v. Society of Sisters, 268 U.S. 510 (1925)

While the *Meyer* case placed a very modest limit on what the state may "qualify" in granting private schools a right to teach, the first case to determine whether a state may "withhold it [the right to teach] altogether" was not heard until 1925.

In November 1922 an initiative was passed by the voters of Oregon amending Section 5259 of the Laws of Oregon known as the Oregon Compulsory Education Act.[10] With exemptions for children who were handicapped, lived too far from school, or had completed the eighth grade, parents or guardians were required to enroll any child between the ages of 8 and 16 in a public school.

Two private schools, a religious school and a military academy, filed suit in district court asking that the state of Oregon be enjoined from enforcing the amended compulsory education law (*Society of Sisters v. Pierce* and *Hill Military Academy v. Same,* 296 F. 928 (D. Ore. 1924)). The district court ruled that the amended statute was unconstitutional because it would deprive private schools of their property without due process and of their right to teach, and would deny parents of the right to direct the education of their children. An injunction was granted prohibiting the state from executing the amendment. The state then appealed the decision to the United States Supreme Court.

In their appeal before the Supreme Court, the state of Oregon defended the constitutionality of the amended education law by arguing two basic points. One, the revised statute was legitimate and lawful. Second, the execution of the statute by the state would not result in any violations of protected rights or liberties.

By virtue of its police power, the state of Oregon has the authority to "enact laws to promote the health, safety, peace and morals, education or general welfare of its people," the Fourteenth Amendment notwithstanding (268 U.S. at 511, 527). This Amendment does not deprive states of their police powers. The Tenth Amendment to the U.S. Constitution secures the right to states in those areas not expressly mentioned. Education is not mentioned in the Constitution. The provision of education is a state function, and compulsory education laws are an expression of the state's interest and duty to promote the general welfare of the public. Under the legal doctrine of *parens patriae,* the state, in the exercise of its police power, has "unlimited supervision and control over their [minors'] contracts, occupation and conduct, and the liberty and right of those who assume to deal with them" (268 U.S. at 512).

The state of Oregon held that an essential part of the state's duty to its citizens was to ensure that they were properly trained to perform their civic responsibilities and obligations so that domestic tranquility and prosperity were secured. The additional proviso, that all children be educated in public schools, was but a logical and legitimate extension of the state's obligation to safeguard its citizens from the " 'moral pestilence of paupers, vagabonds, . . . convicts,' " to avert "internal dissentions" along religious and ethnic lines, and to prevent the ignorant from being seduced by "certain economic doctrines entirely destructive of the fundamentals of our government," as advocated by "bolshevists, syndicalists and communists" (268 U.S. at 524–526). Unless all are trained to be "patriotic and law-abiding citizens," the state would not be fully "prepared for war . . . in times of public danger" (268 U.S. at 524–526, 528).

Although none of the social dangers and disorders listed by the state of Oregon had actually transpired, the fact that they might occur was sufficient reason to justify the amended statute. Private schools were the primary target of the state for two reasons. One was that they were not under the control of the state and thus constituted a potential breeding ground for socially divisive and unpatriotic ideas. The state argued that if the amended school law was not declared constitutional, "there will be nothing to prevent the establishment of private schools, the main purpose of which will be to teach disloyalty to the United States" (268 U.S. at 528). The second reason was that most of the children who had not enrolled in public schools (and presumably had enrolled in private schools) were immigrants or their parents were. In the mind of the state, private schools represented the worst possible situation. What they taught was beyond the control of the state and a majority of their students were those most susceptible to dangerous ideas and in the greatest need to be American-ized with proper social and political values. The statute, therefore, was rational and reasonably related to the interests of the state in perpetuating itself and the establishment of a moral and productive society.

The state's position, as summarized by the Court, also maintained that the revised education law did not unnecessarily deprive any legiti-mate party of its constitutional rights. There was no deprivation of prop-erty without due process. The government is not liable for business losses incidental to legislation, and if the state decides to "engage in any field, the question of the effect upon private business is immaterial" (268 U.S. at 522). Besides, private schools may teach students during times that students are not required to be in attendance at public schools. Further-more, private school teachers who are qualified may be employed in the public schools.

No person, the state insisted, was being deprived of any liberties. The two private schools as corporations are "artificial" not "natural" persons and, therefore, do not fall under the protections offered by the Four-teenth Amendment. The parents and students are "natural persons" and thus come under the liberty protections of the Fourteenth Amendment, but they have no legal standing or "recognized legal interest" in this case as third parties. In addition, parents can still have their children partici-pate in religious and ethnic education outside of public school hours. The statute in question does not infringe on the religious liberty of anyone (268 U.S. at 512). Furthermore, there is no violation of the Equal Protec-tion Clause. The statute is not discriminatory and is applicable to all stu-dents in the same manner.

Finally, in response to allegations by the private schools that the new education law violated the "obligation of contracts" clause in Article 1, Section 10 of the *United States Constitution,* the state argued that the char-ters of the schools had not been changed or amended by the state action. The private schools were quite free to offer instruction. The only restric-tion was the availability of students during certain times of the year and day. Moreover, any charters, contracts, or agreements entered into by the private schools "are subject to modification and annulment under the police power" (268 U.S. at 512).

In asking the Court to affirm the lower court ruling, the two private schools argued that the amended statute was "arbitrary and oppressive . . . having no reasonable relation to . . . promot[ing] the public welfare" (268 U.S. at 528). It would not change or improve the effects of the compulsory education laws. The same number of children would be attending school. It was not necessary to ensure an educated citizenry. It was excessive in its effort to address public concerns such as the Americanization of immigrants and the teaching of subversive and un-American ideas. The state could pass specific legislation making the teaching of subversive and disloyal ideas a criminal act if such a threat to public safety existed. Furthermore, the state had the power to require teachers to be licensed and meet certain standards of conduct in order to teach, and to regulate private schools to ensure that students received a proper education. Americanization was not sufficient justification for the enactment of a "prohibitory statute" (268 U.S. at 516, 519). Furthermore, only seven-and-a-half percent of the state population were unnaturalized, and only a small percentage of those had children who attended private schools. In addition, there was no evidence that private schools were any less effective than public schools in Americanizing the foreign population or in providing an adequate education. The need for such a draconian measure simply did not exist—other less drastic remedies were available to address the concerns raised—nor would it result in any discernible improvement in the education of Oregon children (268 U.S. at 517).

In the opinion of the private schools, the statute was a "wanton abuse of power" (268 U.S. at 516). It not only failed to serve any rational or advantageous purpose, but it arbitrarily infringed on the liberties of private schools, private school teachers, parents, and children. The "true purpose of the act, as well as its plain and intended practical effect, was the destruction of private, primary, preparatory and parochial schools" (268 U.S. at 514). The freedom of private schools to engage in a lawful business would be denied, and their property would be lost without due process. Private school teachers would be unable to enjoy their right to pursue a legitimate profession, and parents and students would be denied the choice of a private education. The statute was clearly an unlawful impairment of the "obligation of contract" embodied in the charters of the two corporations. The laws of Oregon, unlike those in Kentucky, did not grant the state authority to "alter, amend, or repeal the charter" (268 U.S. at 520).

In addition to the institutional concerns of the schools themselves, the two private schools viewed the amended compulsory education law as a massive and serious invasion of parental rights. The child belongs to the parent and not the state. The right of parents to direct the education of their children "is a most substantial part of the liberty and freedom of the parent" (268 U.S. at 518).

In addition to refuting the state's arguments about the pressing need for, social benefits of, and absence of any unlawful infringement on protected liberties in the revised compulsory education law, the private schools pointed out the positive and valuable contributions of private education to American society. Private schools have always played an important part of our national history. They not only educated our founding fathers but have served as sources of education innovation and experimentation. The statute goes against this long tradition of educational and social pluralism in Oregon public policy and "embodies the pernicious policy of state monopoly of education" (268 U.S. at 514–515, 519).

Mr. Justice McReynolds, in delivering the unanimous opinion of the Court, affirmed the district court ruling, striking down the amended statute as unconstitutional. This opinion of the court is the landmark decision for private schools and has been referred to by some as the "Magna Carta" for private schools.[11]

After a brief recital of the facts, the Court agreed that the practical consequences of the statute would be the destruction of the two schools and probably all other similar schools. The Court judged the bill to be an excessive and improper use of police power by the state. The supporting rationale for the decision came from a substantive due process interpretation of the Fourteenth Amendment and the lack of sufficient and substantial evidence by the state of Oregon justifying the breach of those protected liberties. Speaking of the parental right and liberty to direct the education of children, the Court declared that

> under the doctrine of *Meyer v. Nebraska,* 262 U.S. 390, we think it entirely plain that the Act of 1922 unreasonably interferes with the liberty of parents and guardians to direct the upbringing and education of children under their control. . . . The fundamental theory of liberty upon which all governments in this Union repose excludes any general power of the State to standardize its children by forcing them to accept instruction from public teachers only. The child is not a mere creature of the state; those who nurture him and direct his destiny have the right, coupled with the high duty, to recognize and prepare him for additional obligations. (268 U.S. at 534–535)

Private schools are corporations and while they technically cannot seek relief under the Fourteenth Amendment, their business and property interests are at great risk and probable loss because of the "arbitrary, unreasonable and unlawful interference with their patrons" and "this court has gone very far to protect against loss threatened by such action" (268 U.S. at 536, 535).

In addition, the Court ruled that the government did not demonstrate a state interest of sufficient magnitude to override the loss of liberties that would be suffered by private schools and their patrons if the amended statute were implemented. "There are no peculiar circumstances or present emergencies," declared the Court, "which demand extraordinary measures relative to primary education." Neither was there any evidence that the private schools were involved in anything "inherently harmful . . . or that they have failed to discharge their obligations to patrons, students or the State" (268 U.S. at 534).

The key issues brought before the Court in *Pierce v. Society of Sisters* were whether private schools had a constitutional right to exist as an alternative to public education and whether parents had a constitutional right to direct the education of their children.[12] The decision of the Court was an unequivocal affirmative response on both counts.

The related matter of the right of the state to regulate private schools was never an issue for either party and thus was not addressed by the Court.[13]

> No question is raised concerning the power of the State reasonably to regulate all schools, to inspect, supervise and examine them, their teachers and pupils; to require that all children of proper age attend some school, that teachers be of good moral character and patriotic disposition, that certain studies plainly essential to good citizenship must be taught, and that nothing be taught which is manifestly inimical to the public welfare. (268 U.S. at 534)

The private schools openly conceded the right of the state to impose "valid" regulations.

> We do not question the right of the state to regulate private schools in the interest of public welfare, to require that proper sanitary and safety precautions be observed, or that certain standards be complied with. (*Oregon School Cases*, 1925, p. 335; see also pp. 653, 659–660, 675, 680 and *Pierce*, 268 U.S. at 519) The Supreme Court acknowledged this in its ruling.[14]

Like compulsory education laws, state regulations are not mandatory but permissive and discretionary legislative acts. Both are circumscribed by the requirement that they be "reasonable" and related to some legitimate purpose of the state. The *Pierce* case provides the touchstone for all cases dealing with rights of parents and private schools in education.

Farrington v. Tokushige, 273 U.S. 284 (1927)

Private schools have the right to operate, and the state has the right to impose reasonable regulations on the conduct of these schools. An important question left unanswered by the *Pierce* decision was what constitutes "reasonable regulations." While *Farrington v. Tokushige* does not fully address this question, it presents an interesting variation on the issues dealt with in the *Meyer* and *Pierce* cases and defines in one instance what is *not* "reasonable."

The legislature of Hawaii passed a bill in 1920 regulating foreign language schools, with subsequent amendments in 1923 and 1925, with the avowed purpose "that the Americanism of the pupils may be promoted." The Department of Education issued regulations pursuant to the implementation of the Act. Among other things the Act and regulations defined a "foreign language school" as "any school which is conducted in any language other than the English or Hawaiian language." The sweeping scope of this definition included not only language schools per se but private elementary and secondary schools (which were "equivalent" to public schools and had to be approved by the Department) that used another language other than English or Hawaiian as the medium of instruction. Owners and teachers in both types of schools were required to obtain an annual permit from the Department of Education and sign an oath swearing they would follow and obey the requirements of the Act and any regulations issued by the Department. In addition, they promised to properly Americanize their pupils. The owners were also required to pay an annual fee amounting to one dollar per student enrolled during the previous year and file a report with the Department of "all pupils in attendance . . . [giving] name, sex, parents or guardians, place of birth and residence." Teachers had to demonstrate to the Department that they were "possessed of the ideals of democracy; knowledge of American history and institutions and [knew] how to read, write, and speak the English language" (273 U.S. at 293). Foreign language schools could not hold classes during the time prior to the beginning of public school classes or during the time public school classes were conducted. Attendance at foreign language schools was limited to a maximum of 1 hour per day, 6 hours per week, and 38 weeks per year. Students who had not completed the first and second grade in a public school or its equivalent or completed the eighth grade or reached 14 years of age could not enroll in a foreign language school (273 U.S. at 294). The *coup de grâce* was that

> in every foreign language school no subjects of study shall be taught, nor courses of study followed, nor entrance, nor attendance qualifications required, nor textbooks used, other than as prescribed or permitted by the department. (273 U.S. at 295)

Compliance with these regulations would be ensured by Department inspectors who had the right to "inspect the buildings, equipment, records and teaching thereof and the text-books used therein" (273 U.S. at 295).

These private schools brought suit against Farrington, the territorial governor, and others asking that the governing officials be prohibited from implementing the Act and the Department regulations. Both the district court and court of appeals granted an injunction against the territory (*Farrington v. Tokushige* 11 F.2d 710). The territorial government then appealed to the Supreme Court, urging a reversal of the lower court rulings.

The territorial government of Hawaii built its case on three main contentions. First, the Act, its amendments, and the regulations were substantively different from those struck down in *Pierce, Meyer,* and *Bartels* because they did not prohibit private schools. They merely set out means by which the territory could "supervise and control" the foreign language schools (273 U.S. at 285). Second, these legislative and regulatory actions were a proper use of police power because the government had a legitimate "interest in the quality of its citizenship" and because of the "extensive power with respect to infants" derived from the doctrine of *parens patriae* (273 U.S. at 286). Third, the enactments served two beneficial purposes by reducing the "evils" caused by these schools teaching their pupils "loyalty to a foreign country and disloyalty to their own country, and hampering them during their tender years in the learning of their own language" (273 U.S. at 286). These government controls would also assist the schools to be more "efficient" in teaching foreign languages, while "not interfering in the least with the proper maintenance of these schools" (273 U.S. at 286).

The foreign language schools attacked the constitutionality of the statute and regulations on the basis that they unjustifiably encroached on the right of parents to direct the education of their children. The enactments intervened to a far greater extent in the educational choice of parents and students than had been allowed by the Court in *Meyer, Pierce,* and *Bartels.* The government's reach into the operations of these schools had resulted in complete "control and direction in the education of [the] child" (273 U.S. at 288). The schools were "prohibited from employing a teacher, teaching a subject, using a book, admitting a pupil, or engaging in any activity of any nature, unless approved by the state" (273 U.S. at 288–289). The consequence of such excessive intervention was "to make them public schools in all but the name" (273 U.S. at 288). Furthermore, these schools were required to pay an "exorbitant fee," which was not required of other private schools. All of this was being done even though there were no "evils" of disloyal teachings taking place in these schools. No evidence was presented showing that anything "un-American is taught in the foreign language schools" (273 U.S. at 288, 296).

The government's position was deficient on two counts. The legislation and regulations contained elements that far exceeded similar statutes that had been declared unconstitutional. The state also had failed to demonstrate that a problem of Americanization existed in foreign language schools and that such a problem, if it had existed, was of sufficient importance to override the liberty claims of the parents and children.

Mr. Justice McReynolds again gave the opinion for the Court, which affirmed the rulings of the lower courts. The statutes were a "deliberate plan to bring foreign language schools under strict government control." In doing so they went

> beyond mere regulation . . . [and gave] affirmative direction concerning the intimate and essential details of such schools, intrust their control to public officers, and deny both owners and patrons reasonable choice and discretion in respect of teachers, curriculum and text-books. Enforcement . . . probably would destroy most, if not all of them; and certainly, it would deprive parents of fair opportunity to procure for their children instruction which they think important. (273 U.S. at 298)

The learning of a foreign language was not "in conflict with any public interest" or "harmful" but "instruction deemed valuable" by the children's parents. The territorial government also failed to demonstrate any "adequate reason" for such stringent measures (273 U.S. at 298). While the Fourteenth Amendment preserves the rights of parents to direct the education of their children free from excessive state control, the Fifth Amendment secures the same protection to individuals from unreasonable intrusions from the "federal government and agencies set up by Congress for the government of the Territory" (273 U.S. at 299).

The importance of the *Farrington* case lies in the fact that while states may not prohibit private schools but can regulate them (*Pierce*), regulations may be unconstitutional if they are too extensive. Not only must there be a *de jure* recognition that private schools can operate, but the situation must be *de facto* as well. That is, a real choice must actually exist for both parents and children. Excessive regulations can result in the same situation and circumstances as legislation prohibiting private schools. It is unconstitutional for states to use regulation as a back-door approach to accomplish what they legally cannot do with an open statute—establish a public school monopoly.[15]

Wisconsin v. Yoder, 406 U.S. 205 (1972)

Wisconsin v. Yoder introduces explicitly an issue that was always lurking in the background of the preceding three cases—liberties protected from government intrusion by the First Amendment.[16] In particular it considers free exercise claims against state approval of an alternative educational program.

In fall 1968, Jonas Yoder, Adin Yutzy, and Wallace Miller, all members of the Amish religion, refused to enroll their children in the ninth grade at the local public high school. Frieda Yoder, Vernon Yutzy, and Barbara Miller had previously attended the public schools and had successfully completed the eighth grade. Wisconsin compulsory education law required the attendance of all children between the ages of 7 and 16 years at a public school or private school or elsewhere where the instruction was "substantially equivalent" to that found in public schools. In an attempt to avert litigation and seek an amicable and fair resolution, the three fathers offered a compromise by suggesting that an Amish vocational training program be considered an acceptable alternative by the state for the 2 years beyond the eighth grade. A similar arrangement had already been approved and established in Pennsylvania. The state rejected the proposal because the vocational training program would not be "substantially equivalent" to the instruction found in the local schools.[17] The trial court subsequently found the three fathers guilty of breaking the law. The circuit court sustained the convictions, whereupon an appeal was filed with the state supreme court (*State v. Yoder*, 182 N.W.2d 539 (Wis. 1971)).

The fathers did not object to having their children receive a basic education and attending public schools up through the eighth grade. Such limited contact with society was acceptable to the Amish religion, which required its members, collectively and individually, to be separate and apart from the world or society as a whole. Elementary schools reflected more of the character and values of the local community. Attendance at a consolidated high school after the completion of eighth grade, however, brought Amish adolescents in direct contact with schools that taught "an unacceptable value system" and sought "to integrate ethnic groups into a homogenized society." This exposure, the fathers felt, would cause the Amish children to become alienated from their religious faith and heritage. In allowing this to happen, the Amish fathers maintained that their salvation as well as that of the children would be lost and the Amish community and religious life eventually destroyed. Thus in the minds of the Amish, the choice was either compliance with a state statute or adherence to religious convictions (*State v. Yoder* at 541–542. Also see Harris, 1972; Herrick, 1972; Karland, 1973.).

In response to the Amish claims of free exercise violations, the state contended that the compulsory education law did not infringe on any aspect of Amish worship or religious practice. Furthermore, in its role as *parens patriae,* the state had the right to supervise children to a greater degree than is allowed over adults. In addition, if an exemption from the statute was granted to the Amish, it would place the state in a position of violating the Establishment Clause of the First Amendment because of the preferred treatment. Also, the exemption would incur "administrative expense and inconvenience" (*State v. Yoder* at 542–543, 545).

In weighing the claims of both parties, the state supreme court reversed the lower court rulings, declaring that the state had not demonstrated an interest of sufficient magnitude to outweigh the obvious encroachment on the rights of the fathers to practice their religion. An appeal was then made by the state to the U.S. Supreme Court (*Wisconsin v. Yoder,* 406 U.S. 205 (1972)).

In delivering the opinion of the Court affirming the decision of the Wisconsin Supreme Court, Chief Justice Burger reviewed in some detail the intimate connection of the Amish religion and way of life with their objection to pursuing a conventional education beyond the eighth grade. The Amish opposed this particular type of education for two basic reasons. First, such education was carried out "in an environment hostile to Amish beliefs" and, second, the kind of knowledge learned in a typical formal educational experience provided by the state had the tendency "to develop values" that "alienate men from God" (406 U.S. at 209–213).

On the other hand, the Court acknowledged the important responsibility of the state to see that all children are provided with an adequate education. Furthermore, "there is no doubt as to the power of a State . . . to impose reasonable regulations for the control and duration of basic education" (406 U.S. at 213). Yet this power "is by no means absolute to the exclusion or subordination of all other interests" but must go through a "balancing process when it impinges on fundamental rights and interests" (406 U.S. at 215, 214).

In balancing the competing claims, the Court emphasized how the "Amish religious faith and their mode of life [were] . . . inseparable and interdependent" and that the Wisconsin compulsory education law requiring "formal education after the eighth grade would gravely endanger if not destroy the free exercise of respondent's religious beliefs" (406 U.S. at 215, 219). The state acknowledged the right of the Amish to believe whatever they desired, but asserted the right to regulate all conduct related to religious practice. The Court held, however, that there are "areas of conduct protected by the Free Exercise Clause . . . beyond the power of the State to control [and that] . . . belief and action cannot be neatly confined in logic-tight compartments" (406 U.S. at 220). The Court further rejected state claims that the compulsory education law applied to everyone, was nondiscriminatory, and was a legitimate state interest. "A regulation neutral on its face," observed the Court, "may, in its application, nonetheless offend the constitutional requirement for government neutrality if it unduly burdens the free exercise of religion" (406 U.S. at 220).

The Court then turned its attention to the more substantive aspects of the state's position. The state asserted that its interest in requiring all children to have a formal education until 16 was a "compelling" one that justified the infringement on the free exercise rights of the Amish. This interest was of sufficient magnitude because of the importance of providing each child with the skills necessary to "participate effectively and intelligently in our open political system" and "to be self-reliant and self-sufficient participants in society" (406 U.S. at 221). While accepting the state's point as valid, the Court declared these interests were "by no means absolute to the exclusion or subordination of all other interests" (406 U.S. at 215). The Court also was not convinced that the additional 2 years of formal education would be of any significant consequence for an Amish child and would be "at best a speculative gain" (406 U.S. at 227). The Amish conducted an informal vocational training program and the child was being prepared not for modern society but for "life in the segregated agrarian community that is the keystone of the Amish faith" (406 U.S. at 222). Apparently, the state's argument would have carried more weight if the child were being prepared to live in modern society.

And finally, the state advanced an intriguing argument under the doctrine of *parens patriae* that Amish children are entitled certain educational rights such as a secondary education and should be allowed to attend high school if they desired. The Court held that such a position was in direct conflict with the "primary role of the parents in the upbringing of their children [which] is now established beyond debate as an enduring American tradition" (406 U.S. at 232). The state's contention becomes even less persuasive when parental rights in directing the education of their children also involve First Amendment claims and the lack of any evidence that the parent's decision would "jeopardize the health or safety of the child, or have potential for significant social burdens" (406 U.S. at 233–234).[18]

The Court concluded that because of the First and Fourteenth Amendments, the state of Wisconsin could not compel the three fathers to send their children to high school for further formal education until they reached the age of 16. The uniqueness of the Amish religion and its way of life, and the marginal difference between the alternative education provided by the Amish and the additional 2 years of formal education required by the state, overcame any compelling interest demonstrated by the state. This did not mean, however, that the state could not establish reasonable standards for the Amish vocational training program that would substitute for the 2 additional years of schooling required by statute (406 U.S. at 234–236).

The uniqueness of *Yoder* lies in the fact that it deals with the question of the free exercise of the religion of parents in directing the education of their children in the face of compelling state interests rooted in a compulsory education law. Before 1990, the usefulness of *Yoder* to other free exercise and state regulation cases was clouded by the many qualifications that the Court attached to its decision. It appeared from Court dicta that a similar outcome in future cases would require that the individual belong to a religious group almost identical to the Amish with its centuries-long religious tradition, the direct and obvious relationship between belief and way of life, and the establishment of a closed society that was literally separate from modern society. In addition, it would have had to be shown that an alternative educational program adequately met the interests of the state in education. It is no wonder that the Court concluded that "few other religious groups or sects" could meet these stringent criteria. Nor is it surprising that such has indeed been the case. Most if not all subsequent lower court cases involving Free Exercise claims and state regulations where *Yoder* is used as a controlling case have failed to sustain the Free Exercise claim (*State v. Shaver,* 294 N.W.2d 883 (N.D. 1980); *State v. Faith Baptist Church,* 301 N.W.2d 571 (Neb. 1981); *Windsor Park Baptist Church v. Arkansas Activities Association,* 658 F.Supp. 618 (8th Cir. 1981); *Jernigan v. State,* 412 So.2d 1242 (Ala. Crim. App. 1982); *State v. Rivinius,* 328 N.W.2d 220, *cert. denied,* 460 U.S. 1070 (N.D. 1983); *Johnson v. Charles City Community School Board,* 368 N.W.2d 74 (1985); *State v. Newstrom,* 371 N.W.2d 525 (Minn. 1985); *Fellowship Baptist Church v. Benton,* 620 F.Supp. 308 (D. Iowa 1985), 815 F.2d 485 (8th Cir. 1987); *Sheridan Road Baptist Church v. Department of Education,* 396 N.W.2d 373 (Mich. 1986), *State v. Patzer,* 382 N.W.2d 631 (N.D. 1986)).[19]

It is not clear why the Court insisted on such an exacting and nearly impossible standard for legitimate religious beliefs when in two prior decisions it accepted a far broader definition of "religion," at least in terms of interpreting a federal statute (*United States v. Seeger,* 380 U.S. 163 (1965); *Welsh v. United States,* 398 U.S. 333 (1970). Also see Herman (1980).). Also, the values listed by the Court that the Amish found objectionable in formal secondary education are not overtly religious values (Arons, 1976).[20] They seem to be just the kind of child-rearing and pedagogical values that the Court condemned later on in the opinion.[21]

Wisconsin v. Yoder was not a case of education versus no education. The Amish wanted education and their society embodied life-long learning. It was a dispute about the content and process of an alternative educational program. The key issue that was forgotten was whether the regulation requiring alternative education to be "substantially equivalent" to public education could withstand First Amendment objections. Was this a "reasonable" and "compelling" regulation in light of free exercise claims, the Amish acceptance of 8 years of formal education in public schools, and their willingness to have two additional years of informal vocational training? The whole issue seems to have been somewhat misconceived from the beginning. The outcome of *Wisconsin v. Yoder* would probably have been the same but without the belabored efforts by the Court to find justification for a special exemption from the compulsory education code through an excessive emphasis on the uniqueness of the Amish religion.

The great value of *Yoder* for cases involving regulation of private schools is that it introduces the concept of freedom of conscience and belief, along with parental rights, into the equation of balancing opposing interests. Since 1990 the *Yoder* case has taken on even greater significance for private school regulation in light of the United States Supreme Court decision in *Employment Div., Dept. of Human Res. v. Smith,* 110 S.Ct. 1595 (1990). In a shocking opinion, the Court eviscerated the Free Exercise Clause of any substantive protections of religious practice by "dismiss[ing] free exercise precedent" (Kelly, 1991, p. 960) and "abandon[ing] the balancing of interest test in those cases where a 'valid and neutral law of general applicability' is being applied to religious practice" (Leahy, 1991, p. 106; see also McConnell, 1990; Rebescher, 1991). The Court did, however, affirm *Yoder* and *Pierce.* It also used *Yoder* and *Pierce* as examples where the traditional "compelling interest" and "least restrictive means" standard could still be applicable in cases where a free exercise claim was raised "in conjunction with other constitutional protections, such as freedom of speech, and of the press . . . or the right of parents . . . to direct the education of their children" (*Smith,* 110 S.Ct. at 1601).

The Supreme Court has yet, however, to fully address the whole issue of private school regulation in a specific and comprehensive manner, especially in light of continued claims of infringement on First Amendment rights by parents (*State ex rel. Douglas v. Faith Baptist Church,* 301 N.W.2d 571, *appeal dismissed sub nom. Faith Baptist Church v. Douglas,* 454 U.S. 803 (1981); *State v. Rivinius,* 328 N.W.2d 220, *cert. denied,* 460 U.S. 1070 (1983); *Johnson v. Charles City Community School Board,* 368 N.W.2d 74, *cert. denied sub nom. Pruessner v. Benton,* 474 U.S. 1033 (1985); *State v. Patzer,* 382 N.W.2d 631, *cert. denied sub nom. Patzer v. North Dakota,* 479 U.S. 825 (1986); *New Life Baptist Church Academy v. Town of East Longmeadow,* 885 F.2d 940 (1st Cir. 1989), *cert. denied,* 110 S.Ct., 1782 (1990)). Supreme Court cases dealing with private schools after the *Farrington* case in 1927 have dealt primarily with public funding or very specific and narrow issues involving federal law and regulations.[22] Any comments about regulation have been incidental to these issues and often refer the reader to the cases reviewed above.

Perhaps part of the reason behind the reluctance of the Court to pass judgment on the maze of private school regulations may be the desire to avoid duplicating the often haphazard and piecemeal results found in its decisions on items and activities of private education that may be legally funded with public monies.[23] A detailed examination of state regulations for private schools may well present another judicial quagmire that the Court would just as soon sidestep.

REGULATION AND THE SUPREME COURT

Summary of Constitutional Parameters

In the landmark cases of the Supreme Court outlining the basic relationship between the state and private schools and in subsequent decisions, it is clear that the state through its police power *may* regulate private schools (*Berea, Meyer, Pierce, Farrington, Yoder*).[24] It is important to notice, however, that the language of the Court in this regard is permissive, not mandatory.[25] The state is under no constitutional obligation or duty to regulate, supervise, or monitor any aspect of the operations of private schools—a choice that several states have elected to take (Randall, 1989).

On the other hand, the state is constitutionally bound by the Fifth and Fourteenth Amendments to allow for the existence and operation of private schools (*Berea, Pierce, Farrington, Yoder*).[26] This includes a *de facto* as well as a *de jure* existence (*Farrington*). It is also forbidden to "contract the spectrum of knowledge" unless it involves teachings and ideas that are "manifestly inimical to the public welfare" (*Meyer*).[27]

If the state chooses to exercise its prerogative to regulate and supervise private schools, the restrictions it places on private schools must be "reasonable," that is, within constitutionally defined limits. The state's power to regulate is not absolute (*Dartmouth, Berea, Meyer, Pierce, Farrington, Yoder*).[28] Regulations cannot "sweep unnecessarily broadly" across the operations of private schools "and thereby invade the area of protected freedoms" (*Griswold v. Connecticut*, 381 U.S. 479, 485 (1965), quoting *NAACP v. Alabama*, 377 U.S. 288, 307). This constitutional limitation on the police power of the state to restrict or direct the activities of private schools in certain areas requires that all regulations at least meet a rational means test and, if fundamental rights are involved, also satisfy a "strict scrutiny" test (*Berea, Meyer, Pierce, Farrington, Yoder*).

The rational means test requires that state-imposed regulations have a rational relationship to a legitimate state objective. They cannot be capricious, arbitrary, and wholly unrelated to a lawful state goal. Legitimate state goals include regulation of incorporated schools (*Berea*), "improv[ing] the quality of its citizens, physically, mentally and morally" (*Meyer* and *Pierce*), concern for a "large alien population" (*Farrington*), citizenship development (*Meyer, Pierce, Farrington*), and a formal system of compulsory education producing students who are politically competent and economically self-sufficient (*Yoder*).[29] Examples of illegitimate goals are homogenization of citizens (*Meyer*)[30] and standardization of pupils (*Pierce*).[31] Unjustifiable means used to achieve legal state objectives include legislation giving near total control of the school to the state (*Dartmouth, Farrington*), suppression of knowledge (*Meyer*), and banning private schools (*Pierce*).[32]

The "protected freedoms" requiring state regulations to satisfy the rational means test are all grounded in the liberties protected by the Fourteenth Amendment. These encompass the right of owners and teachers of private schools to pursue a lawful business and occupation (*Meyer, Pierce*), the right of parents to direct and control the education of their children (*Meyer, Pierce, Farrington, Yoder*),[33] and the right of children to learn and acquire useful knowledge (*Meyer*).[34]

Even if a regulation passes the minimal rational means test, it may still be unconstitutional if it fails examination under the "strict scrutiny" analysis. A strict scrutiny test is required if the regulation infringes on a fundamental right protected by the constitution (*Skinner v. Oklahoma*, 316 U.S. 535, 541 (1942)). In this instance the state is obligated to show two things. First, that the regulation serves not only a rational relationship to a legal state objective but that it serves a compelling or crucial state interest (*Yoder*, 406 U.S. at 233).[35] Second, that the particular regulation selected by the state is the "least restrictive" means available to accomplish its "compelling state interest" (*Thomas v. Review Board, Indiana Empl. Sec. Div.*, 450 U.S. 707, 718 (1981)).[36] The major exception to this level of judicial review was created with the 1990 *Smith* decision discussed earlier with *Yoder*. Even though religious actions are protected by the First Amendment, the Supreme Court declared that when "neutral, generally applicable regulatory law" (*Smith*, 110 S.Ct. at 1605) places a burden on free exercise rights, the legislation would have to meet only the minimum rational means test to be constitutional. However, if state action were challenged on free exercise claims *and* additional grounds involving fundamental rights, then this "hybrid situation" would require such government action to review under the traditional strict scrutiny standard with its compelling interest and least restrictive means components (*Smith*, 110 S.Ct. at 1601, 1602).[37]

That the state has a legitimate and even compelling interest in the education of its citizens cannot be denied.[38] Education has been acknowledged as a matter of "high responsibility . . . [that] ranks at the very apex of the function of the state" (*Yoder*, 406 U.S. at 213) and that is "perhaps the most important function of state and local governments" (*Brown v. Board of Education*, 347 U.S. 483, 493 (1954)) because of its "vital role" (*San Antonio Independent School District v. Rodriguez*, 411 U.S. 1, 30 (1973)), "supreme importance" (*Meyer*, 262 U.S. at 400), and "fundamental role" (*Plyler v. Doe*, 457 U.S. 202, 221 (1982)) in preserving our society and assisting each child in the acquisition of basic occupational and citizenship skills. The state's interest in circumscribing the liberty of parents and children through compulsory education laws and regulations is itself limited. It is limited to providing a basic education that will enable children to "participate effectively and intelligently in our open political system" and to "be self-reliant and self-sufficient participants in society" (*Yoder*, 406 U.S. at 221). In short, the state's interest is to empower children with "political and economic competence" (Strike, 1982a, p. 105).[39]

Areas of Permissible Regulation

The decisions of the Supreme Court have specified some areas that the state may regulate and monitor. The state can mandate that the instructional language be English (*Meyer*). The state can require private schools to provide an education that is "basic," "equivalent [to public education]" (*Yoder*, 406 U.S. at 213), or an "adequate education" (*Wolman v. Walter*, 433 U.S. 229, 240 (1977)) that meets "minimal educational standards" (*Yoder*, 406 U.S. at 239).[40]

The state can regulate the "quality and nature" (*Board of Education v. Allen*, 392 U.S. 236, 245 (1968)) of the curriculum consisting of "elemental skills" (*Wolman v. Essex*, 342 F.Supp. 399, 411, *aff'd*, 409 U.S. 808 (1972))[41] and "prescribed subjects of instruction" (*Allen*, 392 U.S. at 246 (1968))[42] "necessary for a productive and valuable life" (*Wolman*, 342 F.Supp. at 411). The state may also set the standards requiring "minimum" hours of instruction (*Allen*, 392 U.S. at 246).[43] Teachers may also be examined to ensure that they have received "specified training" (*Allen*, 392 U.S. at 246).[44]

The state may also inspect schools to ensure that they are in compliance with "fire inspections, building and zoning regulations" (*Lemon v. Kurtzman*, 403 U.S. 602, 614 (1971)), and "safety standards" (*Wolman*,

342 F.Supp. at 406).[45] In addition to prescriptive regulations, the state may also prohibit racial discrimination in admission decisions of private, commercial, nonsectarian schools (*Runyon v. McCrary*, 427 U.S. 160 (1975)).

On the other hand, the state is specifically forbidden to regulate the "acquisition of knowledge" (*Meyer*, 262 U.S. at 400)[46] by dictating what *cannot* be taught and "religious training" (*Yoder*, 406 U.S. at 212). Private church schools also cannot be required to pay unemployment compensation taxes as mandated by the Federal Unemployment Tax Act, and their teachers do not fall within the jurisdiction of the National Labor Relations Board (*St. Martin Evangelical Lutheran Church v. South Dakota*, 451 U.S. 772 (1981); *National Labor Relations Board v. Catholic Bishop of Chicago*, 440 U.S. 490 (1979). Also see Worthing (1984) for additional discussion on related topics.).

SUMMARY AND CONCLUSION

A review of statements in Supreme Court decisions about the nature or character of regulation of private schools in fulfilling the legitimate interest of the state in education reveals several common themes. One is the emphasis on the ends instead of the means. The Court's focus is on acquisition of knowledge and skills and academic achievement and far less on how they are accomplished. The final product is far more important than the methods used to produce it. In fact, there is some uneasiness about being too prescriptive and detailed about how a student receives a basic education.[47] Second, the Court is concerned with the possession of basic skills and essential knowledge—the minimum required to function in society. Third, cautionary flags are placed around areas that may result in the intrusion on fundamental rights such as freedom of religion, speech, and conscience. And fourth, the state is given wide latitude and discretion in developing appropriate regulations to ensure that its legitimate interests in education are protected.

While the comments by the Court about specific educational activities of private schools that the state may legally regulate do provide some general guidance to states in the construction of appropriate regulations, their usefulness is severely diminished by several factors. One is the fact that all of the statements are court dicta. They are remarks made about issues that are peripheral to the central concern of a particular case. Not since *Farrington* in 1927 has the Court decided a case where the *central* issue was state regulation of private schools. Even here the Court simply declared that near or complete control of private schools through state regulation was unconstitutional. No clear and identifiable standard or boundary was given that would mark the entrance by the state into forbidden territory. In addition, the Court does not supply any rationale for its comments. They are simply assertions, supposedly self-evident in nature, and even so, there is a suggestion of conflicting and contradictory statements.[48]

Second, terms used by the Court are vague rather than precise, ambiguous instead of exact. This simply begs the question of appropriate regulations. What is a "basic" or "adequate" education? How literal is the term "equivalent" supposed to be taken?[49] What does the Court mean by "elemental" skills? What constitutes "minimal" educational standards? What "specified" training should teachers be required to have?[50] What are the ingredients of a "productive and valuable life" that the curriculum should revolve around? What does it mean to be a "self-reliant" and "self-sufficient" person and at what point is one considered so? What makes a regulation "reasonable" or "unreasonable"? Although the ambiguity of the language could be beneficial in some ways, its positive effect would depend on those who enforce the regulations. All of this suggests, however, that attempts by the Supreme Court to provide assistance to states in formulating appropriate regulations for private schools have been inadequate, raising far more questions than answers.

There has been a significant increase in the amount of litigation by private schools challenging various efforts of the state to regulate their programs and activities. This is particularly true for the past 20 years. A review of Supreme Court rulings revealed some general guidelines and principles that shape the relationship between the state and private schools. Private schools have a right to exist as an educational alternative, and the state has the right to regulate them in a reasonable manner. The term "reasonable" has never been given a precise meaning except that regulation that allows private education in name only is unjustified. The imprecise nature of the Supreme Court rulings and present decisions to not review current controversies have left state and appellate courts on their own to determine what is reasonable in the context of competing rights, especially in light of claims that state regulations violate freedoms protected by the United States Constitution.[51] The reluctance of the Court to furnish clearer guidelines imposes on state legislatures an even greater burden of formulating appropriate regulations that will serve the interests of the state and yet protect the rights of parents, students, and private school officials (Smolin, 1986).

The key point of the Supreme Court cases was that a legitimate choice of an alternative educational program cannot be denied by the state. The crucial questions still remain, however. Where is the point where government action is able to protect its legitimate interests and yet leave the private education option with sufficient internal integrity to still be a real choice? If this point cannot be located with sufficient precision to be of any practical use in constructing a regulatory algorithm, what should be the proper policy in the regulation of private schools?

Chapters 4 and 5 suggest a useful strategy for assisting public policy to sail safely between the Scylla of state tyranny and the Charybdis of educational promiscuity in private schools.

4 ✝ PRIVATE SCHOOLS AND STATE REGULATION

> Freedom unrestrained by responsibility becomes mere license; responsibility unchecked by freedom becomes mere arbitrary power. The question, then, is not whether freedom and responsibility shall be united, but how they can be united and reconciled to the best advantage.
> —Carl L. Becker, *Freedom and Responsibility in the American Way of Life*

Chapter 3 reviewed decisions by the United States Supreme Court touching on the relationship between the government and private elementary and secondary schools. This relationship obviously draws in legitimate and significant third parties such as parents who have exercised their legal right of educational choice and the children who are private school pupils.

While the excursion into this judicial thicket was informative, it did not reveal the kind of specific guidelines necessary to develop proper educational policy and appropriate regulations. It often raised more questions than it answered as new issues such as religious belief and the liberty of parents to direct the education of their children were added to the problem.

One major contribution that the legal foray did produce was a heightened sense of the complexity of the issues involved. What are the essential interests of both the state and the private schools? What is the proper mix of responsibility and freedom? In what manner can the integrity of both positions be simultaneously preserved to the advantage of all? And on a more practical level, two additional questions arise. One, is it even possible to draft a blueprint to guide the fashioning of regulations that are equitable to both parties? Second, even if the regulatory pattern can be satisfactorily drawn, is our current state of educational technology and expertise capable of successful implementation?

The purpose of this chapter is to explore these questions by examining more closely some of the basic issues unveiled in Chapter 3. These

An earlier version of this chapter entitled "Private Schools and State Regulation" appeared in *The Urban Lawyer, 24,* Spring 1992, pp. 341–378. Permission to use material from that article in this chapter was granted by the American Bar Association, Section of Urban, State, and Local Government Law and is gratefully acknowledged.

include such things as liberty interests, the precise justification for state intervention in private schools, the inherent difficulties such restriction produces, and whether the knowledge and capacity actually exist to develop and implement proper regulations.

This chapter is divided into three major sections. The first introduces some basic concepts of rights and liberty. These concepts are essential in evaluating the state's desire to regulate private schools to ensure a minimum education for all students.

The second section examines the state's position, its justification for regulating private schools, and what it hopes to achieve by such measures. To appreciate the dilemma that state intervention in private schools creates for both parties, it is critical to understand why the government insists that it must supervise private school functions.

The third portion of the chapter analyzes the utility of regulation as a public policy approach in achieving government objectives. It considers some major difficulties faced by many states that have chosen to regulate private schools. These significant challenges to state regulation can be grouped into five broad, interrelated categories: (1) goal-related questions, (2) strategic issues, (3) moral complications, (4) constitutional concerns, and (5) educational or practical problems. The value of examining the costs and benefits associated with regulating private schools lies in the conceptual directions it provides for evaluating a highly controversial educational policy and the feasibility of alternative approaches.

RIGHTS, LIBERTIES, AND STATE ACTION

An important part of our national heritage, as expressed or implied in the Declaration of Independence, American Constitution, and many state constitutions, is the idea that everyone possesses natural and unalienable rights that secure the opportunity to choose and pursue his or her own notion of the good life (Hafen, 1984; Hirsch, 1992).[1] Implicit in this idea is that a human being, by nature, is a rational and autonomous being. He or she is also a moral agent who can independently arrive at reasoned choices and is accountable and responsible for them.[2] In addition to the qualities of rationality, liberty, and moral conscience, our tradition of liberalism also asserts a sense of equality or equivalency (Rawls, 1979; Wasserstrom, 1979). One person is not inherently superior or sovereign to another.[3]

Linked to these fundamental rights are corresponding responsibilities or obligations. One has the responsibility to exercise his or her rights in such way as not to interfere with or encroach upon the rights or liberties of others (Rawls, 1979). Often in the course of events, conflicting choices arise between individuals or between the individual and the state in the fulfillment of an individual's communal obligations to society. A successful resolution often requires accommodation, compromise or coercion and is usually done under the auspices of the state.

The exercise of these rights does become circumscribed somewhat. Liberty becomes an "ordered liberty" (*Yoder,* 406 U.S. at 215). The general principle undergirding liberal political thought and our system of government, however, has been the maximization of individual liberty to the fullest extent possible. If restrictions are placed on individual liberty, they cannot be arbitrary but must be based on justifiable reasons (Locke, 1979; Lyons, 1979; Mill, 1980; Strike, 1982a).

The formulation of justifiable reasons for interfering with the liberty interests of others as individuals or as a group has always been and continues to be an area of much discussion and sharp disagreement. The question of the "nature and limits of the power which can be legitimately exercised by society over the individual," observes John Stuart Mill, "has divided mankind almost from the remotest ages" (1980, p. 3). Most often this issue is couched in terms of what is the proper role of the state in society.

The Preamble to the *United States Constitution,* along with the Declaration of Independence, is an embodiment of liberal political thought that sets forth the basic rationale for the American nation and the purposes for which it was established.[4] The articles and subsequent amendments to the Constitution, along with state constitutions, specified in greater detail the limited role of government in American society, and its relationship to individuals and groups. The fundamental principle supporting the concept of the American state was "that all lawful power derives from the people and must be held in check to preserve their freedom." This principle is, according to Laurence Tribe (1978), "the oldest and most central tenet of American constitutionalism" (pp. 1–2).

Just as individuals have inalienable rights, so is police power inalienable to the state. The use of this power to coerce, however, is bound by constitutional and statutory enactments. State action must be legally authorized and justified. On the other hand, the individual or any other nongovernment entity may act *unless* a particular action is forbidden. In other words, the individual or private group does not need permission to pursue its own interests, but the state always needs authorization before it takes any course of action. The state must justify its actions through legislation, but the individual or group need not. In conflicts arising over state intervention in private affairs, therefore, the state must justify its curtailment of basic liberty rights (Rawls, 1979).

Parental Rights and *Parens Patriae*

The state is a social artifact constructed by individuals who preceded it. They possessed pre-existing rights and responsibilities inherent in their nature as human beings. One of these basic human rights is the right to bear children, raise them, and direct their upbringing.

This parental right is derived from two primary sources. First, it is a natural right because the child is the offspring of his or her parents. This gives them the inherent right and responsibility to care for him or her. The second source is positive law—constitutional and statutory provisions. There exists "the time-honored right of a parent to raise his child as he sees fit. . . . *Yoder* and *Pierce* hold that parents, *not* the government, have the right to make certain decisions regarding the upbringing of their children" (*FCC v. Pacifica Foundation*, 438 U.S. 726, 769 (1978), J. Brennan, dissenting opinion); *Yoder*, 406 U.S. at 232, 233).

Constitutional and statutory law formally acknowledge a prior and primary right of parents to direct the educational experience of their children.[5] The Court has declared that "it is cardinal with us that the custody, care and nurture of the child reside first in the parents" (*Prince v. Massachusetts*, 321 U.S. 158, 166 (1944)) and that the "primary role of parents in the upbringing of their children is now established beyond debate as an enduring American tradition" (*Yoder*, 406 U.S. at 232; *Pierce*, 268 U.S. at 534, 535). These parental rights are protected from unjustified state abridgment. "There does exist a 'private realm of family life which the state cannot enter,' *Prince*, 321 U.S. at 166), that has been afforded both substantive and procedural protection" (*Smith v. Organization of Foster Families*, 431 U.S. 816, 842 (1977)). The parents are entitled to a right of privacy from state interference in fulfilling their parental responsibilities. This right of "family privacy has its source, and its contours are ordinarily to be sought, not in state law, but in intrinsic human rights" (*Smith v. Organization of Foster Families*, 431 U.S. at 842).

This right of privacy also includes the right of parents to direct the education of their children. The Court has declared that "the Constitution extends . . . special privacy rights such as those of marriage, procreation, motherhood, childbearing, and education" (*United States v. Orito*, 413 U.S. 139, 142 (1972); *Akron v. Akron Center for Reproductive Health*, 462 U.S. 416, 426, 427 (1983)).

The state's acceptance of these parental rights in constitutional and statutory provisions does not invest the parent with ownership of the child or grant absolute immunity from state interference.[6] It does, however, bestow a legal fiduciary responsibility upon parents to provide for the well-being of their children—food, clothing, shelter, medical care, education, and so on. This right and legal stewardship cannot be taken from parents unless specific neglect is proven (*Smith v. Organization of Foster Families,* 431 U.S. at 842).

The state has a right, under the doctrine of *parens patriae,* to intercede in family life on behalf of the child if parents fail to fulfill their responsibilities.[7] *Parens patriae,* "parent of the country," "originates from English common law where the King had a royal prerogative to act as guardian to persons with legal disabilities, such as infants, idiots, and lunatics" (Black, 1979, p. 1003). This legal concept is at best a metaphor and simply gives the state "standing" to protect the interests of the child from abusive or neglectful parents. Many proscriptions by the state on the rights of parents to direct the rearing and education of their children require substantiated proof of parental neglect (Baskin, 1974; Thomas, 1972; Wald, 1975).

REGULATION OF PRIVATE SCHOOLS: THE STATE'S POSITION

State Rationale for Involvement in Education

Education is a critical sphere of human activity in which the American state is deeply involved. The federal constitution does not contain any specific provisions concerning education. The rudimentary rationale for government involvement in education does begin to appear, however, in various state constitutions[8] and federal legislation such as the Northwest Ordinance of 1785.[9] While espousing noble sentiments about the importance of education, however, federal and state constitutions do not specify the nature of the state's involvement. In order to justify state-sponsored schools, a rationale would have to be deduced and an ideology would have to be created.

As was discussed in Chapter 2, the rationale for the state as an educator initially came from the primary premises of self-preservation and perpetuation.

> The primary purpose of the maintenance of the common school system is the promotion of the general intelligence of the people constituting the body politic and thereby [to] increase the usefulness and efficiency of the citizens, upon which the government of society depends. (*Fogg v. Board of Education,* 82 A. 172, 174 (N.H. 1912); also see Dubay, 1959, pp. 3–14)

This public interest rationale for state schooling is to maximize the competency of each citizen for the benefit of society and includes the elimination of "all things hurtful to its comfort or inimical to its existence" (*Berea College v. Commonwealth,* 94 S.W. 623, 625 (Ky. 1906)). While efficiency demands a state school system, effectiveness requires that it be universal and compulsory.

> Free schooling furnished by the state is not so much a right granted to the pupils as a duty imposed upon them for the public good. If they do not voluntarily attend the schools provided for them, they may be compelled to do so . . . they [free schools] are governmental means of protecting the state from the consequences of an ignorant and incompetent citizenship. (*Fogg v. Board of Education,* 82 A. 172, 175 (N.H. 1912))

The public interest or "general welfare" justification of state involvement in training citizens to be politically competent and economically productive was expanded further to include the importance of building a common culture. "Social order and stability" (*Plyler v. Doe,* 457 U.S. 202, 222, n. 20 (1982)) required a sense of community and "national unity" (*Minersville School Dist. v. Gobitis,* 310 U.S. 586, 595 (1940)) that would be created by the socialization of all students in schools teaching a set of "shared values" (*Plyler,* 457 U.S. at 222, n. 20).

Another dimension of the public welfare argument is a concern focused on the individual—a personal development notion. The state's involvement in education is not just to "provide a mass of educated, and, hence taxable citizens, but . . . to educate for life" (*Yoder,* 406 U.S. at 239). It is an effort to "nurture and develop human potential of its [the state's] children . . . expand their knowledge, broaden their sensibilities, kindle their imagination, foster a spirit of free inquiry, . . . increase their human understanding and tolerance" (*Yoder,* 406 U.S. at 239). It is a concern for the "social, economic, intellectual, and psychological well-being of the individual" (*Plyler,* 457 U.S. at 222). It is an interest in the quality of life for the individual and society as a whole.

The final component of the public interest position is one of individual rights and justice. Each child has a "birthright" (*State v. Trucke,* 410 N.W.2d 242, 245 (Iowa 1987)) or a "substantive right" (*Yoder,* 406 U.S. at 205) to a basic education that will empower him or her to lead a productive and fulfilling life.[10] "In these days," stated the Supreme Court, "it is doubtful that any child may reasonably be expected to succeed in life if he is denied the opportunity of an education" (*Brown v. Board of Education,* 347 U.S. 483, 493 (1954)). Closely connected with this right to an education is the issue of equal opportunity and social justice. In a meritocratic society, a sense of fairness requires that each child be given an equal opportunity to develop his or her talents and skills, an equal opportunity to exercise his or her right to a basic education. A "deprivation" of this opportunity for all "make[s] it most difficult to reconcile . . . with the framework of equality" inherent in the Fourteenth Amendment (*Plyler,* 457 U.S. at 221–222).

The interest of the state in education for personal development and the right to receive a basic education springs, in part, from the legal doctrine of *parens patriae.* This doctrine confers upon the state the responsibility to look after children who have been neglected by their parents. In assuming this guardianship for neglected children, who, in addition to belonging to a family, are also members of society, the state functions as a substitute parent in ensuring the well-being of the child. A substantial part of this well-being is an adequate education (*Quigley v. State,* 5 Ohio CC 638, 655 (1891), *aff'd* 27 WL Bull 332 (1892); *State v. Bailey,* 61 N.E. 730, 732 (Ind. 1901); *Pierce,* 268 U.S. at 512; *Farrington,* 273 U.S. at 286; *Prince,* 321 U.S. at 165–168; *Ginsberg v. New York,* 390 U.S. 629, 639 (1968); *State v. Yoder,* 182 N.W. 2d 539, 543 (Wis. 1971); *Wisconsin v. Yoder,* 406 U.S. at 222, 234).

State Rationale for Regulating Private Schools

Except for the responsibility to ensure that public monies are spent in a manner consistent with legislative mandates, the justification for state regulation of public as well as private schools is basically the same—quality control to ensure a minimum standard or level of education. If education is an integral element of individual and social well-being, then the *quality* of the educational experience is of vital interest to the state.

> Nonpublic schools perform, in substantial part, a strictly secular function. They teach a portion of the state's school population those elemental skills necessary for a productive and valuable life. It is nearly tautological that the state has a legitimate interest in requiring minimum standards in all its schools. (*Wolman v. Essex,* 342 F.Supp. 399, 411, *aff'd* 409 U.S. 808 (1972)[11]

If nongovernment means are used to educate, the state "has a proper interest in the manner in which those schools perform their secular educational function" and where "it can be known, by reasonable means, that the required teaching is being done" (*State v. Hoyt,* 146 A. 170, 172 (N.H. 1929); *Smith v. Donahue,* 195 N.Y.S. 715, 202 A.D. 656, 662 (1922); *Board of Education v. Allen,* 392 U.S. 236, 247 (1968)). If there are no standards, children could be denied any education whatsoever. Furthermore, even those parents who really want to provide an adequate education for their children, may not be sufficiently trained or have the proper educational resources or facilities (*State v. McDonough*, 468 A. 2d 977 (Me. 1983)).

Of fundamental and specific interest to the state is "knowing . . . its children are attending school" (*Fellowship v. Benton*, 620 F.Supp. 308, 313, 815 F.2d 485 (8th Cir. 1987)) in a "safe and healthy environment," where the child is being properly prepared "to be a productive worker and effective citizen in our democracy" (*New Life Baptist Church Academy v. East Longmeadow*, 666 F. Supp. 293, 307 (D. Mass. 1987)).

Other important interests are to protect parents and children from educational and business fraud (Sanders, 1969), prevent the teaching of anything "manifestly inimical to the public welfare" (*Pierce*, 268 U.S. at 534; *People v. American Socialist Society*, 202 App. Div. 640 (N.Y. 1922), promote Americanization (*Farrington*, 273 U.S. at 289), and deter racial discrimination (*Runyon v. McCrary*, 427 U.S. 160 (1975)).

From these general declarations about the social value and role of education, states have constructed an assortment of regulations to ensure compliance by private schools in one or more of these state interests.[12] This action by the government, however, has often been met with both noncompliance by many private schools and litigation.[13] The reasons behind this reaction by private schools are many and complex (see Chapter 3). But the underlying rationale seems to be the perception on the part of private schools and parents that the government has unnecessarily, arbitrarily, and brazenly intruded upon their liberty interests. A closer examination of the way the state regulates private schools suggests that the disagreement with many state controls may be warranted and reasonable.

REGULATION OF PRIVATE SCHOOLS: SOME PROBLEMATIC ISSUES

Goal-Related Issues

The review of American education and court cases in Chapters 2 and 3 revealed little, if any, disagreement by those in private education with the importance and broad role of education in society. Private schools have never denied the importance of education in the "promotion of the general intelligence of the people," preventing "ignorant and incompetent citizenship," ensuring "social order and stability," and providing for the "social, economic, intellectual, and psychological well-being of the child." It would be untrue to say that private schools and parents are not interested and concerned with society, education, and children.

While the state and private schools share the same general goals, disagreement arises over their meaning. What is meant in practical terms by the "happiness of mankind," "good government," "usefulness and efficiency of the citizens," "all things hurtful to . . . [society's] comfort or inimical to its existence," "incompetent citizenship," "productive worker and effective citizen"? Whose "unity" should be nationalized or in whose image should immigrants be Americanized? The ambiguity of these phrases in the general premises on the importance of education lends itself to any number of reasonable interpretations. The state seems to presume that there exists only one correct interpretation—the one it devises. But even this interpretation has varied over time and among states, depending on which group and political party is in power (see Chapter 2).

Another major weakness in the state's position is the general absence of educational objectives in its statutes that are explicit, clearly articulated, and widely accepted in the professional community.[14] What kind of knowledge is of most worth? What are the basic skills all should have, and what comprises an adequate education? What constitutes an effective school and a competent teacher? It is true that state departments of education have educational goals. These goals, however, are not always explicit and are often formulated by unelected officials in the state's educational bureaucracy (McCarthy & Deignan, 1982).[15]

In addition to exegetical difficulties and the lack of educational objectives, there is also the problem of nonsequiturs. What are the connections between the specific regulations imposed on private schools and the educational objectives of the state? For one thing, if these objectives are not always explicit and do not have wide consensus, it is difficult to see what principles lie behind private school regulations other than conventional wisdom and/or the personal preferences of state education officials. This potentially confusing condition increases the likelihood that decisions about the adequacy of private education will be based on vague and arbitrary criteria (Smolin, 1986).

Even if the state has educational objectives, the implementation process is not obvious.[16] When regulations are formulated, where is the empirical evidence linking them to the state's educational objectives? The causal link between certain regulations and the educational goals of the state are often based on unstated, unproven assumptions.

In essence, educational adequacy has been defined by the standards imposed, even though such standards may be based on faulty assumptions regarding for what and for whom educational programs should be adequate. Solutions have been implemented without thorough exploration of the problems they are designed to solve or the outcomes they are intended to achieve. Until the incongruities between means and ends are addressed, the proliferation of legal mandates establishing educational input and output standards will not assure that educational programs are indeed *sufficient* for a *given purpose.* (McCarthy & Deignan, 1982, p. 98)[17]

It should not be surprising, then, that many private schools sense a great deal of subjectivity, personal preference, and arbitrariness in private school regulations and feel they have been dealt with unfairly. Donald Erickson (1984) concludes that state

> regulations seldom reflect any defensible rationale, specifying the good things to be walled in and the bad things to be walled out. As one frequent result of this confusion, the regulations encourage what should not be encouraged, discourage what should not be discouraged, punish people who deserve no punishment, and create much avoidable animosity. (p. 227)

Strategic Issues

There are a variety of public policy techniques available that help to reduce risk or ensure the general welfare of society. Sound policy decisions require a careful analysis of whether such a decision is right, its effectiveness in achieving its objective, and an assessment of the costs as well as the benefits it seeks to obtain (Stone, 1982). Whatever the specific decision, the choice will be: to what degree will the policy tool be based on (1) "anticipation" or risk prevention, and (2) "resilience" or enhancing the ability to respond to actual problems (Wildavsky, 1983, pp. xv–xvii)?

Regulations are a classic example of "anticipation" or risk prevention and are selected quite frequently. While risk prevention may have an immediate intuitive appeal as the best approach, it may not be the best upon closer examination. Wildavsky suggests this is the case when it is not known what evil or harm will actually result, or because what appeared to be dangerous may turn out to be harmless, or when the cost of trying to prevent the dangers may be greater than the damage they would cause if they occurred. Wildavsky (1983) concludes that

> the most likely eventuality by far is that whatever happens will be unexpected. We might be better off, then, increasing our capacity to respond, our resilience, rather than dissipating our strength in efforts to ward off we know-not-what. (p. xvii)

State intervention into private elementary and secondary schools is an anticipatory approach. Although it is well-intentioned, it poses several substantial problems by raising questions about its moral and legal legitimacy, as well as its effectiveness and efficiency in achieving its objective.

Moral Issues

Introductory Premise. Restriction of choice and personal liberty is a fundamental moral concern because "interference with another's freedom requires a moral justification" (Hart, 1979, p. 24). If a person is a rational, moral, autonomous being, possessing an inherent "right . . . to be free" (Hart, 1979, p. 14), on what basis do others, who are his or her equals, prohibit certain actions?[18] It would have to be on the grounds that such an action would restrict or inhibit the right of another person to be a rational, moral, self-directing individual (Haggard, 1983). In education it would require a showing by the state that those having primary responsibility for educating children—parents and guardians—are derelict in their duty and incompetent in their fiduciary capacity.[19] The rationale for coming to such a conclusion would have to be based on substantial, objective reasons. To limit the liberty of another on a subjective or arbitrary basis would be morally wrong because it violates the basic human right of equality with its entitlement to be dealt with fairly.

Unsubstantiated Means, Ends, and Connections. The right of parents to direct their children's education is a "natural" as well as legal right (Hart, 1979, p. 22). Therefore, any state intervention in parents' educational decisions must be justified. A sense of fairness dictates that regulations should flow from state educational goals that are clear and explicit. There must also be some objective connection between the regulation and what is it attempting to achieve.[20] There must be a demonstrated need that requires the regulation in the first place. The regulation must be objectively substantiated in order to be a proper restriction of personal liberty. Otherwise the regulation could be based on subjective criteria, faulty assumptions, and misconceptions. Such a regulation would unjustly impose the state's preference and thus become "ethically problematic" (Brock, 1988, p. 559). The action becomes arbitrary and the limitation a violation of personal liberty.

The previous section pointed to a lack of clarity in educational objectives as well as their scarcity in state statutes. An explicit connection between educational objectives and a specific regulation is often missing in legislation. Furthermore, the state is rarely required to demonstrate such a connection in litigation other than the almost meaningless assertion that the state has an interest in education, thereby justifying whatever the state requires. In *State v. Faith Baptist Church*, the church school objected to the state's requirement of teacher certification. The court "believe[d] that it goes without saying that the state has a compelling interest in the quality and ability of those who are to teach its young people" (301 N.W. 2d 571, 579 (Neb. 1981)). From this, the court assumed that teacher certification was the only acceptable way to ensure quality instruction. In a dissenting opinion, however, J. Krivosha considered such a conclusion "unjustified" because "no evidence was offered that, absent a baccalaureate degree, one is not qualified to teach" (*State v. Faith Baptist Church*, 301 N.W. 2d at 583). He also stated, "I find nothing either in our statutes or in logic which compels a conclusion that one may not teach in the private school without a baccalaureate degree if the children are to be properly educated" (301 N.W.2d at 582).

In addition, there is no empirical evidence presented by the state that parents with children in private schools or private schools themselves have harmed the children by providing an inadequate education. The argument might be advanced that there is no evidence of harm *because* of state regulations. While this point does have some merit, it does not account for those private school students in states with little or no regulations, or students attending *un*approved private schools that are contesting the legality of the regulations.

The question may well be asked, do private schools engage in activities that are harmful to their students? Have children received an inferior and inadequate education? What evidence can the state produce to demonstrate that private schools are endangering students' lives, teaching dangerous doctrines, defrauding parents, or turning out students who are ill-prepared to be productive members of society or have been inhibited in their personal development?

The available evidence suggests that private schools, almost without exception, have demonstrated a concern for the child and provided an adequate education. Otherwise, how does one explain the continued existence and popularity of private education and the departure of many students from public to private schools in recent years? In fact, research claims that students in private schools achieve as much or more than students in public schools (Coleman, Hoffer, & Kilgore, 1982; Koos, 1931).

Private schools have a historical legacy of providing a quality education. This study has not found, in the review of court cases or readings, any documented evidence that attendance at a private elementary or secondary school has ever harmed a student, educationally or physically.[21] Empirical evidence is, however, often presented to the court that students receiving private education are making satisfactory progress and, in some cases, better progress than they were making in the public school.

A typical example is found in *Sheridan Road Baptist Church v. Depart-*

ment of Education. A church school was found to be in compliance with all state regulations except teacher certification. Results from achievement tests submitted to the court indicated "acceptable and, indeed, above average levels of scholastic achievement" (396 N.W. 2d 373, 418, n. 54 (Mich. 1986)). In fact, the state admitted that "there [was] no allegation on [its] part that the children were being deprived of an education or being miseducated" (396 N.W. 2d at 417, n. 53). The petition of the private school, whose teachers all held college degrees, that testing be accepted in lieu of teacher certification was denied and the conviction was sustained.[22]

The state's justification for regulating private schools appears to be primarily based on opinion and conjecture rather than empirical evidence. The danger of this is that "if we allow speculation to support the justification of emergency or decisive benefit, then . . . we have annihilated rights" (Dworkin, 1979, p. 102). Sometimes the state's justification for the regulations is based on speculation of what might happen. Many private school regulations, such as teacher certification, class size, and specific textbooks, have not been empirically substantiated as essential and closely linked with explicit state educational goals, or proven capable of achieving their intended objective. Neither has it been shown that the mandated action is the only way to reach the goal.

The dearth of objective evidence by the state justifying private school regulations suggests the distinct possibility that they are based on conventional wisdom, subjective criteria, faulty assumptions, and undeclared presuppositions. At this point, private school regulations are indeed "ethically problematic."

Conflict of Interest. Regulation of private schools is carried out by the state, which also has its own educational system. Private schools are, therefore, regulated by their competitor—a competitor not only for students and financial support but a rival in educational paradigms and world views.[23] For example, in the *Yoder* case, the court record revealed that

> there is strong evidence that the purpose of this prosecution was not to further the compelling interests of the state in education, but rather the reprehensible objective, under the facts of this case, to force the Amish into [public] school only for the purpose of qualifying for augmented state aids. (*State v. Yoder,* 182 N.W.2d 539, 550 (Wis. 1971), J. Heffernan, dissenting opinion)

Since those individuals employed by the state owe much of their control and influence to claims of expertise and special knowledge, alternative claims present a threat to their position and power. This presents a classic conflict-of-interest case where decisions made by state and local education officials regarding the content and enforcement of regulations have great potential for bias and prejudice (West, 1983).

One need not stoop to a conspiracy theory on the part of the state to control private schools and parental decisions affecting their children's education. Self-interest, professional arrogance, and ideological incommensurability[24] will suffice (Arons, 1986).[25] "As a method of social control [regulation] helps those who get there 'firstest with the mostest,' because they decide in whose interest regulation is to be implemented" (Wildavsky, 1983, p. xvii).[26] Whatever the specific motivations, the important thing is that state regulations can masquerade under the pretense of serving the interests of society and the students, but in reality are serving the personal interests of education officials.[27] For example, some states require that teachers in private schools be certificated. But is teacher certification the *sine qua non* of a competent teacher?[28] Or is it a way the teaching profession, like other professions, has used to enhance professional status and salary by restricting entry? Must a private school meet all of the requirements imposed on public schools before it can be considered capable of offering an adequate education? Yet it is public education that has come under severe condemnation during the past 30 years for poor performance. The policy of having state and local education officials supervise private schools is morally suspect. It subjects private schools and parents to arbitrary and subjective restraints on their natural liberty to engage in a legitimate occupation and direct the education of their children.

Many regulations placed on private schools have questionable linkages with state educational objectives, create a conflict of interest because they are composed and enforced by state education officials, and impose undeserved burdens on private schools and parents. This strongly suggests that private school regulations are open to the charge of being arbitrary and somewhat capricious. To the extent this is the case, private school regulations are unethical. They lead to "a morally impermissible incapacitation of some people as moral agents, undermine their distinctive human nature, and violate their basic human rights. [They are], in short, a form of injustice" (Machan, 1983, p. 280).

Constitutional Issues[29]

The landmark case for parental rights in education was the *Pierce* decision in 1925. The Court declared that parents had a constitutional right under the Fourteenth Amendment to an alternative educational choice besides a school sponsored by the state. The state could not require parents to enroll their children in state schools only. Although state regulation was not an issue per se in *Pierce*, the Court has referred to *Pierce* as precedent that the state may, if it wishes, require that nonstate schools comply with reasonable regulations (*Yoder*, 406 U.S. at 213, 233). There is an important fact here that is sometimes overlooked. There is a constitutional mandate for reasonable choice in education but there is *not* a similar mandate for state regulation of private schools. The state *must* allow for educational alternatives besides state-sponsored schools. This is not optional. What *is* optional is the imposing of reasonable regulations on private education. These obligatory/optional elements suggest a primacy, a prioritizing of rights, constitutional concerns, and regulatory content. That which is required is more important than that which is voluntary. Proper public policy should, therefore, seek first to ensure that that which is constitutionally mandated is implemented and guaranteed before that which is constitutionally permissible. In addition, higher order rights should not be at the mercy of rights of a lower rank. The receipt of an education is not a fundamental right protected by the federal constitution, but many aspects of the parental right to direct the education of children are (*San Antonio Independent School District v. Rodriguez*, 411 U.S. 1, 35 (1973)). Overzealous state officials may be trying to enforce a secondary right through regulations at the expense of a primary right of parental direction in the education of their children.

The *Pierce* decision clearly compels educational pluralism in public policy. The *Farrington* decision 2 years later explicitly requires that parental choice in education, that is, educational pluralism, be both structural and substantive. Even though private schools actually exist, the state is prohibited from restricting parental choice in education through imposing extensive regulations on private schools. The essence of these decisions centers around the liberty of parents to choose alternative educational experiences for their children. The choice must be a real one, a bona fide option. Attempts by the state to emasculate the option of private education do not take seriously the right of parents to direct the education of their children. Much of the controversy between private schools and the state would be avoided if this fundamental fact was not dismissed or overlooked so quickly by the state.

The determination whether, in fact, a real and substantive choice exists is, admittedly, somewhat problematic. It seems, however, since the right to choose was given to parents and not the state, that they, rather than the state, should initially be allowed to pass judgment on the acceptability of the choice. Any narrowing of choices, shaping of alternatives, or restrictions on parental agency that the state might elect to do, would need to be justified, having a "reasonable relation to some purpose within the competency of the State" (*Pierce*, 268 U.S. at 535).

The regulation of private schools and the current standard of judicial review pose a potentially significant threat to this fundamental right of parents to govern and manage the education of their children. They come uncomfortably close to infringing upon rights clearly classified as "fundamental," such as freedom of religion and conscience and the right to privacy. This section on constitutional issues examines the various ways in which parental rights in directing the educational experience of children are often trivialized and marginalized by state action and by some judicial decisions.

Judicial Standards of Review for State Action. Parents are not required to justify their right to choose various forms of private education. The state, however, is supposed to demonstrate just cause for its intervention into private schools. A review of many court cases involving private school regulation reveals, however, that just the opposite seems to be the case. Much of the reason for this lies in the changing standard of judicial review.

The standard of constitutional review used by the courts has undergone two significant changes since the turn of the century that have had a profound impact on the efforts of individuals and private organizations such as schools to contest federal and state legislation and regulation. The selection of the particular "test" used by a court to evaluate the constitutionality of state action is of critical importance to the type of supporting evidence each side must present, which side has the responsibility for proving the veracity of its position, and the final outcome of the case. It is important, therefore, to understand these changes in the standard of judicial review.

The first major modification was the relaxation of the standard of review for state action. Prior to 1937, the court employed a stricter means–end test for all state and federal legislation. The Court interpreted the Due Process Clause of the Fourteenth Amendment as having a significant "substantive" as well as a "procedural" dimension. Legislation not only had to follow "lawful procedures" but also could not infringe on the liberty interests of others unless there was a "substantial and real" relationship between a government objective and the particular means selected by the state to achieve that goal. Both means and ends were given careful scrutiny to ensure legitimacy and closeness of fit (*Lochner v. New York*, 198 U.S. 45 (1905)). Furthermore, the burden of demonstrating the close connection between a state goal and specific legislation was placed on the state. The state had to justify its restriction of individual rights and freedoms if state actions were challenged.

Under no small pressure from the economic difficulties of the Depression and political forces such as President Franklin D. Roosevelt's threat to "pack" the Supreme Court with justices who would approve his economic and social legislation, the Supreme Court abandoned this standard of review for a far more lenient measure of constitutionality in *West Coast Hotel v. Parrish,* 300 U.S. 379 (1937) (Tribe, 1978, pp. 446–455). The "substantive" component in the Due Process Clause was significantly reduced for all economic and social legislation, which included education (*San Antonio Independent School District v. Rodriguez,* 411 U.S. at 35).

With the new standard of review, this type of legislation and regulation only had to be rationally related to a legitimate state objective. The requirement for a close fit between ends and means was reduced to simple rational or plausible relationship between the two. Furthermore, state action was still considered *presumptively* rational and thus constitutional until proven otherwise (*McGowan v. Maryland,* 366 U.S. 420 (1961)). In addition, the burden of proving that a specific piece of legislation was not rationally related to some proper state goal was placed on the individual or private party. This presented a nearly impossible feat,[30] for what legislature comprising elected representatives does not act in a rational manner?[31] This new "rational basis test" is, states John Ely (1980), an "essentially meaningless requirement" (p. 19). Laurence Tribe, a scholar of constitutional law, considers the new standard of review with its nearly complete deference to the state as "virtually complete judicial abdication" where the Court began to "resort to purely hypothetical facts and reasons to uphold legislation or . . . to uphold it for virtually no substantive reason at all" (1978, pp. 450–451). Speaking of the *West Coast Hotel* decision and its impact on American jurisprudence, Norman Karlin (1983) concludes that "in what can only be described as an Orwellian *tour de force* in reasoning, 'liberty' became subject to restraints of due process, and regulation . . . [became] due process" (p. 67). Substantive due process was retained, however, for rights designated as "fundamental" and is part of the second major departure from traditional American jurisprudence.

The second significant change was the incorporation of "fundamental personal rights" specified in the first eight amendments in the Bill of Rights into the Due Process and Equal Protection Clauses in the Fourteenth Amendment (*West Virginia Board of Education v. Barnette,* 319 U.S. 624, 637 (1943); *Griswold v. Connecticut,* 381 U.S. 479, 488 (1965); *Duncan v. Louisiana,* 391 U.S. 145, 148 (1968)). The specific liberties found in these amendments, protected from abridgment by the federal government, were extended to individuals confronted with similar action by state and local governments. The parameters of permissible action by the states were reduced in some respects by this addition of protected liberties.

In addition, the Court has identified several fundamental rights not specifically mentioned in the first eight amendments but that are derived from "penumbras" and "emanations" that flow from the Bill of Rights (*Griswold v. Connecticut*, 381 U.S. 479, 484 (1965)). These implicit but fundamental rights now include those of privacy, marriage, having children, having one's child learn a foreign language, choosing to enroll one's child in a private school, voting, travel, and freedom of association (*Pierce*, 268 U.S. 510 (1925); *Roe v. Wade*, 410 U.S. 113 (1973); *Seone v. Ortho Pharmaceuticals, Inc.*, 660 F.2d 146, 149 (1981); Tribe, 1978). These fundamental liberties found in the Bill of Rights, both explicit and implicit, cannot be encroached upon by the state unless there is a state interest that is vitally important or "compelling." Furthermore, the specific means selected by the state to fulfill its compelling interest must be the "least restrictive alternative." (The major exception is Free Exercise claims, as discussed in Chapter 3. See *Employment Div., Dept. of Human Res. v. Smith*, 110 S.Ct. 1595 (1990).) The individual or private party need only to demonstrate that a relevant liberty is being denied or infringed. The burden of proving the presence of a compelling state interest and the least restrictive means rests with the state.[32] This higher standard of review or "strict scrutiny" test resembles somewhat the "real and substantial" test used before 1937.[33]

The implications of these profound changes in judicial review for legislation are obvious. Unless a state regulation touches upon some narrow and specific right guaranteed in one of the first eight amendments, or is one of the few implicit fundamental rights discovered by the United States Supreme Court, the chances for judicial relief are virtually nonexistent. Many state courts have considered parental rights to direct the education of their children as a general liberty right protected only by the Fourteenth Amendment. Assertion of this liberty right, outside of the general private school option, is practically worthless in these instances because the rational basis test is the applicable standard of review for the regulations in question.

Parental Rights in Education: A Fundamental Right to Privacy. A good case can be made that parents' right to direct their children's education receives its legal viability from a bundle of *fundamental* liberties protected by the First, Fourth, and Ninth Amendments in the Bill of Rights. This would require the courts to use the strict scrutiny test as the standard of review. This bundle of fundamental liberties is part of a more "comprehensive" right of privacy,[34] which is to have "independence in making certain kinds of important decisions" (*Whalen v. Roe*, 429 U.S. 589, 599–600 (1977)). This right of personhood (Tribe, 1978) is simply the "'right to be let alone'" and is the "'right most valued by civilized men'" (*Stanley v. Geor-*

gia, 394 U.S. 557, 564 (1969)). The United States Supreme Court explains that

> our other "right of privacy" cases, while defying categorical description, deal generally with substantive aspects of the Fourteenth Amendment. In *Roe* the Court pointed out that the personal rights found in this guarantee of personal privacy must be limited to those which are "fundamental" or "implicit in the concept of ordered liberty" as described in *Palko v. Connecticut,* 302 U.S. 319, 325 (1937). The activities detailed as being within this definition were . . . matters relating to marriage, procreation, contraception, family relationships, and childrearing and education. In these areas it has been held that there are limitations on the State's power to substantively regulate conduct. (*Paul v. Davis,* 424 U.S. 693, 713 (1976))[35]

The right to privacy in child-rearing decisions is not absolute (*Roe v. Wade,* 410 U.S. 113, 154 (1973); *H.L. v. Matheson,* 450 U.S. 398, 449 (1981)). The child is not a "mere creature" of the parents nor is "the family . . . beyond regulation" (*Moore v. East Cleveland,* 431 U.S. 494, 499 (1977)). Parental decisions regarding their child's education cannot be made completely "unfettered by reasonable government regulation" if the state so chooses (*Runyon v. McCrary,* 427 U.S. 160, 178 (1975)). On the other hand, the power of the state to regulate is not absolute (*Mercer v. Michigan State Board of Education,* 379 F.Supp. 580, 585, *aff'd* 419 U.S. 1081 (1974)). The child is not a "mere creature" of the state, nor is there constitutional authority for "unfettered state control of child rearing" (*Parham v. J.R.,* 442 U.S. 584, 637 (1979), J. Brennan, with J. Marshall and J. Stevens, concurring and dissenting in part; *Meyer,* 262 U.S. 390 (1923); *Pierce,* 268 U.S. 510 (1925); *Yoder,* 406 U.S. 205 (1972)). However, all of this is but to state the obvious. The ubiquitous dilemma of what the proper relationship should be between the state and the parent (or private school) is still before us.

A substantial contribution to this legal morass has been puzzling statements by the Court that seem to hedge or "cheat" on the privacy right of parents to direct the education of their children.[36] These statements are again court dicta lacking any clear explanation or rationale of why the position they are advocating should be the case. These statements, coupled with the curious zeal with which some states regulate private schools, suggest that this aspect of the fundamental right to privacy in family life is not taken very seriously. While declaring that child-rearing decisions about choices concerning education are part of the right to privacy (Tribe, 1978), various court dicta appear to marginalize it.

A person's decision whether to bear a child and a parent's decision concern-

ing the manner in which his child is to be educated may fairly be characterized as exercises of familial rights and responsibilities. But it does not follow
that because the government is largely or even entirely precluded from regulating the child-bearing decision, it is similarly restricted by the Constitution
from regulating the implementation of parental decisions concerning a
child's education. (*Runyon v. McCrary,* 427 U.S. 160, 178 (1975)

The parental right in educational choice is limited (except in the most
extreme case, e.g., *Farrington*) to a choice of public versus private school
and not to a particular private school. The choice is narrowly confined to
the general source of education and not a specific educational experience.
If this actually represents the size of the "private realm of family life
which the state cannot enter" (*Prince v. Massachusetts,* 321 U.S. at 166) in
educational decisions, then it is so small as to be of questionable value in
many cases. The practical consequence of such interpretations has been to
severely weaken this aspect of the right to privacy and leave inadequate
protection for this fundamental liberty. The very restricted application of
the privacy right in educational decisions reduces this liberty almost to a
"mere shadow of freedom" and illusion of choice.[37]

Such a narrow application of the right to privacy has the obvious
result of restricting the range of choices open to parents. Yet in other right
of privacy cases involving family decisions, statutes and regulations were
declared unconstitutional because they "clearly burden the freedom to
make such decisions" and "imposed a heavy, and unnecessary burden"
(*Akron v. Akron Center for Reproductive Health,* 462 U.S. 416, 438 (1983)) on
the decision-making process. This is a substantial part of the family choice
ethos found in the *Meyer, Pierce,* and *Farrington* cases.[38]

Parental Rights in Education: First Amendment Protections. Another area of constitutional concern in state regulation of private schools deals with fundamental liberties protected by the First Amendment—freedom of conscience, exercise of religious belief, and freedom of association. Although
First Amendment protection from governmental intrusion is not absolute
(*United States v. Lee,* 455 U.S. 252, 257 (1982)), "the discretion of the States
and local school boards in matters of education must be exercised in a
manner that comports with the transcendent imperatives of the First
Amendment" (*Board of Education v. Pico,* 457 U.S. 863, 865 (1982)). State
intervention in the operations of private schools and in restricting parental choice in education has the real and profound potential of infringing
on liberties protected by the First Amendment. In addition to the right to
privacy, current analysis of *Pierce* and *Meyers* places these decisions in the
context of fundamental rights protected by the First Amendment.

Today those decisions would probably have gone by reference to the concepts of freedom of expression and conscience assured against state action
by the Fourteenth Amendment, concepts derived from the explicit guarantees of the First Amendment against federal encroachment upon freedom of
speech and belief. (*Poe v. Ullman,* 367 U.S. 497, 544 (1961) (J. Harlan, dissenting opinion) but which is quoted approvingly in *Moore v. East Cleveland,*
431 U.S. 494, 501–502 (1977). The association of people is not mentioned
in the Constitution nor in the Bill of Rights. The right to educate a child in a
school of the parent's choice—whether public or private or parochial—is
also not mentioned. Nor is the right to study any particular subject or any
foreign language. Yet the First Amendment has been construed to include
certain of those rights.

By *Pierce v. Society of Sisters, supra,* the right to educate one's children as
one chooses is made applicable to the States by the force of the First and
Fourteenth Amendments. By *Meyer v. Nebraska, supra,* the same dignity is
given the right to study the German language in a private school. In other
words, the State may not consistently with the spirit of the First Amendment, contract the spectrum of available knowledge. The right of freedom of
speech and press includes not only the right to utter and print, but the right
to distribute, the right to receive, the right to read . . . and freedom of inquiry, freedom of thought, and freedom to teach . . . indeed the freedom
of the entire university community. (*Griswold v. Connecticut,* 381 U.S. 479,
482 (1965))[39]

The Court has openly acknowledged "that a state law interfering with a
parent's right to have his child educated in a sectarian school would run
afoul of the Free Exercise Clause" (*Committee for Public Education v. Nyquist,*
413 U.S. 756, 788 (1973)). More important, the coexistence of "commu-
nicative activity or parental right" with a Free Exercise claim creates just
the kind of "hybrid situation" that would require the strict scrutiny test
for many state regulations for private schools (*Employment Div., Dept. of
Human Res. v. Smith,* 110 S.Ct. 1595 at 1601, 1602, 1604).

Many of the recent court cases involving private schools and state
regulations have centered on claims of infringement regarding free exercise and freedom of association.[40] The objections range from opposition to
any form of state interference at all to allegations that specific regulations
impose a significant burden on First Amendment rights and that a less
restrictive alternative should be allowed. The opposition to state regulation in general is based on the claim that private schools sponsored by
religious organizations are an integral part of the church's ministry in
assisting parents to fulfill their biblical mandate to properly educate their
children.[41] Private school regulations represent, therefore, state intervention into religious affairs and, ultimately, into the private realm of belief,
conscience, and the parent–child relationship.[42]

The state requirement of teacher certification is one of the most common regulations challenged by private schools. Since teachers play such a key role in the educational process, state approval is viewed as an excessive intrusion of state control that virtually destroys the institutional integrity of the private school. There are three ways in which the requirement for certified teachers may offend First Amendment rights. One, there could be a general opposition to state regulation per se because the school is considered an integral part of the church ministry. The requirement would be akin to state regulations governing qualifications for ordination to the ministry (*State v. Shaver,* 294 N.W.2d 883, 887 (N.D. 1980)). Second, the courses required to receive certification could contain offensive material (*Sheridan Road Baptist Church v. Department of Education,* 348 N.W.2d 263, 268 (Mich. App. 1984) or there could be, as in the case of the Amish, a religious belief forbidding higher education. And third, there may not be a sufficient number of certified teachers who also meet the religious requirements of the private school (*State v. Patzer,* 382 N.W.2d 631, 635 (N.D. 1986)). The proposed "least restrictive" alternative has been standardized testing, which has often been rejected by the courts.[43]

Regardless of which particular regulation(s) is at issue, the fact remains that private school patrons perceive their religious beliefs being attacked and compromised in a fundamental way. They feel a strong sense of alienation from the moral, educational, and cultural values of the public schools and of American society. The significance of these perceptions and beliefs is confirmed by private school patrons' willingness to litigate, often at great personal cost and sacrifice. The courts have, however, for the most part, been quite unsympathetic to the claims of Free Exercise violations by private school patrons. While the sincerity of the religious belief has never been questioned in these cases, the amount of burden that a particular regulation(s) has placed on the exercise of religion has been discounted by the courts as incidental or "minimal," an assessment obviously based on a great deal of subjectivity. Because of this the state is never required to prove its assertion that a particular regulation has a close and substantial means–end fit.[44] Whether the new "hybrid situation" announced by the Court in *Employment Div., Dept. of Human Res. v. Smith* will have any effect on private school cases in the future remains to be seen.

There are several options for private schools and parents when such rulings go against them. One is to compromise their beliefs and violate their personal consciences by accepting state regulations. Another is to refuse to accept the regulations and thus be subject to fines and jail sentences. A third option is to move to a state that will allow them to exercise their religious beliefs. Such alternatives do not speak well for the right to free exercise of religion, freedom of conscience, and freedom of association.[45]

Aside from the legal technicalities of the private school litigation, there seems to be a more fundamental issue involved if one is to make some sense out of the intensity of the litigation and court rulings. In opting for the private school choice, parents are clearly demonstrating their strong disapproval of government schooling. Whether their disapproval is based on more traditional religious grounds or moral foundations or cultural roots, they are all dissenting from a state-established orthodoxy and the imposition of majoritarian values. They are seeking personal and institutional autonomy to abandon a particular world view they consider as educationally, morally, and culturally bankrupt and to pursue their own vision of the good life (Arons, 1986). They recognize what courts and state officials fail to confess, that education is not and cannot be neutral. The secular/religious dichotomy employed by the courts is a false one and more self-serving than self-evident.[46]

Private school litigation, whatever the particular issue, is over values, meaning, and world views. It is a contest over which ideology will be allowed to exist (*West Virginia Board of Education v. Barnette*, 319 U.S. 624, 640–642 (1943)). At its center it is an issue of conscience and belief. Attempts by the state, through regulations, to shape the form that religious and cultural dissent may take in an educational setting will, by the very nature of the enterprise, result in the imposition of the very values, child-rearing practices, and cultural norms that private school patrons are trying to escape. Freedom of conscience then becomes more illusory than real, freedom of choice in the rearing and education of children more imaginary than genuine.[47] This resultant "despotism over the mind" (Mill, 1980, p. 129) comes about, states Stephen Arons (1986),

> because of a flawed understanding of the problem of family/school value conflict. Most judges and legislators have not perceived the centrality of school socialization to the lives of families and the raising of children; neither have they acknowledged the relationship between the formation of world views in children and the expression of opinion protected by the First Amendment. And finally, the courts have been so preoccupied with preventing religious impositions in publicly supported schools that they have virtually ignored the more significant imposition of ideology by the state in public schools and through regulations governing private schools (p. 198).

This occurs in spite of past statements by the Supreme Court that

> if there is any fixed star in our constitutional constellation, it is that no official, high or petty, can prescribe what shall be orthodox in politics, national-

ism, religion, or other matters of opinion. (*West Virginia State Board of Education v. Barnette,* 319 U.S. 624, 642 (1943))

The other disturbing factor in these private school cases, besides the marginalizing of religious beliefs and "flawed understanding" of the socialization and acculturation elements in education, is that the court does not require the state to demonstrate a substantial means–end relationship between the regulation(s) in question and the legitimate state goals. This is often justified by reducing the currency of First Amendment contentions, thereby allowing the court to use the rational basis test, or by allowing specific regulations to piggyback on the state's claim that education is a compelling state interest, which then overrides any violations of First Amendment rights. For example, in the *Sheridan Road Baptist Church v. Department of Education* cases, the court misconstrues these points by stating that

> the issue is not whether there is a compelling state interest in any individual regulation, but whether the individual regulations are reasonable means to give effect to a broader compelling state interest—in this case the provision of education to all children. (348 N.W.2d 263, 274 (Mich. App. 1984))

Such a line of reasoning would give every state regulation a compelling state interest and therefore be impervious to any kind of constitutional assault.

The burden on First Amendment rights was declared "minimal" because one can fulfill teacher certification requirements at religious or nonreligious schools, and there was no evidence of any shortage of qualified people. The court completely missed the point of the private school. It was not against competent teachers per se, but was against the "requirement that no one may carry out a teaching ministry without a government license to do so," which was in "direct conflict with their religious belief" (396 N.W.2d 373, 381, 414 (Mich. 1986)).

These approaches do not take rights protected by the First Amendment seriously (Pierce, 1982; Rosen, 1978).

Parental Rights in Education: Establishment Clause. Another dimension showing arbitrariness and contradiction in court decisions involving the First Amendment involves the issue of public aid to private schools, especially those sponsored by religious institutions. The three-pronged *Lemon* test— it serves a secular purpose, its primary effect is neutral toward religion, and it avoids excessive entanglement—is used to determine constitutionality of public aid (*Lemon v. Kurtzman,* 403 U.S. 602, 612–613 (1971)). It is the third prong—excessive entanglement—that often spells defeat for such legislation. The state is forbidden to give a particular form of public aid to private schools because it would require an unacceptable level of state supervision and monitoring of the aid program.[48] Such extensive government intervention would result in an "establishment of religion" by the state.

It is curious that the Court applies different standards of acceptability of state supervision and control for the Establishment Clause than for the Free Exercise Clause.[49] If a somewhat minimal level of state supervision and oversight in the provision of public funds creates excessive entanglement between the state and the private school, why does it not do the same when claims of infringement on free exercise are alleged in the face of state action dictating the educational programs of private schools?[50] As a matter of fairness, the Court cannot have its cake and eat it too. It cannot deny aid to private schools on the basis of excessive entanglement and yet turn around and claim that such involvement is permissible when it comes to regulating the operations of private schools. It cannot be a private affair in one circumstance and public affair in another, more religious in one situation but secular in another. Kurland (1978) observed that the

> entanglement part of the Court's triad is either empty or nonsensical. If entanglement means intercourse between government and religious institutions, then no law is more entangling than that which imposes government regulation on private schools as all compulsory laws do. *Pierce v. Society of Sisters* forbade state monopoly of lower school education but implicitly commanded that the state set and enforce proper standards of secular education for parochial schools. The oversight demanded by these laws is certainly far greater than the public aid to private school statutes that the Court has struck down. (p. 19)

It is not clear what substantive differences exist in the degree of state control between government supervision of expenditures of public monies in private schools and government regulation of private school functions. Yet, the former is pronounced illegal and the latter is declared constitutional. A principal reason for the use of two standards for permissible state intervention could be the constraints it would place on state action. In a moment of refreshing candor, Justice Rehnquist stated that

> the entanglement test as applied in cases like *Wolman* also ignores the myriad state administrative regulations properly placed upon sectarian institutions such as curriculum, attendance, and certification requirements for sectarian schools, or fire and safety regulations for churches. Avoiding entanglement

between church and State may be an important consideration in a case like *Walz*, but if the entanglement prong were applied to all state and church relations in the automatic manner in which it has been applied to school aid cases, the State could hardly require anything of church-related institutions as a condition for receipt of financial assistance. (*Wallace v. Jaffree*, 472 U.S. 38, 110 (1985), dissenting opinion)

This would be even more so if the private religious school did not receive any state aid at all. To avoid impaling itself on the horns of either the Free Exercise Clause or the Establishment Clause, the Court uses a different criterion for defining permissible state interference. This allows the state to intervene much more extensively in Free Exercise cases (especially since *Employment Div., Dept. of Human Res. v. Smith*, 110 S.Ct. 1595 (1990)) than in Establishment Clause cases. What this suggests is that state regulations can and do impose significant burdens on liberties protected by the First Amendment. In *New Life Baptist Church Academy v. East Longmeadow*, 666 F.Supp. 293, 324 (D. Mass. 1987), the court ruled that the requirement of observing private school teachers in the classroom would "involve the state in the church's educational ministry" in violation of the Establishment Clause. But often these claims of infringement are not given the careful consideration that they deserve as varying standards of constitutional review and application are applied. Such actions suggest that the rights of private school patrons to freedom of conscience and religion often are not taken seriously.

Absence of Genuine Harm or Danger. Restrictions can be legally placed on individuals and institutions in spite of violations of First Amendment rights. Interference in personal liberties is often justified on the basis that a significant harm or danger will be avoided or reduced. This constitutes an important part of the "compelling interest" argument for state intervention. The Court has ruled, however, that "conclusive presumptions" about potential dangers are not sufficient (Tribe, 1978, p. 1078). The harm must be a "grave and immediate danger" (*West Virginia Board of Education v. Barnette*, 319 U.S. 624, 639 (1943)) or involve "conduct or actions . . . [that] posed some substantial threat to public safety, peace, order . . . or abuse or danger . . . [with] proof to warrant such fears" (*Sherbert v. Verner*, 374 U.S. 398, 403, 407 (1963)). The evidence cannot be in the nature of a "general, speculative fear" (*Heffron v. International Society for Krishna Conscience*, 452 U.S. 640, 662 (1981)) with "no specific evidence" (*Wisconsin v. Yoder*, 406 U.S. at 224).

Part of the rationale supporting the landmark decisions affecting private schools was the acknowledgment by the Court that the activity the state was seeking to restrict could not "reasonably be regarded as harmful . . . [and that] no emergency exists" (*Meyer v. Nebraska,* 262 U.S. at 400, 402; *Farrington v. Tokushige,* 273 U.S. at 298) or that

> these schools were not unfit or harmful to the public . . . nothing in the present records indicate that they have failed to discharge their obligations to patrons, students or the State. And there are no peculiar circumstances or present emergencies. (*Pierce v. Society of Sisters,* 268 U.S. at 534)

In the *Yoder* case, the Court observed that

> this case, of course, is not one in which any harm to the physical or mental health of the child or to the public safety, peace, order, or welfare has been demonstrated or may be properly inferred [nor is there evidence of anything that] will . . . impair the physical or mental health of the child, or result in an inability to be self-supporting or to discharge the duties and responsibilities of citizenship, or in any way materially detract from the welfare of society. (406 U.S. at 230, 234)

In other words, the danger or harm must be real. "There must be . . . a clear and present danger, and the danger must be one of magnitude" (Dworkin, 1979, p. 102).

Again, where is the evidence that supports the need for regulation of private schools? The rationale given by the state in the various court cases is one of the general importance of education and the compelling interest that the state has in ensuring that all receive an adequate education for economic and political competency. A leap of logic occurs when the means chosen by the state to accomplish this compelling interest automatically assumes a compelling nature. Regulations become "compelling" only by association. Because they have been selected by the state as the means to achieve a legitimate state objective, they are illegitimately given the same status as the goal.[51] Also implied in the state's position and the court's often facile acceptance, is that the structure and content of education are self-evident. That is, they are not defined by the state or explicated. It seems to be a given that the kind of education that takes on a compelling nature can be whatever the state wants to define as such. A good example of this is found in *Sheridan Road Baptist Church v. Department of Education.* The request by the church school to replace the teacher certification requirement with standardized testing was denied. The court unjustifiably held that "to the extent that certification of teachers furthers education, it can be considered a compelling state interest" (396 N.W.2d 373, 381 (Mich. 1986)).

The key points, however, are, first, that means are not the same as ends and thus should not be treated as equivalents. Nor should disagreement about the means, for example, private school regulations, be interpreted as a disagreement about the end goal. Second, the "causal connection" between the goals of the state and the means it has selected is at best "obscure," and "if rights mean anything," states Dworkin (1979), "then the government cannot simply assume answers that justify its conduct" (p. 108). In his theory of justice as fairness, Rawls (1979) states that

> liberty of conscience is to be limited only when there is a reasonable expectation that not doing so will interfere with the security of public order; this expectation must be established by evidence and ways of reasoning acceptable to common sense, that is, by observable and provable consequences and by modes of thought which are generally recognized as correct. (p. 41)[52]

This has simply not been the case in litigation involving regulation of private schools, except in the most general and abstract sense. Instead of supporting documentation there has been speculation, rhetoric in place of a reasoned presentation of the facts.[53] When this occurs and the courts accept the state's assertions as presumptively valid and sufficient, then the fundamental rights of religious freedom, freedom of conscience, freedom of association, and parental rights are not taken seriously.

Pragmatic or Educational

Effectiveness and Efficiency: Evaluating Regulations. The last major area of concern in state regulation of private schools examines regulations in terms of effectiveness and efficiency. Do private school regulations actually accomplish what the state says they are intended to do, namely, provide private school pupils with economic and political competencies? Are they cost-effective? That is, are there other, alternative means that could achieve at least the same result but with less social and financial cost? Substantive answers to these critical questions constitute major areas of research and reach far beyond the scope of this study.[54] What can be accomplished in this limited setting is to set forth some preliminary thoughts and observations and raise some important issues.

The basic strategy for evaluating regulations seems straightforward enough—considering whether the means (regulations) achieve their intended goal. However, the exact process of arriving at a conclusive determination is not so clear. The first major problem is discovering what the intended objectives are. Nearly all statutory language in this area is devoid of explicit objectives. Even if objectives are specified, it is often left to state agencies to devise (divine?) the specific purpose behind the particular regulation. The near universal lack of articulated goals and objectives for regulations is probably a major reason why this study did not find a single evaluation of the instrumental value of current private school regulations.

An additional problem of no small proportions is the absence of any objective criteria within the general goals that are given. What does it mean to be politically and economically competent and how does one know when pupils have achieved these two important goals? What is the "common core" of knowledge that is vital for social and cultural renewal and at what point has a student acquired a sufficient portion? A scarcity of specifics suggests either ineptness on the part of policy makers and/or an implicit confession that many private school regulations may ultimately be subjective and thus arbitrary curtailments of individual liberty. Lacking any reasonable objective foundation, they thereby constitute an abuse of state power.

Means and Ends: Making the Connection. Let us assume, however, for the sake of argument that clear and objective goals were to be articulated. For example, students in private schools should be learning basic cognitive skills such as reading, writing, and mathematics. Standardized tests could be given to determine the level of academic achievement in these three areas, and a minimum score selected to indicate a required level of learning. These scores would represent the specific outcomes deemed by the state as necessary if one is to have the abilities to function effectively in our political system and be self-supporting. Current regulations flowing from legislation would be the means through which these essential outcomes would be secured for each private school student. The assumption to be tested is whether there is indeed a causal connection between these regulations and the achievement outcomes. If there isn't, then the regulations not only perform a useless function, but also are a waste of public resources and impose a significant burden on the liberty interests of private school owners and parents and should therefore be repealed.

Private school regulations are very similar if not identical to those regulations governing public schools. They are primarily programmatic in character and focus on the ingredients that conventional wisdom says must be present to ensure quality education—items such as instructional time, teacher certification, teacher/pupil ratio, class size, curriculum, adequate physical facilities, and so on. Empirical research, however, reveals that there is little if any correlation, let alone causal connection, between these specific types of educational "inputs" and academic achievement or other educational outcomes such as "student attitudes, school attendance rates, and college continuation or dropout rates" (Hanushek, 1986, p. 1150).

In a review of 112 studies looking at class size and achievement, Hanushek (1986) found that 89 were statistically insignificant, while 9 were positively significant and 14 negatively significant. The same general result was uncovered for the educational level of the teacher (95 of 106 studies statistically insignificant, 6 positively significant, 5 negatively significant) and years of teaching (69 of 109 studies statistically insignificant, 33 positively significant, 7 negatively significant). While teacher experience was the only factor that tended to give some support to conventional educational wisdom, even it could be questioned with the possibility of selection bias. Teachers with more years of experience often are given the choice of the best schools, classes, and students (pp. 1161–1162). Other factors such as the

> organizational aspects of schools, of specific curricula or educational process choices, of such things as time spent by students working at different subject matters . . . detailed information on teachers—their cognitive abilities, family backgrounds, where they went to school, what their majors were, their attitudes about education or different kinds of students . . . school facilities and school administrators and other personnel have not met with much success in producing desired outcomes. . . . The closest thing to a consistent finding among the studies is that "smarter" teachers, ones who perform well on verbal ability tests, do better in the classroom, but even for that the evidence is not very strong. (p. 1164)

Rather than being able to identify general, systematic factors affecting educational outcomes, it appears that factors (outside of the student) that lead to academic achievement are teacher specific and thus reflect the individual teacher's own "idiosyncratic choices and teaching style and methods" (Hanushek, 1986, p. 1164).[55] This does not mean that schools do not make any difference (Heyns, 1978; Murnane, 1981; Rutter et al., 1979). It does mean, however, that the current state of educational research has been unable, so far, to identify those specific factors or inputs that will lead to educational outcomes such as academic achievement.

> When we turn to the available evidence, however, there is little to support the conventional wisdom. Over the past two decades . . . schools have consistently spent more on education each year; this added spending has resulted in smaller classes, more experienced teachers, and teachers with more education. . . . Thus it is difficult to ascribe any deterioration in school quality to decline in resources available to schools. More importantly, a review of a wide range of sophisticated and comprehensive studies of student per-

formance indicates that there is no consistent relationship between school expenditures and student performance. . . . Yet, while wanting to "do good," policymakers have had an inadequate understanding of the determinants of scholastic performance. . . . Our understanding of what makes for effective performance in schools is astonishingly primitive. (Hanushek, 1981, p. 20; see also Cibulka, O'Brien, & Zewe, 1982, pp. 180–184; Kirst, 1981–1982, p. 298; McCarthy & Deignan, 1982, pp. 99, 102; van Geel, 1987, p. 264)

Hanushek (1986) concludes that "the entire area of state certification and educational regulation is open to considerable question, particularly given the evidence above" (p. 1169).

Another major factor that severely undermines any pretense that current private school regulations have any instrumental value in achieving legitimate state goals is the student him- or herself. Again, assuming that objective goals exist and that specific educational inputs having a causal effect on educational outcomes have been identified, how would the state disentangle the contributions of the private school in the realization of these outcomes from the innate abilities and family background influences that individual students bring to the educational process? At what point could the state accuse the school or the parents of not providing an adequate educational experience for the child and neglecting their public stewardship? How much of the responsibility for low achievement scores could be assigned to the private school? The amount of variation in achievement is of major magnitude. In a meta-analysis of 101 studies investigating the influences of family background variables on achievement, White (1982) discovered that family characteristics such as "home atmosphere" on the average accounted for at least 33% (r = .577) of the variance in achievement among students (p. 470).[56]

The problematic character of teasing apart and identifying the factors and the magnitude of their contributions to the educational experience of the student is again illustrated in litigation claiming "educational malpractice" on the part of public school officials (*Peter W. v. San Francisco Unified School District*, 60 Cal. App.3d 814, 131 Cal. Rptr. 854 (1975); *Hoffman v. Board of Ed. of City of N.Y.*, 400 N.E.2d 317 (1979); *Donahue v. Copiague Union Free School Dist.*, 391 N.E.2d 1352 (1979); *D.S.W. v. Fairbanks No. Star Bor. Sch. Dist.*, 628 P.2d 554 (1981); *Hunter v. Bd. of Ed. of Montgomery County*, 425 A.2d 681 (1981); *Doe v. Board of Education*, 453 A.2d 814 (1982); *Poe v. Hamilton*, 565 N.E.2d 887 (1990)).[57] Even though many of the students in these cases were obviously deficient in their level of educational achievement, they have not won a single case (Brown & Cannon, 1993; Dye, 1987–1988; Jamieson, 1991; McCarthy & Deignan, 1982). Malpractice suits are "based on a negligence tort theory" that requires successful plaintiffs to demonstrate that a "cause of action" exists. This is done by meeting four criteria: proving that education officials have a legal obligation to the student, that the "standard of care" or specific educational experience was not given to the student, that the student suffered an injury as a result, and that the injury was caused by the school personnel (Dye, 1987–1988).

It is interesting to note that few if any of the cases have been successful in meeting even one of the four criteria, let alone all of them. What is even more surprising is that the one criterion that would appear to be the easiest to meet—namely, that education officials have a legal obligation to provide a particular educational experience—"has traditionally been the downfall" of most educational malpractice suits (Dye, 1987–1988, p. 501).[58] In the other three areas, the absence of any clear standard as to what constitutes good education, tort law defining poor academic progress as a "deprivation of benefits" rather than a "legal injury," and the inability to determine the cause of poor achievement all preclude any successful outcome for educational malpractice suits (Dye, 1987–1988).

When private school regulations are viewed in the context of educational malpractice litigation, it raises serious questions about the wisdom of such state intervention, which also may have some legal implications. The overall rationale for private school regulations is to prevent "educational malpractice" on the part of providers of private education. It is to ensure that students attending private schools receive an adequate education and that parents properly fulfill their natural and legal responsibility to direct the education of their children.

But there is no way of really knowing whether private schools or parents are in fact guilty or not guilty of providing an inferior and unacceptable educational experience for the child. Yet private schools and parents are prosecuted by the state, have fines levied against them, and are sentenced to jail for allegedly doing what is impossible to prove—neglecting a child's education. On the other hand, it has been impossible to indict public school officials for similar irresponsibility in cases where students under their care and direction have emerged as functional illiterates and with poor academic achievement.

Part of the answer to this glaring inconsistency and the contradictory legal outcomes in educational malpractice cases can be found in the legal technicalities of tort law and statutory enactments. Yet the fact remains that the legal outcomes in educational malpractice litigation and litigation involving state regulations of private schools, contradict each other. Such inconsistent results in educational law reveal the presence of contradictory policies and a regulatory approach lacking some degree of rationality. It also raises legitimate questions of fairness. What moral and legal justification exists for holding private schools and parents entirely responsible for something over which they have limited and ambiguous control? Furthermore, why are public school officials not held accountable when some of their students graduate as functional illiterates?

The absence of specific articulated goals containing objective criteria and the "primitive" state of educational research lead to the undeniable conclusion that current private school regulations do not and cannot have any causal linkage with legitimate state educational objectives. Conventional wisdom in education is not supported by extant empirical evidence. Many regulations governing private schools are based on unprovable presuppositions growing out of subjective and speculative criteria.[59] They do not appear to accomplish what they are intended to do and they incur both a financial and social cost. It is quite likely that they are ineffective and inefficient and, therefore, are irrational public policy devices. Furthermore, recent research on effective schools points to such factors as "strong administrative leadership, high expectations for achievement, an orderly learning environment, emphasis on basic skills, . . . frequent monitoring of pupil progress . . . clear curricular goals . . . [and] dedicated teachers" as characteristic of successful schools (Doyle & Hartle, 1985, pp. 13, 52). Several of these important factors seem quite elusive to any attempts to ensure their presence through regulation.

Quality of Private School Education. While causal connections between educational achievement and progress cannot be linked with any practical precision to educational inputs and resources, it is valuable from a policy perspective to examine the level of academic accomplishment and educational experience in private schools. Perhaps most of the fears of illiterate, poorly educated private school students are unfounded and based on mere speculation.

A major objective of educational research in unveiling the learning process and discovering the character and configuration of educational resources that will best enhance this process, has yet to be realized. This lack of empirical evidence constrains policy makers to be modest in their descriptive summaries and most circumspect in any prescriptive claims. This holds true for public as well as private schools.

While there is little research on educational achievement in private schools, what is available shows a rough equivalency, if not occasional superiority, in academic achievement as compared with public schools (Abramowitz & Stackhouse, 1980; Cibulka, O'Brien, & Zewe, 1982; Coleman, Hoffer, & Kilgore, 1982; Koos, 1931).[60] A comprehensive comparative study of public and private education was done by Coleman, Hoffer, and Kilgore (1982). Their study revealed that students in private secondary schools generally tend to have higher academic achievement (as measured by standardized tests for reading, vocabulary, and mathematics), higher levels of self-esteem, better attendance, fewer discipline problems, and somewhat higher aspirations for postsecondary education; take more demanding academic classes; and are less racially segregated.[61]

Conventional wisdom in education would suggest that private schools appear to be doing a more than adequate job in providing good education to their students. If private schools have done and are still doing so well, why the need to regulate? The argument may be advanced that they are doing well *because* they are regulated. If this is true, then why did private schools do so well before regulation began at the turn of century, and currently appear to do quite well in states with little or no regulation at all? This again raises the question of the utility and value of the current regulatory approach to private schools. Regulatory measures taken by state agencies do not appear to have any appreciable effect on ensuring that children receive an adequate education. They seem to secure little if any real benefits to the state, yet can be quite costly in terms of litigation and implementation.

Credibility of Public School Officials. On a final note, the public side of American education has been under an almost relentless barrage of severe criticism for the past few years for declining test scores, graduates who are functionally illiterate, an upsurge in violence and drugs, lack of public confidence, significant defections to private schools—and the litany of deficiencies goes on and on (Chubb & Moe, 1990; Harnischfeger & Wily, 1976; Lerner, 1982; Levine, 1983; Powers, 1984; Ravitch, 1985).[62] Public education in America has deteriorated to such an extent that in the opinion of a national commission, it has placed our "nation at risk" (National Commission on Excellence in Education, 1983). This report on the sorry state of American education was followed by hundreds of additional commissions and studies, each painting a somewhat different picture of what is wrong with public education and what should be done to set it right.

Yet what is interesting about all of this is that the same government and educational officials who presided over this dramatic decline in the quality of American education still insist on being qualified to tell private schools what is required for a good education and enforcing such opinions through regulations. This unfortunate situation is a classic example of the "beam in the eye" problem. The state should be concentrating its efforts on resolving the immense problems it has with its *own* educational system rather than harassing a few private schools that by all indications are doing a good job of educating their pupils.

In addition, comments by public school partisans downplaying the significance of the Coleman, Hoffer, and Kilgore (1982) study, comparing public and private high schools, is a sword that cuts both ways. Albert Shanker (1987), president of the American Federation of Teachers, cautioned that "we are not very skilled at controlling for all the variables affecting student outcomes, we actually know less than meets the eye about whether attending private schools results in greater achievement" (p. 644). This observation must also hold true for outcomes in public education and those in state governments who write private school regulations.

When it comes to pinpointing exactly what is necessary to ensure an adequate education, clearly we "see through a glass, darkly." The kinds of helpful conclusions, gleaned from years of educational research, that can be drawn for policy-making purposes are limited and sketchy, especially concerning appropriate regulations for private schools. Daniel Levy (1986) observes that

> there is ample reason for humility when tackling the subject of private education and public policy. Even if we knew much more about the former than we do, ramifications for the latter would not flow unambiguously. Private education and public policy are subjects not for mastery but for serious and continued attention. (p. 24)

In this somewhat agnostic condition, the state must proceed with great caution in formulating private school regulations on substantiated evidence, if it is to escape valid charges of constructing and enforcing public policy on personal opinion and bias. In summarizing the inherent difficulties in developing sound educational policy and the indeterminate condition of education, Hanushek (1981) warns policy makers that

> the fact that school policies are so hard to evaluate makes it easier for teachers and school officials to be influenced by their personal interests. There is a lack of consensus about how to measure educational output; there are technical difficulties in separating the various influences on school performance; and there is a reluctance or incapacity to engage in experiments in order to evaluate programs. Without direct evaluations, teachers and school officials need not confront the possibility that their privately preferred policies may be useless for the student and bad for the community. (p. 33)

SUMMARY AND CONCLUSION

Restriction of personal liberty and institutional autonomy through state intervention into private schools raises serious and significant questions about its moral justification, its legality, and its usefulness in achieving legitimate state objectives. The current state of our knowledge about education and learning casts deep doubts on the ability and competency of the state to construct a regulatory algorithm that is not substantially based on the opinions, personal preferences, and speculative ideas of state officials. This pervading sense of arbitrary restrictions on significant personal decisions and liberty suggests an unethical dimension of significant proportions in current policy. The likelihood of infringing on basic constitutional rights such as right of privacy and First Amendment rights of free exercise of religion and freedom of conscience and association, along with violations of the Establishment Clause through regulatory entanglement, demonstrates that the field of private school regulation is heavily mined with legal explosives. And finally, there is simply no way in which the state can know if its regulations are indeed accomplishing legitimate state objectives.

One thing that does appear evident is that any increase toward statism in private education will not unite freedom with responsibility but destroy the former and make a mockery of the latter. It is also clear that the knowledge and technology do not exist to guide the state in its efforts to ensure responsible action in any great detail on the part of private schools. Henry Levin (1987) summarizes the issues facing the state's effort to regulate private schools and concludes that

> at the heart of this view [public benefits of private education] is a substantial involvement of the state in private education to meet the public interest. Somehow the state must assure that at least a minimum set of public outputs are produced. Whether this can be done through mandating minimum personnel, curriculum, or output requirements is problematic. Surely personnel must be competent to impart the values and knowledge to produce public benefits efficiently, the curriculum must include the subjects and experiences that will contribute to this end, and the result must be reflected in the outputs of the schools.
>
> Yet to assure this is so would require an unusual amount of regulation, and this would be costly, cumbersome, and probably unconstitutional to the degree that the state would need to become entangled in religion when evaluating whether schools meet these regulations. Furthermore, it is not clear that many of the public benefits of schooling can be measured for purposes of public accountability. (p. 635)

Regulating private schools appears to be highly problematic and often beyond the competency of the state to effect. Most regulations are probably neither effective nor efficient. A lack of clearly articulated state educational goals, an explicit connection between legislation and ensuing regulations, and a substantive means–end relationship with most regulations constitute fundamental if not fatal flaws in the state's justification for intervention.

Most regulations do not appear to offer any tangible benefit to the public. They are, however, a source of considerable tangible costs—expenditures for implementation and litigation and social conflict—both to the state and to the private school and its patrons. Furthermore, even if some tangible benefit could be ascertained, it is questionable if the magnitude of the benefit is of any practical consequence to society. The costs of state intervention are very narrowly localized (i.e., a particular private school and small group of parents), yet the benefits are distributed throughout the entire American society. The net societal benefit may very well be imperceptible. The costs to the individuals directly affected, however, can be enormous, especially when liberty interests and rights of conscience are involved. In such an ambiguous and complex area, prudent public policy would suggest the need to carefully weigh generalized societal benefits against particularized individual costs.

If the point where the interests of the state end, and the interests of private education begin, cannot be identified with any degree of certainty, what should be the proper policy in regulating private schools? If most state intervention into the operation of private schools is impractical and of a highly questionable moral and legal character, in what way can "freedom and responsibility . . . be united and reconciled to the best advantage" (Becker, 1953, p. 3)?

5 ✛ PRIVATE SCHOOLS AND PUBLIC POLICY

> In essentials unity, in doubtful matters liberty, in all things charity.
> —Simon Episcopius, (Haley (1972))

Before proposing possible ways to "reconcile freedom and responsibility," it is important to highlight the basic points presented in the previous chapters. Chapter 1 introduced the issue of state regulation of private schools with two striking accounts of private schools being closed by the state. The harsh manner in which the state forced these schools to close was, for one state supreme court justice, more characteristic of Nazi Germany than America. Chapter 1 also presented the dilemma of the need for both order and liberty, both common values and ideological pluralism in a democratic society. State regulation of private schools is of course but one of the many visible manifestations of this dilemma in public life.

The purpose of this book is to carefully examine government intervention into private schools in order to determine whether a more satisfactory approach might be found.

Chapter 2 revealed the historical and legislative roots of private school regulations as they developed in a social context. That chapter also presented substantial evidence to suggest several important findings. First, there has been an enormous shift of power from the private to the public sector in education since the colonial era. A most disturbing aspect of this shift of power has been its usurpation by various interest groups to transform, through legislation, their private values and ideologies into public values. These "public" values have then been imposed on the rest of society, particularly minority groups. Second, the existence of both state and private schools—educational, cultural, and ideological competitors—has given rise on occasion to suspicion and hostility.[1] Private schools, for example, have good reason to be wary of the state. The historical record contains many examples of the state's animosity toward private education. The position of the private schools and their patrons is a very precarious one because only the state has the legal power of coercion.

Third, the social and legislative history of private education in America strongly suggests that the fence separating government and private education has not been sufficiently strong to prevent the state from breaking through and trespassing on the liberty interests of private schools and their patrons. This is not to say that the state does not have any legitimate interest in the welfare of the children attending private schools. The state should intervene if the occasion requires, but the measures must be based on a justifiable cause. The historical analysis in Chapter 2, however, did not reveal any documented negligence on the part of private schools. Nearly all of the state action appeared to be based on what *might* happen or on cultural, religious, or ideological bias. All of this seems far more despotic than democratic, and it raises serious questions about the preservation of basic individual rights, especially for members of minority groups.

The courts have often been a place of refuge for private schools upon state encroachment. The court records are a rich source of information about the character of the conflict and the merits of each position. Consequently, Chapter 3 examined the rate and use of litigation by private schools to protect their interests from state interference that was allegedly illegal. The rate of litigation in absolute terms has increased. This suggests a deepening conflict and an even more urgent need to find a more satisfactory solution.

Perhaps the most significant contribution of Chapter 3, however, was to more clearly define the complex nature of the problem. The questions and issues raised in that chapter about parental rights in education, state interests in education, and fundamental rights of religion and conscience were valuable in conceptualizing the problem of state regulation of private schools.

A review of all the United States Supreme Court cases touching on private schools did not reveal very much in the way of legal guidelines to assist in adjudicating disputes between the state and private schools. Private schools have a right to exist and the state has the right to regulate them in a reasonable manner. While that does permanently fix the general location of the fence separating the state from private schools, it leaves an immense area ill-defined and open to differing interpretations. This ambiguity often leads to further litigation and social conflict.

Litigation and disagreement about state action and legislation are not in themselves proof that the government has acted in any illegitimate way. For example, laws forbidding physical harm or death and the placing of convicted felons in prison are considered not just legitimate actions by legislatures and state officials, but necessary and essential for the welfare of society. Nearly all those accused of such crimes either take their case to court or enter into a plea bargain agreement. These governmental measures, however, have universal acceptance and justification. The necessity for such protective action is clear. There is an obvious and tight connection between the means and a specific social welfare goal.

A strong possibility exists, therefore, that any state action outside of banning or taking over private schools is legitimate state action and in the best interests of society. In that case, Chapters 1, 2, and 3 would have served nothing more than to review a current social and educational problem. The fence defining the relationship between the state and private schools should, perhaps, simply be left as is—a barrier that the state may cross for almost any reason, a wall with more symbolic meaning than practical significance.

It is most difficult, however, to let the issue rest here. When a state official pries the fingers of a crying child off the desk in an unapproved private school as he and his classmates are forcibly relocated to a public school, or when state troopers bodily remove people worshipping in a church used as a site of an unapproved private school, the matter requires further consideration.

In addition, there are those nagging historical events chronicling the use by the state of both public and private education to control and indoctrinate immigrants, the poor, and other minority groups into the world view and beliefs of the majority group. And there are also those nettlesome questions about personal liberty, freedom of religion and conscience, parental rights, private groups, and the need for structural and substantive pluralism in order for a democratic society to be just that—democratic. The state has sometimes been an abusive neighbor. Avenues must be pursued that may lead to a more harmonious and productive relationship between the state and private schools, one in which the vital interests of both are protected.

Since the state is the only party with regulatory power, it is the one that initiates the action that then often develops into a conflict. In order for it to legitimately use its police powers, the state must justify its actions on the basis of legitimate goals and means (*Meyer, Pierce, Farrington, Yoder*).[2] The question of whether this is indeed the case concerning the regulation of private schools is central to any resolution of the issue. If a careful examination of the rationale for state regulation of private schools reveals sufficient uncertainty about state intervention then a search for an alternative or modified approach is necessary.

The objective of Chapter 4 was to carefully scrutinize the state's interest in education that theoretically allows, but does not require, it to intervene in private education. A fundamental premise of that chapter was that our constitutional and legal system was established to maximize freedom in a responsible way and that the state had to adequately justify any restrictions on personal liberty. Another premise of Chapter 4 was that an adequate justification of state action must meet two tests: the end and the means must be legitimate in and of themselves, and there also must be some reasonable relationship between the two. An important part of the reasonable connection between goals and means was whether the methods selected by the state actually achieved their legitimate purpose. If they did not, then there was no rational connection between the two. Legislation is presumed constitutional, however, until proven otherwise.

The research presented in Chapter 4 suggested serious reservations about the strength of the state's position. There was an absence of clearly articulated state educational goals and of substantive means–end relationships in most types of regulations. Another significant discovery of the chapter was the highly problematic nature of assessing responsibility for achievement, or the lack thereof, with current educational technology. There was also no indication that most types of regulations produce any tangible public benefit.

Besides the lack of any substantial benefits, most regulations exact a high cost from private schools. Just as important, research conducted in connection with this study did not discover a single documented case in which attendance at a private school had harmed a child in any way. The basic conclusion of Chapter 4 suggested that state intervention in private schools is not only impractical for the most part, but raises significant moral and legal questions. Perhaps Chester Finn (1982) quite accurately described the relationship between the state and private schools as one marked by "confused policy, schismatic philosophy, and stalemated politics" (p. 6). It would appear, therefore, that there is a substantial basis for looking at some alternative approach that will properly revitalize the relationship between the state and private schools along more compatible and fruitful lines.

The remaining task of this study, which becomes the major objective of this chapter, is to construct and justify an alternative approach for state regulation of private schools that is viable and, arguably, superior to the current regulatory strategies of using programmatic controls. The fundamental premise of this alternative policy option is that the state's regulatory approach to private schools should be minimal and allow for the greatest degree of educational diversity possible. Such a position is required because of ethical, legal, and practical difficulties created when the government intervenes into the operations of a private school. Whatever real benefits, if any, accrue to the state through extensive regulation are outweighed by the individual and social costs involved. A more pluralistic approach, it is argued, will at least maintain the advantages of the state's approach while drastically cutting the costs.[3]

This chapter has three major sections. The first introduces the general concept of pluralism and its valuable contributions to a democratic society. The second section examines the important role of private schools in our pluralistic society with a state-sponsored and -controlled educational system. The third section looks at the policy implications of educational pluralism in defining the proper relationship between the state and private schools and in deciding which private school functions ought to be regulated by the state. The advantages and disadvantages of a more pluralistic posture by the state toward private schools are discussed and assessed.

PLURALISM

Theoretical Foundations

Broadly speaking, pluralism sees reality as being multifaceted. One source of supporting evidence for such a viewpoint is based on the extraordinary diversity observed in the world we live and participate in. John Chapman (1969) writes that

> men, on the basis of their experience, presume there exists a plurality of values, no one of which is ultimate in a sense that would make all others its derivatives. Justice is not simply a means to happiness or reducible to equality, and all stand to some degree in a relation of tension with liberty. This pluralistic structure in the realm of value is the philosophical foundation of pluralism. (p. 92)

Opposed to pluralism is the idea of monism—that reality is grounded in a single element or is one-dimensional in character.

Flowing from these two diametrically opposed explanations of the world are particular subsystems such as political and cultural pluralism and monism (Jackson, 1977). While political pluralism/monism is a relevant issue in examining the proper relationship between the state and private schools, the cultural element is also an important factor in providing the social context for such an examination.

Political pluralism is not a well-defined theory but is a "current of ideas" (King, 1974, p. 20), which is "assigned numerous meanings" (Ehrlich, 1982, p. xi). Ehrlich (1982) describes pluralism as a trend

> oppos[ing] uniformation of social life, namely authoritarian rule, bureaucratic centralism, totalitarianism, technocratic ideology, and all tendencies toward monolithism. In a word, endeavours to monopolize social initiative are opposed by respective forms of pluralism. (p. 234)

The fundamental problem of how power should be allocated among individuals, private groups, and the state is a universal and central concern of any theory of political pluralism. A driving force behind articulated versions of political pluralism in the nineteenth and twentieth centuries was the emergence of the positive state—high levels of government intervention and coercion—and the problems it posed for individual and institutional integrity and autonomy.[4] The problem of intensive state intervention was further aggravated by the pervasiveness of Lockean liberalism and individualism in our political and legal culture and the high degree of social diversity in America.

Although there are many variations of political pluralism, there are three basic principles or "pillars" upon which these theories reside.

> (a) an insistence that liberty is the most important political value, and that it is best achieved in a state where power is distributed and dispersed, rather than being concentrated at one point; (b) a rejection of the idea of sovereignty; legal, political, and moral; and (c) a notion of the real personality of groups. (Nichols, 1975, p. 11)[5]

Political pluralism, while unequivocally opposed to any form of totalitarianism, is not, however, anarchism but sees the state performing an important and vital role in keeping order in society.[6] It also does not embrace the extreme position of the "ethical pluralists" who insist that "there can be no single right course of action in any situation" but affirms that the objectives of political action must be ethically based (Ehrlich, 1982, p. 16). The ethical basis for state action should be "to ensure a maximum of individual [or group] freedom in any given set of circumstances" (Nichols, 1974, p. 6).

What the basic tenets of political pluralism do espouse, then, are liberty coupled with moral agency as the primary social and political values and thus the ethical norm in the formulation of public policy. These values can best be achieved with the presence "of a multiplicity of power centers" in society (Baskin, 1971, p. 176). This dispersion or fragmentation of power will prevent one group from dominating all the others. In asserting these principles, pluralism requires a repudiation of the absolute sovereignty of the state as the ultimate source of moral, legal, and political values and power.[7] There are other legitimate sources existing naturally independent of the state or state action. These other legitimate sources of moral, legal, and political values and power are individuals and, in particular, voluntary groups that individuals create and with which they associate. Associations *qua* associations have rights. Pluralism is simply against any notion that the state is somehow omnipotent, omniscient, and "omnicompetent."

Individual and Societal Benefits

The political pluralist orientation offers valuable individual and social benefits.[8] There is a clear regard for the dignity of the individual and his or her capacity to rationally direct his or her life in a morally responsible way. These voluntary associations provide avenues through which individual rights can be both exercised and preserved. Pluralism offers great sensitivity and protection to fundamental issues of conscience, formation of life-directing values, and ethnic and religious diversity. It prevents the unwarranted imposition of majoritarian world views on minority groups and requires mutual toleration and respect. An ethos of pluralism encourages the creation of private groups that perform an indispensable function as "mediating structures" or buffers between the individual and the state (Berger & Neuhaus, 1977).

A high degree of pluralism also strengthens the ability of a society to survive. It provides a wide range of views that could potentially contribute to better, more informed decisions. It enhances the capacity of society to respond rapidly to a constantly changing world. Arons (1986) considers tendencies toward cultural monism as "cannibalizing culture," where the "points at which a culture might regenerate itself become points of destruction. Cut off from these sources of regeneration, an already collapsing culture becomes further ossified and brittle" (p. 196).

Pluralism can also add to the stability of our society by reducing social conflict and strife. Through the availability of more choices, individuals can choose alternatives that are most compatible with their needs and desires as self-directing individuals. Just the opposite often occurs when the state mandates more uniformity and standardization through legislation. Arguments begin to sharpen over *whose* personal choices become public requirements (Williams, 1978). In addition, the autonomy to direct one's life in a meaningful manner can often engender respect and loyalty toward the state. One is far more willing to give consideration and support when it is reciprocated. In speaking of attempts by governments to assimilate individuals and groups into a national culture, Nichols (1975) observes that such actions are "often seen by minority groups as constituting a threat to their existence or their way of life" and that a "state may well bring upon itself that very disintegration which it was the purpose of the policy to avoid" through eventual directions toward "totalitarianism or to civil war" (pp. 122–123).[9]

Potential Problems and Solutions

Political pluralism is not without its dangers and "darker side" when carried to excess. Groups can "capture" governmental and political processes for their own private use (McConnell, 1970, p. 3).[10] In addition, there could be near or complete paralysis in arriving at solutions to major social problems needing immediate attention (Kelso, 1978), the fostering of parochial outlooks in civic responsibilities and common societal concerns (Dahl, 1982, 1986), the potential loss of personal liberty by virtue of group membership (McConnell, 1969), and social inequality (Arons, 1986). Furthermore, it is obvious that pluralism is *not* to be desired in many situations. It would be counterproductive to have several systems of public education, measurement, legal codes, coinage, national government and defense, and so on.

While pluralism can lead to social inefficiencies, it does offer a greater potential for effectiveness by increasing the knowledge base for decision making. The threat of social segmentation and balkanization is reduced by the fact that individuals often are members of several different groups rather than a single entity. Many people feel a loyalty and commitment to a number of different social groups, which creates a greater sense of social interdependency. If a person feels that his or her personal liberty is being compromised by membership in a particular group, he or she is free to withdraw at any time and find another more compatible group. That some regulatory bodies are largely controlled by those they regulate is a reflection more of corrupt political practices than of the dangers of pluralism. Unacceptable aspects of pluralism that attack or diminish the integrity of the individual, such as racism, can be prohibited by law.

In the specific area of private education, the potential dangers from pluralism are decreased further by the predominate presence of a state-sponsored educational system. The state has already been "captured" by its own agents in the state educational department. The small proportional size of private education and the intrasector variety will also work against any concerted effort by private schools as a group to gain control of the regulatory process or influence policy decisions. Private commercial schools are already forbidden to discriminate in admission decisions on the basis of race.

The potential and actual dangers of pluralism must be acknowledged. The value of such recognition allows society and the state to take precautionary measures that can preserve the great benefits of pluralism and minimize its dangers. In the final analysis, however, some degree of risk is part of the price of a democracy. Kilpatrick (1979) reminds us that "occasional abuses are part of the price we willingly pay for freedom of religion, freedom of thought, freedom of mind to seek the truth and happiness in individual ways. The benefits of diversity far exceed the supposed advantages of uniformity" (p. 4a).

PLURALISM AND PRIVATE SCHOOLS

Private schools, like other voluntary groups, are a vital source of institutional diversity and "in many ways contribute to the vitality and pluralistic nature of the state" (*Wolman v. Essex*, 342 F.Supp. 399, 418, *aff'd*, 409 U.S. 808 (1972)). But unlike many other private groups, private schools are engaged in the transmission of culture in a formal educational setting. They, like their public counterparts, are helping to shape the minds, hearts, and actions of impressionable young people. In either setting, these children are a captive audience because of compulsory education laws. Because of this distinctive role in providing an alternative to state-sponsored education and socialization, private schools make unique and indispensable contributions to our democratic society.

The educational pluralism engendered by the presence of a nonpublic educational alternative provides an

> opportunity for experimentation, innovation, and a healthy competition for educational excellence. . . . No area of social concern stands to profit more from a multiplicity of viewpoints and from a diversity of approaches than does public education. (*San Antonio Independent School District v. Rodriguez*, 411 U.S. 1, 50 (1973))[11]

The organizational diversity found in the private school sector allows it to find different and innovative ways to adapt educational practices to our changing society. This educational pluralism not only enriches society as a whole but, ironically, may well prove to be the salvation of the public educational system by demonstrating alternative approaches and solutions to common educational problems.

Private schools are also an alternative source of education for those dissatisfied with the quality of public education.[12] This not only diversifies the educational menu but can be an important force for social justice and equal educational opportunity. Those children caught in public schools providing a poor educational experience have the option to leave, if they can afford it, and obtain an education that will better prepare them to be economically self-sufficient and more productive contributors to society. The private school alternative can help alleviate the socioeconomic stratification that can occur when attendance at a particular public school is a function of where one can afford to live. Another critical factor in promoting choice in education and equal opportunities for education is the provision of funds for those who cannot afford to pay both property taxes to support public schools and tuition for private education.

In addition, parents most often want to raise their children according to their own belief system. The problem arises when other individuals or institutions charged with the responsibility of assisting parents in their child-rearing obligations present ideas and values to children that are contrary to the fundamental values and beliefs of the parents. This becomes especially problematic when it discredits some beliefs and exalts others in a setting where the children are a captive audience, and parents are financially unable to place their children in an educational environment that is compatible with their personal beliefs (Arons, 1986).

It is here that private schools make one of their most significant contributions to a pluralist democracy. They greatly attenuate any indoctrinating tendencies that may occur in government schools (Hirschoff, 1977; Moskowitz, 1978; Rice, 1978).[13] They neutralize any attempts by various groups or individuals to dominate and control the socialization and education of children.[14] They provide an escape and a protection for those who feel their basic values are being attacked and replaced with repugnant alternatives. Private schools perform an essential role in preserving and protecting the fundamental rights and cornerstones of a democracy— freedom of conscience, free exercise of religion, freedom of association, and freedom of speech—through providing a setting for religious education as well as for those with cultural, sociological, political, and ethnic concerns and differences in educational philosophy (Hirschoff, 1986).[15] The importance of such educational and socialization alternatives is heightened by the fact that much of the "family/school conflict . . . is not resolvable by technical or professional judgments. Instead, these are questions of values, of conscience, of the definition of the good life," which often are based on "irreconcilable world views and matters of personal and cultural identity that are not amenable to compromise or resolution through political process" (Arons, 1986, pp. 193–194).

Drawing upon the work of three noted First Amendment scholars— Alexander Meiklejohn (1961), Thomas Emerson (1966), and Justice Douglas (*Griswold v. Connecticut,* 381 U.S. 479 (1965))—Stephen Arons (1976; 1986) gives three additional and interrelated reasons for the need for organizational pluralism in American education and the critical position private schools occupy in protecting First Amendment rights and safeguarding democracy. Meiklejohn focuses on a person as a "political individual" who is the basic governing element in a democracy. Self-expression is an essential facet of political participation. This fundamental

prerequisite for exercising political responsibilities and any activity necessary for its development, such as education, is protected by the First
Amendment from unjustified limitations by the state. Arons surmises that
Meiklejohn's "theory seems to imply that government control of the content of education is tantamount to infringement of the individual's governing powers." This is because the "originating point of the consent of
the governed would be controlled by the government, and all communication, learning, speech, voting, and assembling would be colored and
distorted by this coercive tampering with individual consciousness" (Arons, 1976, p. 94). Such action "threatens to make that individual politically impotent" (Arons, 1986, p. 203).

Emerson expands the political individual of Meiklejohn into the social individual, the basic component of society. As a self-directing individual, one is entitled to seek "individual self-fulfillment," which includes
the development of his or her personal consciousness and personality.[16]
Central to this development is the formation of beliefs and values. "Even
though belief is not identical to expression," observes Arons, "the system
of freedom of expression protected by the First Amendment could not
operate without freedom of belief" (Arons, 1986, p. 201).

Justice Douglas's contribution of specific First Amendment rights and
implied rights from the *Griswold* decision "provides a framework capable
of incorporating Emerson's and Meiklejohn's thinking and adding a case-
hardened vision of the amendment's central commitment to the protection of the individual" (Arons, 1976, p. 96). Arons (1986) concludes that

> if the government were able to use schooling to regulate the development
> of ideas and opinions by controlling the transmission of culture and the so-
> cialization of children, freedom of expression would become a meaningless
> right; just as government control of expression would make the formation
> of belief and opinion a state-dominated rather than an individually based
> process. If the First Amendment protected only the communication and not
> the formation of ideas, totalitarianism and freedom of expression could be
> characteristics of the same society. In modern times the opportunity to co-
> erce consciousness precedes, and may do away with, the need to manipu-
> late expression. . . .
>
> Thus the First Amendment's concern for the formation of individual
> belief and for individual self-fulfillment in schooling is joined to a concern
> for the exercise of individual political sovereignty and the legitimate forma-
> tion of political majorities. (pp. 206–207)[17]

The United States Supreme Court has extolled the virtues of educational pluralism but has warned the state against trying to "standardize
its children" (*Pierce v. Society of Sisters,* 268 U.S. at 511) or "foster a homoge-

neous people" (*Meyer v. Nebraska*, 262 U.S. at 402) or create "enclaves of totalitarianism" (*Tinker v. Des Moines School District*, 393 U.S. 503, 511 (1969)) in its efforts to implement the state's vital interest in education. Justice Douglas voiced his uneasiness over government schools that "may attempt to mold all students alike according to the views of the dominant group and to discourage the emergence of individual idiosyncrasies" (*Lemon v. Kurtzman*, 403 U.S. 602, 630 (1971)).[18]

The private school option offers just the kind of protective buffer needed, if adequate funding is available, to ensure that First Amendment rights are authentic and available to all (McCarthy, Oppewal, Peterson & Spykman, 1981).

There is little doubt of the essential and often unique contributions of private schools to a genuine pluralism. Our democratic society is greatly enriched and strengthened by the assistance private schools give to improving public education, promoting social justice through equal educational opportunities, providing an indispensable means of preserving and protecting First Amendment rights, and helping children develop into competent citizens and self-fulfilled individuals. The magnitude of these valuable contributions to society, however, is greatly diminished by the degree of control exercised by the state through statutory and administrative regulations.

PLURALISM, PRIVATE SCHOOLS, AND PUBLIC POLICY

In defining the relationship between the state and private schools, *Pierce* established two basic points. One, there would definitely be a fence between the private and public sphere in education. Private schools had a constitutional right to exist. Second, *Pierce*, as interpreted in subsequent cases such as *Yoder*, indicated the general location of the fence. The state had a right to regulate private schools in a reasonable manner if it chose to do so. *Meyer* and *Farrington* specified that the fence had to meet some minimal construction requirements. The fence was to be at least strong enough to prevent the state from crossing over to forbid the teaching of useful knowledge or from tearing it down by gaining near complete control of private schools through extensive regulations.

As this book has pointed out, these judicial decisions have not resolved the problem of determining the proper relationship between the state and private schools. The debate still rages on over the exact location of the fence and how strongly it should be built to ensure state interests and yet prevent unjustified trespassing on individual liberty rights. The purpose of this last section is to propose a proper and precise location for the fence and the specificities of its construction. It is to suggest an appropriate mix of freedom and responsibility in state regulation of private schools.

If a better approach exists than the programmatic one presently used by many states, it will have to come from justifiable alternatives that are built on less, not more, state intervention into private schools. This seems to be a logical assumption based on three observations of this study. One, increased state intervention into the affairs of private schools would most likely result in additional conflict and litigation. Second, the continuing ambiguity surrounding the objectives of education and the crude state of educational technology argue against the wisdom of more state controls. And third, decisions of the Supreme Court indicate that a step toward increased state regulation is a step closer to the constitutionally forbidden, albeit ambiguous, zone of excessive regulation. On the other hand, there are no similar constitutional proscriptions in the opposite direction. States can elect to not regulate at all or even pass legislation prohibiting any of their agencies from supervising any aspect of private school functions.

The thesis of this book is that control of private schools by the state should be kept to an absolute minimum. The maximum level of permissible state intervention is that amount which is clearly justified and necessary in protecting the state's essential interests in the education of all children. Essential interests are those which are imperative and indispensable to the preservation of a democracy and, as such, would justify coercive action by the state to ensure their protection. Legislation and accompanying regulations must clearly reflect this. Any attempt to go beyond this regulatory threshold is unethical and violates fundamental rights protected by First, Fourth, and Fourteenth Amendments. It also does not provide any discernible public benefits. Furthermore, inappropriate restrictions placed on private schools unnecessarily diminish the pluralistic character of our society and could very well be counterproductive. The significant and indispensable contributions that private schools make to the well-being and stability of our democratic society could be sharply curtailed.

A policy approach based on the three basic principles of pluralism has much to offer toward resolving the dilemma of realizing a proper blend of freedom and responsibility in the regulation of private schools. The first principle of pluralism, the maximization of liberty, reduces the complexity of the difficulty by eliminating some of the more fundamental problems of infringement on the personal liberties of private school personnel, parents, and children.

The autocratic nature of a more statist approach leads to standardization, uniformity, and "bureaucratic centralism" in making educational policy and formulating private school regulations. This carries with it the very real possibility of unjustified violations of liberty rights. It also faces the difficulty of proving that a regulation has a sufficient means–end relationship with a legitimate state objective. State intervention, therefore, has to simultaneously contend with significant aspects of both freedom and responsibility.

The second principle of pluralism rejects the legitimacy of the state as the Sovereign Parent. It recognizes that private schools, parents, and children have basic rights against unjustified state action and constitute independent and legitimate sources of educational values and decision making. The third principle of pluralism affirms the "personhood" of voluntary associations such as private schools and families. "Pluralism," explains Charles Burgess (1982), "is not merely a question of unity versus diversity or small versus large; it has to do with the essential vitality of communities of loyalty beyond the paternal reach of the state" (p. 64).

The complexity of the problem thus is greatly reduced for pluralism. By entrusting private schools and parents with much of the decision-making power in educational matters, pluralism need not be concerned with infringing on personal liberties. It can concentrate almost exclusively on the important issue of how to ensure that autonomous groups and individuals do not abuse their freedom and act in irresponsible ways by causing harm to others.[19] What assurances are there that private schools and parents will provide an adequate education for children who enroll? And if some harm is done, unintentionally or not, what remedial or compensatory measures are available? What is the role of the state with pluralism as a guiding principle in its educational policy?

Public, Private, and Familial Interests

Defining Parameters. In all the discussion of rights, liberties, public and parental interests, Supreme Court decisions, and educational research, it is easy to lose sight of the single most important element: the child, not the aggregate of American children, but the *individual* child. What essential interests of the child do the state, private schools, and parents have a fundamental obligation to protect? An a priori assertion is that parents, because of the natural relationship already existing between them and the child, have a more comprehensive interest and obligation toward their children than does either the state or the private schools. This comprehensive interest on the part of the parents could be broadly defined as wanting their children to find self-fulfillment in life and to develop into rational, self-directing individuals who are morally responsible for their actions.

The essential interests that the state and private schools have in the welfare of the child are smaller in scope and magnitude than those of the parent. Their relationship to the child is more of a social and legal artifact and more contractual in nature. Since parents freely choose which private school they want to assist them in their child-rearing responsibilities, the essential interests of the private school become coterminous with those delegated to it by the parents. If they do not coincide, parents will simply withdraw their children from the private school, which then must either make the necessary changes or be forced eventually to close its doors because of economic pressures.[20] The state's essential interests center around the child as a member of a democratic society and the fulfillment of basic membership obligations and responsibilities. Those mandatory societal duties relating to education have been broadly defined by the United States Supreme Court as political competency and economic self-sufficiency (*Wisconsin v. Yoder*, 406 U.S. at 221; *Lemon v. Kurtzman*, 403 U.S. at 655, J. Brennan, concurring opinion; and *Plyler v. Doe*, 457 U.S. at 221).[21] A strong democracy requires that its members intelligently use their governing franchise and be able to sustain themselves. The state's essential interests in the education of each child are those dealing with the acquisition of basic occupational and citizenship skills. The state would be justified in taking appropriate measures to ensure that these fundamental interests are satisfied. This does not mean that the state cannot or does not have any additional interests in the educational development of the child. These other interests, however important and useful they may be, do not take on the fundamental and primary character of essential interests. Noncompliance with these less fundamental interests would not justify the deprivation of personal liberty by the state.

It should become apparent that the integral interests of the state and private schools are often but subsets of parental interests and responsibilities for the welfare of the child. In this essential fact there is unity. The objections raised over state intervention into private schools have not been disagreements over these fundamental educational concerns of the state for the child. The disagreement has been over the substantive and detailed nature of what constitutes these occupational and citizenship skills, who is to make the decision and with what criteria, and the best way to teach the skills. The dispute thus far is not over general goals but over ways of interpreting the meaning and substance of those goals and the best ways of achieving them (*Minersville School District v. Gobitis*, 310 U.S. 586 (1940); *West Virginia Board of Education v. Barnette*, 319 U.S. 624 (1943)).[22] These have been and continue to be problematic issues. In these matters there is considerable doubt and uncertainty as to who is right. Although the actions of both sides could appear misguided at times, both the state and private schools have the same object in mind—the welfare of the child.

Primacy of Parental Interests. Since parental interests harmonize with the essential concerns of the state, as broadly defined by the Court, who should have primary responsibility to see that the individual child actually does become a productive and responsible citizen?[23] A good case can be made that the responsibility should rest primarily with the parents rather than with the state. There are many reasons why this assumption is a valid one. First, it has presumptive validity because the state has legally recognized the pre-eminent status of the parent–child relationship, its centrality in the development of the child, and the primacy of parental authority in child rearing. The state cannot interfere with the child-rearing practices of the parent without justification such as protecting the child from physical abuse at the hands of the parent.[24]

Second, parents love their children and have a greater feeling of concern because of the natural rather than legal relationship.[25] Third, parents are far more knowledgeable about the changing needs of the child. They can customize solutions to respond to the diverse and often idiosyncratic problems of children, who grow and develop in a variety of ways and rates. Fourth, in addition to being more knowledgeable, the close proximity of the parent to the child allows the parent to be even more effective in addressing the needs of the child without unnecessary delay.[26]

Fifth, parents have made a personal investment, often at a great sacrifice of time, energy, money, and other resources, in the care and nurture of the child. They care deeply about what happens to the child. Sixth, the emotional well-being of both parent and child are tied up in their natural relationship. Their individual sense of identity, self-esteem, and self-fulfillment come in large measure through the parent–child relationship.[27] "Protecting these relationships," declared the Supreme Court, "from unwarranted state interference therefore safeguards the ability independently to define one's identity that is central to any concept of liberty" (*Roberts v. United States Jaycees*, 468 U.S. 609, 619 (1984)).

Seventh, many parents feel an ethical and even a religiously compelling obligation to direct the development and education of their children (Chapter 4). Eighth, allowing parents freedom to raise their children "ensures the preservation and diversity in our culture" (*Franz v. United States*, 707 F.2d at 598). The parents "act as critical buffers between the individual and the power of the state" (*Roberts v. United States Jaycees*, 468 U.S. at 619). A federal appeals court concluded that

we rely on parents to instill in their offspring the values and motivations necessary to develop them into "mature, socially responsible citizens." We assume that this is a function the state cannot effectively perform; only parents (or some close substitute) are sufficiently sensitive to the myriad, constantly fluctuating needs and drives of children to be able to provide them the combination of support and guidance necessary to prepare them for later life. Such preparation, in turn, is essential not only to enable each child to think and act independently when he comes of age, but to preserve and promote our system of government and way of life. (*Franz v. United States,* 707 F.2d at 598).[28]

The maximization of parental liberty in raising children and directing their education is essential to the proper growth and development of the child into a competent adult and responsible citizen. A major way to maximize parental liberty in directing the education of their children is to allow for as many responsible educational alternatives as possible. Thus this expansion of educational options could result in the preparation of more competent and productive individuals.

State regulations for private schools limit parental choice in education and child rearing. They tend to take away in one hand what the other hand of the state has given to parents—the primary responsibility for raising children. The procrustean character of regulations and their enforcement often homogenizes and standardizes the educational program for youngsters and parents who have different and diverse educational goals and needs.[29] This becomes the case especially when state statutes or regulations contain some sort of "equivalency" requirement.[30] The wholesale application of public school regulations to private schools "is but to require that the same hay be fed in the field as is fed in the barn" (*Kentucky State Board of Education v. Rudasill,* 589 S.W.2d 877, 884 (Ky. 1979)).

The arbitrary nature of regulations is antipluralistic, attacks the dignity of parents and private school personnel as persons, intrudes into the delicate and sensitive parent–child relationship, violates the parents' sense of moral and religious duty toward their children, and calls into question the parents' competence and motivation without justification. The centralized decision-making process—individuals far removed from the "front lines" producing educational regulations—takes on an air of arrogance and unwarranted state paternalism that is foreign to the democratic ethos of our society. To restrict parental choice and discretion in educational practices with unjustified regulations is to harm both the child and the parent in significant ways.[31] It prevents the parent from meeting the needs of the child and the family in the most effective and efficient manner possible. It also represents an unwarranted abridgment of the right of privacy in family life by interfering with parental decisions regarding the education of their children and the intimate relationship between parent and child.

As Chapter 4 suggested, the state has not provided sufficient evidence to justify many of the regulations governing private schools. Many regulations are means in search of a goal, and there is no realistic hope that current educational technology can determine whether most regulations do indeed accomplish what they are supposed to do. In addition, there is little if any evidence that children have been harmed by attending private schools. This would suggest a very reasonable and plausible assertion: that most regulatory efforts by the state, at the very least, do not make any positive contribution to the child's welfare and may even cause harm to parents and children involved in private schools.

The basic argument advanced by the state for the existence of regulations is to protect those children whose parents are abusive and/or incompetent. The state claims that some parents do not know whether their children are receiving an adequate education or do not care if their children are educated or may even prevent their children from having any educational experience altogether. The state also claims that some private school operators are incompetent and try to deceive the public.[32] In any of these examples, significant harm could be done to the child and unnecessary burdens would be imposed on society. This point is a very important one and must be taken seriously. The state does have a responsibility to protect children from parental and other private decisions that cause serious injury to the children.

A great part of the difficulty lies in the fact that the state does not know which parents and private schools may act in irresponsible ways causing significant harm to the child. The virtue of regulations, then, is their pervasive sweep, which anticipates irresponsible acts and hopefully prevents harm and injury from occurring.[33] The real and staggering cost this imposes on the great majority of parents and private schools that are competent has already been discussed in Chapter 4. But are there not ways in which public policy in education can reduce these costs and still provide at least the same level of protection against potential harm to children? Is there not a way in which "freedom and responsibility . . . can be united and reconciled to the best advantage" of all (Becker, 1953, p. 3)?

Internal Regulators

While the state's rationale for issuing regulations carries considerable weight, the force of its argument is significantly reduced when applied to the private school setting. There are several self-regulating features inherent in private education that accomplish most of what state regulations are supposed to do. Furthermore, these internal regulators perform their protective function through a natural selection process at little or no cost in limiting personal liberty or otherwise. If this is the case, then regulations become at best superfluous, and at worst wasteful, unethical, and unconstitutional.

The enrollment of children in private schools is *prima facie* evidence that their parents are vitally concerned about their upbringing and education. The decision not to enroll a child in the state school system often comes after careful study and reflection. Private education is not the cultural norm. Attendance at a private school is a gesture of dissent from the predominant public school ethos in American society. Also, it often requires, observes William Ball, significant financial and personal sacrifices "in the face of high taxation, inflation, and sometimes job loss" (U.S. Congress Senate, Committee on Labor and Human Resources, 1984, p. 50). These significant barriers would be more than sufficient deterrents to those few parents who do not care about their children's educational development.

Parents who select private education for their children also demonstrate *prima facie* evidence that they know the basics of a quality education. They have not only done a comparison between the public and private sector but have selected a particular private school. This would strongly suggest that they are sufficiently competent to direct the proper education of their children. In a study by Donald Erickson (1986) comparing preferences of parents in private and public schools, the "top-priority reason" given by parents preferring private schools was Religion/Spirituality (22%), followed by Academic Quality/Emphasis (20.5%), and Discipline (16.8%). In contrast, parents preferring public schools listed their main reason as Don't Know (13.6%), followed by Cheapness (13.3%) and Proximity, Convenience (12.5%) (pp. 93–94).[34] It is little wonder that Erickson could suggest that

> parents who actively seek out schools that fit their preference are unusually well informed, sophisticated, thoughtful, and concerned about their children's schooling. In exercising their preferences, these parents sort themselves out into schools with different emphases and obtain much greater satisfaction than do the parents who do not actively choose. If the ratings by these people may be taken seriously, the quality of their children's schooling might have been inferior if the options in question had not existed. (p. 98)[35]

A second way in which the private school choice naturally operates against the possibility of educational deprivation for private school students is the vested interests of the parents. They not only have great concern about the proper development of their children, but they also have made significant emotional and psychological investments, as well as investments of time and money, in the private school choice. They have a vested interest to see that their child succeeds and does well. They will want to have a much closer and substantive involvement in their child's educational progress. In doing this they perform the dual function of providing quality control and being a source of support, help, and encouragement to the child. Studies by James Coleman (1966, 1982) and Karl White (1982) have suggested that family variables account for a good portion of the variance in academic achievement. Because of this active involvement by parents, private school students have a better than average chance of receiving a more than adequate education.

A third internal regulator is the economics of private education. The market for the educational dollar is a tight one. If parents cannot find an educational experience superior enough to that offered in the public schools, what rational incentive is there for them to pay school taxes *and* private school tuition for an inferior or even equivalent educational program? Private school operators are aware of this. Their potential customers are knowledgeable and aware of what constitutes a good education. "Parents *will* withdraw their children," notes William Ball, "from schools which are poor in quality, or poor in discipline. That in fact is why so many parents have removed their children from public schools" (U.S. Congress Senate, Committee on Labor and Human Resources, 1984, p. 50). It is not in the best interests of private schools to offer a shoddy educational program. If they do not satisfy a clientele that is concerned and knowledgeable about their children's education, the students will be withdrawn and the schools will be forced to close or respond to the demands of the parents. Private schools simply must produce acceptable results, or else. Furthermore, private elementary and secondary schools, unlike private trade or technical schools, have a long-term interest in the educational career of the child. It is to their advantage to provide quality education year in and year out in order to keep students coming back.

This interest in self-preservation is also manifest in the admission and dismissal policies of schools. A private school will not be inclined to admit students, or permit them to stay, who are disruptive to the learning environment or do not have a good chance of succeeding.[36] A good reputation has great monetary value for a private school.

A fourth intrinsic factor working against harm occurring to children in private schools is the educational milieu of the school. This happens in two major ways. One, private schools have the institutional autonomy to exercise a greater amount of control over the educational environment of the school. They have a driving incentive to develop the kind of characteristics found in effective schools. These include such things as "clear sense of purpose, an institutional ethos, [and] team spirit" (Frymier, 1986, p. 648), along with "curricular goals, high expectations for students, dedicated teachers, effective discipline . . . strong emphasis on academic subjects" (Doyle & Hartle, 1985, p. 52), "strong educational leadership" (Chubb & Moe, 1985, p. 5), a shared " 'belief structure, a value system, a consensual rather than hierarchal governance system, and a set of common goals that blur the boundaries between . . . private and organizational lives'" of the school community (Doyle & Hartle, 1985, p. 53).[37] This has led several researchers to suggest that the difference in achievement found in the Coleman, Hoffer, and Kilgore (1982) study between public and private school students might be partially explained by the freedom private schools have to construct and customize an educational environment conducive to excellent education (Chubb & Moe, 1985, 1990).[38]

Another means by which the private school environment reduces the possibility of a student receiving an inferior education is the influence of his or her classmates. Richard Murnane (1986a, 1986b) contends that private school students have higher achievement scores than public school students in part because more capable students attend private schools than public schools. The selective admission policies of private schools create a more homogeneous student body "com[ing] from more advantaged homes and consequently bring[ing] more skills to school with them." Having such "fellow students," states Murnane, "plays a significant contributing role in determining student scores" (1986a, p. 142; see also Murnane, 1983, 1986b, pp. 153–169; Willms, 1983). Cookson and Persell (1985) report that the susceptibility of youngsters to peer pressure "can have an impact on even an indifferent student" surrounded by classmates "who are academically interested and ambitious." As one student observed, " 'It isn't cool to be dumb around here'" (p. 95).

Thus the private school environment, both in terms of institutional ethos and the students who constitute the student body, functions as an additional intrinsic governor greatly moderating the possibility of a child receiving an inadequate education.

And finally, there is another factor that helps to blunt possible harm coming to a child attending a private school. Much of the child's education takes place outside the four walls of the school, either public or private. There are a variety of sources for learning, such as "the parent, the family, its friends, the church, books, television, radio, newspapers, correspondence courses . . . 'on the job training'" (West, 1965, p. 10), magazines, libraries, and museums, to mention just a few. Our dependence on schools for information may be lessened, especially in an age of electronic media and interactive computer programs. These provide an important source of instruction to supplement what the child receives in school.

External Regulators

Justification and Approach. Like the state, parents and private school personnel are not infallible. There is the remote possibility that parental interest and the internal regulatory features inherent in private education will not be sufficient in every instance to protect the interests of the child. But what should be done in these rare cases? What policy approach can replace the indiscriminate effects of the regulatory cannon with the specific impact of a rifle shot? What would be the most effective types of external regulators?

The regulatory approach, which "assume[s] with perfect impartiality that every parent [and private school official] intends to defraud his child, and can only be supplied with a conscience at the police court," is a most "cynical assumption of the weakness and selfishness of parents [and private school officials]" (Herbert, 1978, p. 65). It is an assumption that lacks empirical support and is further refuted by the vast majority of parents who properly care for their children and provide for their needs and wants. The available evidence from several court cases and research on private schools suggests that concerned and competent parents do try very hard to ensure that their children are receiving a good education in the private sector (Chapter 4). The use of regulations still remains attractive to the state, however, but perhaps more for reasons of administrative ease and convenience for the state's educational bureaucracy in complying with state law than for providing demonstrable benefits to the child.

The first principle of pluralism calls for the optimization of liberty. In the case of private schools, this basically means increasing the quantity and quality of educational choices open to parents. State restrictions of educational choice through direct means such as prescribing the educational content, or indirect means such as health, safety, fire, zoning, and tax-exempt status requirements,[39] are often the very antithesis of pluralism. The state, however, does have an essential interest and role in protecting the liberty rights of *children* from parents and private school officials who may be ignorant, incompetent, and abusive. State intervention, paradoxically, could be consistent with the principles of pluralism in those rare instances where the child's liberty was obviously being limited unjustly by parents and/or private school officials not fulfilling their delegated responsibilities. Keeping in mind the general axiom that "externally imposed requirements do not contribute to good education" (Doyle & Hartle, 1985, p. 52), what would these rare instances be and in what manner should the state step forward to prevent the unjustified infringement of the child's liberty?

One approach to answering these important questions is to look at all the state regulations governing private schools and begin to select those which appear to be essential in protecting the basic liberty rights of children. This approach does have some merit but is exceedingly burdensome and complex, somewhat analogous to searching for four-leaf clovers in a football field. One must first gather all the pertinent regulations, then sort through them and by some predetermined criteria select the ones that appear to be essential. One potential flaw in this approach is the assumption that the current body of private school regulations contains all the essential regulations.

A more effective approach may be to rephrase the question in terms of identifying those things which would definitely *prevent* a child from receiving a basic education, rather than trying to identify all of the contributing ingredients of a basic education. The distinction here is somewhat subtle but most important. The avenues leading to failure are far fewer than the many different paths to a successful educational program. By identifying and removing factors causing failure, parents and private schools are free to develop a variety of productive and effective educational programs that are in closer harmony with the needs of children and parents. These failure factors would be proper areas for state regulation.

Appropriate Areas for State Regulation. The first, most obvious way in which a child can fail to be properly educated is through loss of life or physical well-being. These events result in a permanent loss of liberty and educational opportunity or inflict devastating handicaps that can last a lifetime. There is little chance for compensation or remedial action to restore lost opportunities to the student. Regulations relating to fire, safety, health, and building codes that serve to ensure a safe and secure learning environment are essential. Along these same lines would be important regulations prohibiting the physical and sexual abuse of children. The protection of the child from physical harm and danger is fundamental to his or her exercise of personal liberty and is a critical area for state supervision in private as well as public schools.

Second, it is obvious that if a parent or private school does not provide any type of formal education, it would be very difficult for the child to be sufficiently educated. To ensure that all children have an opportunity to learn and grow in fundamental and essential ways, the state has a duty to require, through compulsory education laws, that such an opportunity be provided by parents and private schools. Reports and reporting procedures needed to account for every single eligible child in the state would be a proper and necessary action on the part of the state. Each private school should be required to notify the state of its existence through some scheme of registration. They should also report the names, addresses, and parents or guardians of those students who have enrolled and those who withdraw.

A third major way in which a child's educational experience could be seriously compromised is through parental ignorance. In private education this could happen in two basic ways. One, the private school could attempt to defraud parents with false and misleading information about the school and the progress of their children. Second, vital information that a parent would need in assessing the quality of the education offered by the school and in finding the right "fit" between various educational programs and the particular needs of their children may not be available. In addition to prohibiting unethical business practices such as "fraud, embezzlement, false solicitation" (U.S. Congress, Senate, Committee on Labor and Human Resources, 1984, p. 51), the state should require private schools to meet in a demonstrable, empirical manner some kind of truth-in-education or disclosure standards. These could include information on such areas as admission requirements (Coons, 1984)[40];

> financial statements; physical facilities; staff, including their education and experience; curriculum requirements for graduation; present students and numbers that have failed or dropped out; average and median scores of students on standardized aptitude and achievement tests; academic placement and performance of students after graduation; statement of the school's basic philosophy and methodology of education (Elson, 1973, p. 4/57)

and policies relating to the internal workings of the school such as discipline, grading, extracurricular activities, liability insurance, tuition and other program costs, and so forth.[41] This type of information would greatly increase the effectiveness and competency of parents in meeting the basic educational needs of their children.[42] This area, however, must be approached in a parsimonious fashion or extensive requirements could violate the Establishment Clause forbidding excessive entanglement by the government in religious institutions (*Lemon v. Kurtzman*, 403 U.S. 602 (1971)).

A fourth and final situation in which the basic liberty interests of all children could be violated in a fundamental way is by being deprived of basic literacy skills. The ability to read, write, and do basic computations is the universal foundation upon which all other learning is built.[43] Take these essential abilities away and the child is almost certain to fail in personal growth and development as well as performing basic citizenship responsibilities in society.[44] The denial of these capabilities would constitute a significant deprivation of the essential liberty interests of the child. The state would be fully justified in mandating that any educational program enrolling children of compulsory schooling age be required to equip each child with these basic literacy and mathematical skills. (This assumes, of course, that the child has the capacity to learn and is not learning disabled.)

These four areas in education represent universal ways in which any child would fail to gain an education essential to his or her personal development and the security of our democratic society. They are, without exception, situations in which the liberty rights of children would be abridged in a fundamental and unjustifiable manner. They constitute, therefore, valid objectives within the overall legitimate state goal of political and economic competency for all its citizens. They qualify as essential areas of state intervention and fall within the realm justified state regulation. The cost that would be imposed on children if the internal regulating mechanism in private education breaks down is of such a magnitude that it warrants state supervision in these essential areas and the curtailment of parental and private school freedoms.

Standards of Judicial Review. The specific form and content of regulations that the state may develop in these four essential areas—ensuring a safe, secure learning environment, universal formal education, ethical business practices and truth-in-education, and basic literacy topics of reading, writing, and arithmetic—are not self-evident. This leaves open the very real possibility of the state issuing regulations "under the guise of protecting the public interest by legislative action which is arbitrary or without some reasonable relation" to these four key objectives in educational policy (*Meyer v. Nebraska*, 262 U.S. at 400). A fundamental principle in our liberal democratic society is that the state is obligated to justify limitations placed on liberty. Justified intervention includes *both* legitimate objectives and legal means.[45] There are both substantive and procedural grounds that the state must meet before it can legally restrict personal liberty. Even in the important area of health, safety, fire, and building codes, regulations could be constructed and enforced in an arbitrary manner and pose a formidable obstacle to parental choice in education through "hypertechnical" codes (*City of Sumner v. First Baptist Church*, 639 P.2d 1358 (Wash. 1982)).[46]

If attempts to modify legislation or the use administrative hearings do not provide a satisfactory resolution of the issue, the only recourse available to parents and private schools in the face of such state action is litigation. As discussed in Chapter 3, the standard of judicial review that the court selects in adjudicating disputes over the constitutionality of legislation and state action is critical to the outcome of the case. If the rational means test is used, then the chance of parents and the private school prevailing is next to nothing. The usefulness of this test would be found only in cases where there was an outrageously clear and blatant invasion of liberty rights such as the banning of the private school option. Yet the other common standard of review, the strict scrutiny test, may impose overly harsh and rigid restraints on the state to act in critical areas of obvious importance such as health and safety. Recently, however, a judicial standard of review has emerged that stands between the rational means test and the strict scrutiny test and that has great potential value in protecting the important interests of both the state and the private educational sector.

The developing third standard of review has been used by the Supreme Court to scrutinize legislation under the Equal Protection Clause of the Fourteenth Amendment where certain suspect classifications did not warrant strict scrutiny review (*Seone v. Ortho Pharmaceuticals, Inc.,* 660 F.2d 146 (1981)). A major function of the Equal Protection Clause is to "operate as an antimajoritarian safeguard which views with suspicion all public actions tending to burden 'discrete and insular' minorities" (Tribe, 1978, p. 1077).

The selection of the intermediate standard usually occurs when "important, though not necessarily 'fundamental' or 'preferred,' interests are at stake . . . [where there has been] either a significant interference with liberty or a denial of a benefit vital to an individual" (Tribe, 1978, pp. 1090–1091).[47] This "heightened standard of review," "intermediate standard of review," or "'second order' rational-basis review" (*Cleburne v. Cleburne Living Center, Inc.,* 473 U.S. 432, 440, 453, 458 (1985)) has been applied directly by the Court to cases touching on classifications based on gender (*Craig v. Boren,* 429 U.S. 190 (1976)); legitimacy (*Clark v. Jeter,* 486 U.S. 456 (1988)); or children of illegal aliens (*Plyler v. Doe,* 457 U.S. 202 (1982)). These areas are "beyond individual control and bear no relation to the individual's ability to participate in and contribute to society" (*Cleburne v. Cleburne Living Center, Inc.,* 473 U.S. at 440).[48]

The application of this third standard by the Supreme Court to important but not necessarily fundamental rights such as parental choice in private education is, I would argue, worthy of consideration. First, there are some good indications that, because private school regulations affect a particular minority group in some important ways, a higher standard of review should be required. In *United States v. Carolene Products Co.,* the Court wondered if

> legislation which restricts those political processes . . . is to be subjected to more exacting judicial scrutiny under the general prohibitions of the Fourteenth Amendment than are most other types of legislation . . . [and] whether similar considerations enter into the review of statutes directed at particular religious, *Pierce v. Society of Sisters,* 268 U.S. 510, or national, *Meyer v. Nebraska,* 262 U.S. 390; *Bartels v. Iowa,* 262 U.S. 404; *Farrington v. Tokushige,* 273 U.S. 484, or racial minorities, *Nixon v. Herndon, supra; Nixon v. Condon, supra:* whether prejudice against discrete and insular minorities may be a special condition, which tends seriously to curtail the operation of those political processes ordinarily to be relied upon to protect minorities, and which may call for a correspondingly more searching judicial inquiry. (304 U.S. 144, 152–153, n. 4 (1938))

It is important to note that many of the court cases referred to in this famous footnote in the *Carolene* decision were landmark cases involving the state and private schools. They were examples selected by the Court of normal political processes not offering sufficient protection for a minority group from majoritarian or state government domination (Smolin, 1986).[49] The history of private schools and the state is a rocky one, with prejudicial attempts by the government to eliminate their presence through prohibition or excessive regulation. The fact that it required three Supreme Court decisions (*Meyer, Pierce,* and *Farrington*) to ensure the private school option attests to the fact that the customary political processes often have not been very effectual in protecting the interests of private schools and their patrons. Tribe (1988) sees the *Meyer* and *Pierce* cases as

> demonstrat[ing] judicial solicitude for the Catholics in Oregon and the Germans in Nebraska against whom the invalidated statutes had evidently been directed because of the inability of those groups to adequately safeguard their interests through the political processes of their states. (p. 1320)

In *San Antonio Independent School District v. Rodriguez,* the Court declared that wealth was not a "suspect class" and did not have any of the traditional "indicia of suspectness: [such as] a position of political powerlessness as to command extraordinary protection from the majoritarian political process" (411 U.S. 1, 28 (1973)). In noting the similarities in language between the *Carolene* footnote and the *Rodriguez* case, "would 'political powerlessness' alone," queries Gunther (1980), "justify a conclusion of 'suspectness'" (p. 864)?

Parents do suffer a loss of parental liberty to direct the education of their children when educational choices are restricted by private school regulations. The benefits of providing a more suitable education to their children from their own perspective, and doing so in a manner that is compatible with their conscience and personal beliefs, are significant. They are the same benefits that public school parents enjoy. The denial of these liberties imposes substantial burdens on parents in their efforts to rear their children and invades the intimate and private sphere of family life.

Many parents with children in private schools claim that state regulations infringe on their religious beliefs and diminish their right to privacy in raising their children according to their conscience. These kinds of assertions begin to touch on areas of fundamental, constitutionally protected rights. This raises another interesting question in terms of judicial review. What would prevent the Court from using the intermediate standard of review under the Due Process Clause of the Fourteenth Amendment for cases that may hover near the periphery of these fundamental, substantive rights?

All of this suggests that the idea of requiring a "more searching inquiry" into state efforts to regulate private schools has currency and must be taken seriously. This study contends that such should indeed be the case. All state regulations governing private schools should be subjected to a "more exacting judicial inquiry," at least at the intermediate level of review. This will offer a more balanced protection of personal liberty rights of parents, private school personnel, and the state. It would also contribute to the pluralistic character of our society and strengthen our democracy.

Laurence Tribe (1988) describes six ways or approaches in which the intermediate standard of review has been used to offer a more substantial protection of liberty interests. First, it requires that legislation be evaluated as to its degree of importance. Second, it requires that there be a fairly close connection or fit between the objective of the legislation and the means selected to achieve it. Third, the judge needs to look at the case from the viewpoint of the aggrieved party. Fourth, it asks that a "current articulation" or rationale be given by the state for the regulation. It must fulfill a contemporary purpose as given by the state. Fifth, the rationale or justification for the regulations cannot be given in hindsight. Principles must precede programs. Regulations should flow from a rationale. And sixth, it requires the opportunity for rebuttal. The state must allow for exceptions to the regulation if the offended party can demonstrate suffi-cient reasons to be exempt.

These six suggested "techniques" for establishing the validity of all private school regulation do not seem overly burdensome or restrictive to the state. They do require that the state exercise much more care and precision in drafting regulations, which would help reduce the potential for capricious legislation and/or arbitrary enforcement. They would also provide a more equitable forum where parents and private schools could contest offensive legislation without having to subject themselves and the state to the much more inflexible, demanding, and difficult strict scrutiny/compelling interest standard. The use of the intermediate stan-dard of review puts "teeth" into what the state is always required to do—justify its restriction on personal liberties. It is more sensitive to those who have a justifiable reason to be exempt from the regulation. To the degree that restrictions on personal liberty are placed on those who actu-ally deserve such treatment, they become more ethical, constitutional, and effective expressions of public policy.

Some might contend that the above criteria for state supervision of private schools are far too conservative and need to be enlarged to include the mandatory instruction in a "common core" of knowledge. Henry Levin (1983) argues strongly that the public interest[50] requires that all children must be exposed to a "common core of educational experience" (pp. 29–30). The curious thing is that he does not specify what that "com-mon core" ought to be. He does suggest, however, some "goals" such as

> provision of equal and appropriate educational opportunities for all children; exposure to ideas, values, political views, and individuals from backgrounds and cultures other than their own; fulfillment of basic requirements in a common language; familiarity with major technological issues; capability in numerical calculations and in reasoning; understanding of our system of government and the rights and responsibilities of individuals; and access to training opportunities for careers. (p. 29)

Furthermore he skirts the issue by naively suggesting that the contents of the "common core" be determined by some kind of "political solutions based upon parliamentary forms of democracy" (p. 30). Kenneth Strike (1982b) takes a more definite position and lists such things as "basic skills . . . instruction in the ideals and practices of a free society . . . history, geography, mathematics, science and language" (p. 159). Justice Brennan would not only agree with Strike's list but would expand it to include "literature and law" (*Lemon v. Kurtzman*, 403 U.S. 602, 631 (1971), con-curring opinion).

The idea of a common core has much intuitive appeal.[51] Every child should not only learn the basic literacy and math skills but should also learn important facts about the world, our culture, and our way of life. An interesting aspect, however, about the "common core" argument is that the common knowledge that should be held in common by all is not commonly known or self-evident. Erickson (1973) points out that the

> educational desiderata of this type can be listed almost indefinitely, far beyond the bounds of student time in the high school and even the undergraduate college. We are forced, then, to confront questions pondered for generations by proponents of liberal education: What knowledge is of the most worth? What knowledge is utterly essential? . . . But if we cannot identify what everyone must master, by what warrant do we specify what everyone must undergo? (pp. 2/7, 2/9)

But a much larger problem than agreement on general topics or categories is defining the substantive details of the common core (Hirsch, Kett, & Trefil, 1988). Which "ideas, values, [and] political views" are to be selected and how will they be taught? Strike's minimal list is far less problematic than Levin's goals, but just what are the "ideals and practices of a free society" that the state should mandate for instruction to every child? A crucial problem with expanding beyond the basic literacy skills is the entrance into dangerous terrain filled with preferences, opinions, values, personal beliefs, and world views. This is a very problematic area because it deals with the content of educational experience upon which there is not much agreement, and yet it is proposed that what is decided be imposed upon all children by the police power of the state. This rather arbitrary action simply creates an "unmanageable conflict over matters of conscience" (Arons, 1986, p. 209) in government socialization of all children. Arons reads the First Amendment as requiring government neutrality "wherever beliefs, world views, or ideologies are at stake . . . as is brought into play with regard to religion" (p. 212).

If the state feels strongly about specifying and mandating a common core of knowledge for all children in both public and private schools, it should prove that such action is constitutional. This burden of proof should be required by the strict scrutiny standard. The fundamental right to privacy, parental rights, and those rights protected by the First Amendment require such a standard and would be ideal components to form a "hybrid" case as required for all Free Exercise claims (*Employment Div., Dept. of Human Res. v. Smith*, 110 S.Ct. 1595 (1990)). The government must give evidence of a compelling state interest and allow a least restrictive alternative if it wants to impose requirements extending beyond the four basic areas of proper state intervention previously outlined. Stephen Arons (1986) contends that

> imposing this well-established constitutional standard on government bodies that attempt to regulate the essentially private function of education would eliminate upwards of 95 percent of the conflicts over schooling reported here. (p. 213; see also Bird, 1979; Devins, 1983; Drake, 1980; Gordon, 1984; van Geel, 1976, p. 167)

The important issue of identifying factors leading to failure rather than all those contributing to educational success needs to be addressed in evaluating the common core argument and other proposals for extending the arm of the state into private school functions. For example, will a child fail to become a good citizen and contribute to the economy if private education does not teach a common core of knowledge above and beyond basic literacy skills? It is not entirely obvious this would be the case. With these basic literacy skills, the student could conceivably manage to acquire whatever "common core" he or she needed to have. In addition, the probability of a viable private school offering instruction in only basic literacy skills does not seem supported by available evidence.[52]

Finally, it is crucial in any discussion of state controls for private schools to keep in mind that a violation of these regulations is usually considered a criminal offense with fines and/or jail sentences attached. Children attending unapproved private schools could be declared as neglected children and removed from their homes and parents by the state. One way to help keep this important perspective in the forefront of any effort to decide which private school activities should be regulated by the state is to pose this question: If a private school refused to comply with a proposed requirement, would the lack of compliance be of such nature as to justify the closing of the private school? If parents enroll their children in a private school not in full compliance with certain state regulations, is that noncompliance of such magnitude as to justify the removal of the children from their home and parents? Is the nature of the penalty proportional to the size of the offense or the potential harm that may result?[53]

The Proper Role of the State

What is proposed here, then, is not total withdrawal or abdication of the state from the supervision of private schools. Through the judicious use of external regulators such as state regulation in only the four essential areas (safe environment, compulsory education, unethical practices, and basic literacy skills), the state can and should play a fundamental role in protecting the liberty interests of the child and the parent. Conflict and disagreement can be minimized if areas of state regulation are limited to those where there is near universal agreement. Conflict can also be reduced by pursuing policies that broaden the regulatory menu and allow for more choices. This includes such things as giving private schools the option of either having a certified teacher or teaching a required curriculum; of choosing between input items such as teacher qualifications or curriculum requirements versus output factors such as standardized tests; of being allowed to seek approval by the state or approval by a private accrediting agency. These are all ways in which liberty can be maximized and harm minimized. Regulatory emphasis on ends instead of prescribing means also allows a much greater breadth for the exercise of responsible choice and the preservation of personal liberties.

There are other ways in which the state can be a positive influence in improving private education and protecting the liberty interests of the child. It can provide information, recommendations, and research results on educational issues and programs to private schools. Private school personnel could be invited to attend inservice workshops sponsored by the state for its teachers. Four states—New York, Florida, Louisiana, and Ohio—have established state advisory boards with state and private school officials where they can work together on matters of mutual concern (Blaunstein, 1986). There is great potential value for the education of children and our society in transforming the usual adversarial relationship between the state and private schools and parents into one of mutual respect and cooperation (Seeley, 1985).[54]

Another area of great importance is the development of alternative approaches to litigation in resolving disputes between the state and private schools, such as arbitration under the auspices of neutral third parties, the full utilization of administrative hearings, and continued efforts to modify offending legislation. The costs of litigation for parents and private schools present a formidable obstacle in their efforts to pursue and obtain judicial relief from state encroachment. The *Whisner* case, for example, cost the small church school over $30,000 in legal fees (Carper, 1982. For additional discussion of the *Whisner* case, see Saltsman, 1977). The state, on the other hand, has almost limitless resources because it is able to externalize its costs upon taxpayers. This raises questions of equity.

To safeguard against the natural tendency of petty despotism, all state regulations must at least pass an "intermediate standard of review." A "strict scrutiny" review should be required for all regulations touching on the actual content and process of the educational program, for example, required courses, textbooks, and specific teacher qualifications. The state must show a substantial means–end relationship between the specific manner in which it wants to limit the liberty of private schools and parents and a legitimate state objective. All this does is to require the state to do what is asked of parents and private schools—act in a responsible, justifiable manner within its prerogatives and authority.

SUMMARY AND CONCLUSION

A natural tendency in our modern welfare state is to increase the presence of the government in private schools to try to reduce even further the slight risk of harm to children. But to what extent, short of taking total control of the child from the parents, should the state go? The Supreme Court has stated that

> the statist notion that governmental power should supersede parental authority in *all* cases because *some* parents abuse and neglect children is repugnant to American tradition.
>   . . . Simply because the decision of a parent is not agreeable to a child or because it involves risks does not automatically transfer the power to make that decision from the parents to some agency or officer of the state. (*Parham v. J. R.,* 442 U.S. 584, 603 (1979))[55]

It is not clear that there would be any real overall advantage of moving to a more statist approach toward private schools. Would we just be trading "abuses of the marketplace" for "abuses of regulations, market failures for political ones" (Machan, 1983, p. 282)? "Is a 'public' bureaucracy independent of democratic controls," queries Dahl (1982), "any more desirable than a 'private' bureaucracy independent of democratic controls" (p. 203)?

Pluralism has much to offer in helping resolve the dilemma of state intervention into the operations of private schools and in preserving the ethos of our democratic society. It argues that the maximization of personal liberty is the central social and political value of our democratic republic. This is not to say that there are not other critical values or that personal responsibility does not go hand-in-hand with personal liberty. What pluralism does maintain is that there are other legitimate sources of moral, legal, and political values and power residing outside of the state. The state is not an absolute sovereign but a servant.

Private schools perform an essential role in our society by providing an alternative environment for those who feel socially, educationally, culturally, or religiously alienated from government schools. The maintenance of this ecological niche for other world views and value systems is critical to the diversity and survival of our democratic biosphere. Inappropriate excursions by the state could destroy or severely damage an essential element in our social, educational, and political world.

The state does have legitimate concerns for the welfare of the child. Although pluralism is not a perfect policy solution to state intervention into private schools, neither is some form of educational statism. Dahl (1982) reminds us that "to say that a solution has disadvantages is never a good reason for preferring the worse to the better" (p. 107).

The rudimentary level of our understanding of such complex processes such as child rearing and education requires a great deal of restraint in any attempts at outside intervention into family life. We simply do not have the knowledge base or the technology to fine tune these intricate and often enigmatic phenomena. With the exception of egregious examples such as neglect and abuse, the resources of the state would be better spent in supporting the efforts of parents to improve family life.

There are several characteristics of the private school world that internally regulate the educational climate to ensure the proper development of students. Parents not only have a knowledge of and deeply personal interest in the child, but have a vested interest in the child's success in school. They are educationally literate about schooling and have made great sacrifices to support their involvement in private education. Other self-regulating features include the marketplace realities of private education, and the private school milieu with customized learning environments for educational success.

There is an essential although limited role for the state in pluralism. The state does have the responsibility to ensure that the obvious barriers to education be removed. These include protecting the child from physical harm and from unethical schools and ensuring that each child is enrolled in school and that each child acquires basic literacy skills.

As the state performs its important role, there will be disagreements with private schools and parents about the degree of government intervention. Since any state intervention will approach sensitive areas such as First Amendment rights and the right to privacy, the standard of review used by the courts in deciding these issues should be the intermediate level of review. This would require a much tighter fit between legitimate state objectives and regulatory activities. Those state interventions that obviously impact the right of privacy in family life and First Amendment rights would require the strict scrutiny standard.

Another way in which the state can fulfill its valuable role is to look for opportunities to work with private schools by providing information and research results in education, making available inservice workshops, and facilitating communication through state advisory boards.

Public policy, grounded in the general principles of pluralism and the specific recommendations of this chapter, offers the best guidance in determining the appropriate relationship between the state and private schools. An emphasis on educational essentials, liberality in educational means, and a cooperative perspective will harmonize freedom and responsibility in education to the benefit of all.

6 ✠ EPILOGUE

Oh, how we love liberty, when it means coercing others into what we choose!
—Bishop John J. Keane

This study began with a chilling and sobering account of the closure by the state of two private schools. These events raised several key questions about the general role of the state in society and its proper relationship with private elementary and secondary schools. What should be the appropriate public policy toward private schools? What legitimate interests does the state possess that would justify government intervention into private schools? Which private school affairs should be regulated and controlled by the government? The purpose of this study is to suggest viable answers to these fundamental questions.

An inquiry into the historical relationship between the state and private schools revealed that education has been used as a tool more of social control than of liberation. This seems to be the case for schools under the English monarchy, the Puritan oligarchy, and American democracy with its changing cast of nationalistic zealots, business interests, nativistic concerns, and professional state educators. Those in positions of social and political power have used the coercive and legal machinery of the state to raise their private values and visions of the good life as universals and applicable to all. This should not be a surprising finding. Education is the means through which social and cultural reproduction occurs. It is the vehicle through which values, ideas, definitions of normative behavior, and world views are inculcated in the young and passed on to the next generation. The stakes in education are simply quite high.

In a political and cultural setting embedded with the ideology of state-sponsored schools, private schools in America have presented a perennial problem to those wishing to standardize American children into a more homogeneous group with similar values and points of view. Private schools have provided an avenue of escape for those individuals (at least those with resources) who find unacceptable attempts by the state through government schools to assimilate all into a more uniform mold of thinking, believing, and acting. Private schools have provided a sanctuary for a dissenting minority from the imposition of a "public" orthodoxy.

The state has pursued three major strategies in attempting to deal with the private school question. It has tried to produce superior government schools, hoping to entice students in private schools to enroll in public schools, and thus causing private schools to fold. It has also tried to ban private schools and, third, to gain near complete control through regulations. The first strategy has not worked. Private schools have survived and are thriving. They have also challenged in court the more active efforts by the state to negate their presence and value. The United States Supreme Court has declared that private schools have a constitutional right to exist and has prohibited the state from engaging in any kind of massive intervention into private school functions. Parents and private school owners have fundamental liberty rights that cannot be abridged by arbitrary and irrational state action.

Private schools have also opposed even more moderate attempts by the state to supervise such functions as health and safety requirements, certification of personnel, required curriculum, reports, and overall approval by the state. The state has contended that it has a duty to ensure the welfare of society and the well-being of the child through the provision of an adequate and proper education. This basic state interest has been defined by the Supreme Court as securing an opportunity for each child to become economically and politically competent regardless of the kind of school in which the child is enrolled.

An analysis of legal guidelines from United States Supreme Court cases did not produce the kind of specific guidelines needed to resolve the issue of what constitutes permissible state intervention into private schools. It did throw light, however, on the complexity of the issue regarding the state and private schools. The state, parents, and private school personnel all have basic, fundamental rights and interests protected by the Constitution.

The dilemma comes into full focus when the fundamental and important interests of the state are juxtaposed with those of the parents and sponsors of private schools. How can the state be sure that parents and private schools are protecting the vital interests of the child and society in a private educational setting? What is the proper mix of responsibility and freedom? What guarantee is there that private schools can act in a responsible manner and yet retain their institutional uniqueness? Where is the point at which government is able to protect its legitimate interests and yet leave the private education option with sufficient internal integrity to remain a real choice, a refuge for cultural, religious, and educational dissenters?

A closer examination of the state's interest in education and the means it has selected to accomplish that interest uncovered some distressing findings. The state has not fully met its obligation to adequately justify its regulatory restrictions on the freedom of parents and private schools. Although the state does have legitimate interests, these interests are not well articulated into clear educational goals. There is a dearth of evidence supporting the link between these goals and the means the state has selected to achieve them. The causal connection between regulations governing private schools and vague or even nonexistent state educational goals is not supported by empirical evidence. Rather, it appears that public policy toward private schools is based more on conventional wisdom and the personal preference and bias of state education officials. Furthermore, extant evidence concerning private schools suggests they are doing a very adequate job in providing a good education to their pupils. All of this raises serious and deeply disturbing moral, constitutional, and educational questions about most state regulations for private schools.

The central thesis of this study is that the indeterminate nature of education and the ambiguity of educational and social goals preclude the state's ability to pinpoint with any practical accuracy where the interests of the state end and those of the private school begin. The magnitude of the imprecision is sufficient to preclude any attempts to fine tune regulations to avoid potential pitfalls and dangers. These pitfalls and dangers are of such magnitude and importance that they require the state to exercise a very cautious and conservative approach toward any kind of control over private schools.[1] The only appropriate alternative is to embrace and protect a more structural and substantive pluralism in American education. A public policy in education grounded on essentials, yet heavily imbued with pluralism, can escape many of the problems and difficulties created by state intervention and yet be able to adequately address the *basic* concerns raised by both sides.

This study contends that a more pluralistic approach in public policy affecting private schools not only is required but could more effectively reconcile freedom and responsibility to the best advantage of *everyone* than could an approach involving extensive state intervention. Important internal regulators such as parental interest and investment, economic realities of the educational marketplace, unique educational environment, and other sources of education are significant barriers to any harm occurring to the child. These internal, self-regulating features of private education are legitimately supplemented with a minimal amount of external regulation. State regulations mandating a safe and secure learning environment, universal formal education, ethical business practices, and curriculum requirements in basic literacy act as a safety net to ensure that children attending private schools will receive an education meeting the essential interests of the state and satisfying the liberty interests of parents and private schools. The key is to require unity on essential matters, allow liberty in matters of a doubtful nature, and do it in a context of charity and mutual cooperation.

An educational policy based on pluralism with its emphasis on the maximization of liberty, the decentralization of decision making, and the recognition of private groups, is, admittedly, not risk free or perfect. But neither is the current regulatory approach used by many states, with its substantial intervention into private schools or massive regulation of public schools, for that matter. The present posture by many states toward private schools is morally offensive, constitutionally unsound, and educationally incompetent.

The pluralistic approach advocated by this study suggests a superior way to maximize choice for parents and private schools and still provide reasonable assurances to protect the liberty interests of children. It defines the appropriate relationship between the state and private schools in a democracy. It offers a valuable model for constructing proper state controls of private schools. It respects the beliefs of all members of society and provides an opportunity for those beliefs to be incorporated into a child's education.

The recommendations of this study, therefore, become imperatives for implementation. Their adoption would resolve much of the current conflict between the state and private schools. They would enrich American education and strengthen our democracy. They represent a feasible solution to preserving both freedom and responsibility in our society.

NOTES

NOTES TO CHAPTER 1

1. One state supreme court justice characterized these actions by public officials as "gestapo tactics" (*State v. Yoder*, 182 N.W. 2d 539, 550 (Wis. 1971)).

2. The term *state* is used in a generic sense and refers to any government entity on any level—local, state, or federal—unless the text specifies otherwise.

3. It might be argued that these increases reflect simply a growing national population and not "real" growth in the private school sector. However, a report from NCES, *Private Schools in the United States: A Statistical Profile, With Comparisons to Public Schools,* shows the proportion of all private elementary and secondary schools in the United States increasing from 22% in 1980–81 to 25.4% in 1985–86 (1991, p. 13). A similar absolute increase is observed in the proportion of students enrolled in these schools. In 1980–81, 11.5% of the nation's elementary and secondary students attended private schools. By 1985–86, the percentage had increased to 12.4% (p. 30).

4. Two exceptions are the studies by McLaughlin (1946) and Romans (1981).

NOTES TO CHAPTER 2

1. Bailyn (1960) describes these writers as "educational missionaries" who attempted to "dignify a newly self-conscious profession" and "with great virtuosity . . . drew up what became the patristic literature of a powerful academic ecclesia" (pp. 7–9).

2. The master stood in place of the father, *in loco parentis,* and was obligated to provide all of the moral and vocational training that the youngster would have received in his own home. The youngster had the mutual obligation to show commensurate respect and obedience.

3. Spring (1986) observes that this is a "good example of how colonial policy viewed education as a means of establishing the superiority of one ethnic group over another. . . . [It] illustrates a continuing theme in American educational history: The use of the school as a means of spreading a particular culture . . . as a means of cultural imperialism" (pp. 12–13).

Lawrence Cremin (1970) points out what is almost a truism in education. "Whenever it took roots, schooling was viewed as a device for promoting uniformity . . . and put to the purpose of the controlling elements of society" (p. 192).

4. Clarence Karier (1986) notes that the "Enlightenment ideology, which

was based on Newton's concept of the universe, a set of assumed natural laws and natural rights, a deistic God and a humanitarian faith in the improvability if not the perfectibility of man, culminated in the idea of progress. The central pillar in the Enlightenment temple of humanity was a theory of progress which itself was based on education" (pp. 23–24).

5. "No State shall . . . pass any Bill of Attainder, ex post facto Law, or Law impairing the Obligation of Contracts, or grant any Title of Nobility" (*United States Constitution*, Art. I, Sec. 10, Par. 1).

6. "Congress shall make no law respecting an establishment of religion, or prohibiting the free exercise thereof."

7. "The Powers not delegated to the United States by the Constitution, nor prohibited by it to the States, are reserved to the States respectively, or to the people."

8. State constitutions contained general statements of encouragement and justification for education. Constitutional provisions found in the Ohio Constitution were typical of the era.

". . . But religion, morality, and knowledge being essentially necessary to the good government and the happiness of mankind, schools and the means of instruction shall forever be encouraged by legislative provision, not inconsistent with the rights of conscience" (*United States Constitution*, Art. VII, Sec. 3; quoted in Samuel Windsor Brown, 1912, p. 99).

9. An ordinance passed by the Regents in 1828 governing incorporated academies reveals a fairly extensive report. Miller (1969) also noted that the scope and detail of the reports grew with the passing of time. By the end of the nineteenth century, the academy report "was composed of no less than one hundred four entries, which were grouped into seven divisions" (p. 26).

10. Additional studies in civil religions can be found in Robert N. Bellah and Phillip E. Hammond (1980).

11. The idea of national or state systems of education was not original with these early Americans. The Englishman William Petty in 1650 advocated a universal, state-sponsored literacy education for all children over age 7. James Harrington contended in 1656 in his work, *The Commonwealth of Oceana*, that the well-being of the state was dependent on the education of young people and therefore education is far more than a parental responsibility but comes under the aegis of the state. He recommended universal, compulsory education for all children aged 9 through 15. Thomas Budd, a Quaker in Pennsylvania, called for universal schooling for 7 years in his pamphlet entitled *Good Order Established in Pennsilvania & New-Jersey in America* (1685). See Cremin (1970, pp. 307, 422, 423). On the Continent La Chalotais wrote an article in 1763 entitled *Essay on National Education*. Turgot followed in 1775 with *Manner of Preparing Individuals and Families to Participate Properly in a Good Social Organization*, and Diderot, in his *Plan of a University for the Russian Government*, pleaded with the Empress Catherine in 1770 to include public education in her social reforms for Russia. Finally, there is the plan for a national public school system embodied in a report written by Condorcet, a close friend of Thomas Paine, Thomas Jefferson, and Benjamin Franklin, for the National Assembly of France in 1792.

12. The "Religion" Rush refers to is Protestantism as interpreted in each locale.

The rise of a strident nationalism juxtaposed to liberalism, with its emphasis on individual rights and liberties, poses a curious combination of political philosophies that are contradictory in nature. The paradox produced in a "search for ordered liberty" required that "the free American was to be, in political convictions, the uniform American" (Tyack, 1966a, p. 31). Americans have been struggling ever since to find the "right" mix of the two in public policy formulations. One of the driving rationales behind the common school movement in the 1830s and 1840s was the need to create and perpetuate a sense of national identity and unity through a common educational experience. Instead of referring to nationalism in public policy discussions today, an appeal is made to the "public interest" or the "public good." The end result is the same. The interests of the individual are secondary to the interests of the state. Benjamin Rush and other educational leaders such as William Smith (1753) in *A General Idea of the College of Mirania* pushed this idea to its logical conclusion in asserting that children "are the Property of the State." (p. 66). Therefore, the state has not only a right but a duty to see that they are properly educated in terms of the state's interest. Nation-states use education to further their own nationalistic interests. One real problem is that the interests of the state are not self-evident and are often determined by the leaders of a particular political party.

13. Horace Mann, better known perhaps for his involvement in the common school movement, was also actively involved in the establishment of insane asylums, temperance movements, religious liberty, antislavery efforts, and the building of public railroads (Karier, 1986).

14. This is a classic example of "blaming the victim" that would be repeated over and over again in American social policy. The poor are accused of causing the very social problems of which they are the victims. See Ravitch (1974, p. 29). It also provided the ideological justification for a continuation of the status quo for those groups and individuals in power and at the same time furnished a relief valve for mounting social tensions by holding out a promise or expectation that this power and social status could be shared if one would become educated.

15. It is a misconception to see private schools at the time of the common school crusade as simply elite schools catering to the aristocratic upper class. In a study of schools in New York City in the 1790s, Kaestle (1972) discovered that they enrolled students from families representing a broad spectrum of economic and occupational groups. "Indeed, New York City's common schools may have been more comprehensive in socioeconomic terms in the 1790's than today, if individual schools are considered. No ideologues promoted the schooling arrangements of New York in the 1790's; they just grew that way" (p. 477).

16. Eighty years earlier, in 1753, a Scottish immigrant, William Smith, published a work entitled *A General Idea of the College of Mirania*. Smith wrote that "nothing could so much contribute to make such a Mixture of People coalesce and unite in one common Interest as the common Education of all the Youth at the same public Schools under the Eye of the civil Authority." (p. 9).

17. Indeed, Daniel Webster in a speech given in 1821 referred to state-

sponsored education as "a wise and liberal system of police, by which property, and life, and the peace of society are secured" (Tyack, 1967, p. 126).

18. Collins (1976) agrees with the cultural conflict model proposed by Spring in that "the solidarity of alien ethnic or cultural groups is the biggest threat to dominant groups. Massive educational systems, then, are control devices favored in conflictual multi-ethnic societies, like the United States and the USSR, and relatively ignored in culturally more homogeneous societies like England, Germany, and China" (p. 248).

19. "Those who dreamed of universal education supported by state funds saw that there was great danger of the realization of their dreams being frustrated through the frittering away of these funds among a horde of petty denominational schools. Economy demanded concentration. Moreover, schools directly controlled by the state could be much more easily maintained at any given standard the state might desire than schools controlled by any ecclesiastical power" (Brown, 1912, pp. 93–94).

20. For reviews of the ethnic, economic, and religious bias of early textbooks, see Ruth Miller Elson (1964) and Jean Anyon (1977).

21. In light of the violent anti-Catholic riots and the burning of some Catholic churches, the First Plenary Council of Baltimore in 1852 suggested that every parish support its own school to prevent exposure of its children to the Protestant indoctrination of the public school. This policy was made mandatory some 30 years later in the Third Plenary Council (Tyack, James, & Benavot, 1987).

22. William Smith in 1753 advocated one system of state education and saw no need for private schools. These schools were to be "suppressed. For such Schools there was now no Use, the Province having, as it were, taken the Business of Education out of private into public Hands, and open'd one general School, calculated for training up all Ranks and Conditions of People, in the surest and least expensive Method, to be good Men and good Citizens in their proper Spheres. Without this Step, the Classes cou'd never have been fill'd; and the whole Intention of the Institutors wou'd have been defeated, had private Persons been suffer'd to teach on a different Plan, and draw off the Youth by their Interest with particular Families, Sects and Parties; or, which is oftener the case by a mean Attention to the Foibles and Weakness of Parents" (pp. 66–67).

23. "Protestant Nationalism became for many the clear statement of the organic concept of the Union [versus the antebellum concept of the nation as a 'legal creation involving contractual rights and obligations'], and majoritarians thus grew confident that this concept justified legal compulsion. Laws to control the behavior of the unorthodox in religion and the unwashed in ethnic and racial background poured from the majoritarian pen between the Civil War and World War I. Compulsion became fashionable on a national scale" (Burgess, 1976, pp. 206–207). Burgess gives some specific examples of political efforts to impose a national conformity: the transformation of the state guard into the national guard, military draft, compulsory voting and arbitration (unsuccessful), uniform standards for child labor and obscene expression (unsuccessful) and several constitutional amendments on such issues as divorce (unsuccessful), suffrage for women (1920) and the Prohibition amendment (1919), which was later repealed.

Additional examples include the outlawing of slavery in 1865 (Thirteenth Amendment), broad guarantee of civil rights in 1868 (Fourteenth Amendment), right to vote regardless of race in 1870 (Fifteenth Amendment), and a national income tax (Sixteenth Amendment).

24. The felicitous phrase "Super Parent" was coined by Donald Erickson (1973).

25. On the federal level, the territories of Montana, North and South Dakota, and Washington were required by Congress to include provisions for the establishment of public schools in their enabling acts of 1889 as a prerequisite for statehood (Tyack, James, & Benavot, 1987).

26. It wasn't until after 1870 that compulsory education laws became widespread. Up to that time only two states, Massachusetts (1852) and Vermont (1867), and the District of Columbia (1864) had compulsory education statutes on the books (McLaughlin, 1946).

For an extensive survey of current compulsory education laws in all 50 states, see Lawrence A. Kotin and William F. Aikman (1980).

27. A most interesting study by William M. Landes and Lewis C. Solomon (1972) examined what effect, if any, the passage of compulsory education laws had on school enrollment and attendance. They concluded that "these laws did not cause the observed increases in levels of schooling in the late nineteenth and early twentieth century . . . [and] that relatively high levels of schooling and probable increases in those levels, preceded the passage of compulsory school laws." The authors suggest that the passage of compulsory education laws was due to school personnel who were "likely to favor and promote legislation that compels persons to purchase their product," served as a "way of giving formal recognition to the community's achievement in committing more resources to schooling," and reflected a decrease in the number of parents opposed to more schooling (pp. 86–87).

28. A good example of this is the positions taken by two state superintendents of education in Wisconsin. A. J. Craig in 1869 felt that unless compulsory education laws were passed, future historians would mark it as the point of "the downfall of a once mighty nation which forgot its origin, derided its destiny, sold its birthright, and ended its career in shame and disgrace." On the other hand, Edward Searing (term of office as state superintendent, 1874–1878) considered compulsory education laws as "essentially opposed to the genius of our free institutions, something essentially un-American. . . . The mere consciousness of the existence of a law compelling the attendance of my children would be intolerable. I want not statute laws telling me how or when to feed, to dress, or to educate my children" (Ensign, 1921, pp. 205, 207).

29. A sampling of statutory language from this early period includes the following: ". . . shall cause child to be enrolled in or to attend some public or private day or parochial school regularly." (Kentucky, *Common School Laws*, 1918, Vol. II, No. 2, Sec. 213, p. 112, as found in McLaughlin, 1946, p. 67).

The compulsory education law passed in New York in 1874 required that children between the ages of 8 and 14 attend "some public or private school for at least fourteen weeks each year." The 1901 compulsory education statute in

Pennsylvania was even less direct. It simply required attendance at "some school where the common English branches were taught" (Ensign, 1921, pp. 120, 187). For reactions to Ohio statute, see *Personal Liberty* (1890).

30. While this requirement may appear entirely reasonable and innocuous, the political fallout from this legislation, which was later repealed in 1891, affected the political scene in Wisconsin for the next 10 years. The large German population saw it as an attack on their language and culture, while the Catholics and Lutherans felt it threatened their private school system. Governor William D. Hoard admitted that the legislation was "aimed at sectarian schools" (Whyte, 1927, p. 377). Also see Mapel (1891), Wyman (1968), and Jorgenson (1987, pp. 187–204).

31. "But who is to decide which set of values takes precedence? Progressive educators quickly reply, the democratic values; but there are no definite value prescriptions in the democratic credo; what the progressives regard as the democratic values somehow resemble their own values closely" (Mehl, 1963, p. 37).

32. See Cremin (1964), *The Transformation of the School*, for an excellent historical treatment of the Progressive movement in American education.

33. "The principal beneficiaries of this side of progressivism were the owners and managers of corporations and the expert who staffed new governmental and educational bureaucracies. . . . It accelerated the demise of small, neighborly communities . . . and brought the domination of a bureaucratic, scientized, depersonalized world, which feeds our bellies so well and our souls so badly. It talked of coercion and the imposition of restraints more effectively than it talked of freedom" (Graham, 1971, p. 137).

David Tyack (1986) labels this period of school legislation as codification. Professional educators "pressed for state legislation to *codify* schooling according to their own 'scientific' administrative models . . . to standardize education . . . to turn educational decision-making over to the experts and to widen the purview of administrative law. In turn such changes . . . lessened the powers of local school boards and parents" (p. 214).

34. In education, the 1920s saw the passage of laws in several states forbidding the teaching of evolution in public schools.

35. Texas was the first state to pass legislation requiring all children to attend public schools. Unlike other states with similar statutes, it did not seem to create any controversy at all (*Butler v. State*, 194 S.W. 166 (Tex. Crim. App. 1917)).

36. The wording of the proposed amendment in 1924 read as follows:

"Sec. 16. From and after August 1, 1925, all children residing in the State of Michigan between the ages of seven years and sixteen years shall attend the public school until they have graduated from the eighth grade.
"Sec. 17. The legislature shall enact all necessary legislation to render said section 16 effective." (McLaughlin, 1946, pp. 111–112)

37. The late 1960s and early 1970s saw many private schools, especially in the South, established to escape the effects of desegregation orders for public

schools. These schools, however, constituted only a very small portion of the new private schools.

38. See the appendix in Randall (1989) for a comparative analysis of private school regulations in 1930 and 1986.

NOTES TO CHAPTER 3

1. For example, American education is still trying over 30 years later to cope with the impact of the 1954 *Brown* decision ordering the desegregation of schools.

2. The appellate court cases were counted from a series of legal digests, *Centennial Digest* and succeeding decennial volumes of the *American Digest System,* published by the West Publishing Company. The same basic categories used by lawyers in compiling the *Digest* were used in the table. An expanded definition of the various category labels was not given in the *Digest* nor was the reason why a particular case was categorized as such or sometimes placed in more than one category. This presented some difficulty as many of the cases are multidimensional and often involved several issues that fell into different categories. A simple numerical count of each category would have inflated the total count. For those cases that were found listed in more than one category, a content analysis was made of the case synopsis to determine which category best reflected the primary issue of the case. The case was then counted as belonging only to that primary category.

Since many regulation cases are prosecuted under compulsory education statutes, the "Compulsory Education" and "Constitutional and Statutory Provisions" categories in the public school section of the *Digest* were also reviewed for applicable cases. Six additional cases pertaining to "Regulation and Supervision" were found and included in that total. This suggests that Table 3.1 is not an exhaustive enumeration of appellate cases for private schools and thus represents a conservative picture.

All court cases before 1907 were collapsed into a single time period to reduce the table to a manageable size. An average was calculated for the nine decennial periods for comparative purposes with the decennial periods since 1907.

Population figures were taken from the U.S. Bureau of the Census, *Statistical Abstract of the United States: 1988* (1987, p. 7). The compilation of court cases in West's *Digest* does not cover the same interval as the census figures. The census year used for the population figure was the census year that fell within the decennial period used by West. For example, for the period 1917–1926, the census figures for 1920 were used.

See a similar review of American educational litigation—private and public combined—in Tyack, James, and Benavot (1987). Compare Lines (1984).

3. It is of some significance to note that these figures do not include cases held at the various trial and circuit courts that preceded appeals to state and federal appellate courts or cases that were never appealed. They are only a partial reflection of the total amount of litigation involving private schools.

4. Nearly one-third of the cases in this category during the past 20 years

dealt with the provision and payment of educational services for the handicapped. They often involved parents seeking state approval and funding for the placement of their child in a private educational institution specializing in education for the handicapped.

5. This has occurred despite the significant decrease in the private school population since the nineteenth century. The pool of potential litigants has contracted in the face of an expanding rate of litigation. This is further evidence of the growing depth and intensity of the dispute between the state and private schools. David Tyack and Elisabeth Hansot (1982) suggest that "much of this increased use of the courts can be traced to a failure of traditional centers of decision making in education to achieve a new political or ethical consensus about education" (p. 247).

6. The pertinent part of the Fourteenth Amendment for this case and references to it throughout this chapter come from Section 1 of the Amendment: "No State shall make or enforce any law which shall abridge the privileges or immunities of citizens of the United States; nor shall any State deprive any person of life, liberty, or property, without due process of law; nor deny to any person within its jurisdiction the equal protection of the laws" (*United States Constitution*).

7. A similar case was brought on appeal to the Indiana supreme court in 1854. Several local residents urged the school district trustee, Mr. Harper, to remove black children who were attending a private school along with white children. He refused to do so. The state supreme court affirmed the lower court ruling in declaring that the school was a private school and that "with such a school Harper had, of course, no right to interfere" (*Polke v. Harper,* 5 Ind. 241 (1854)). Unlike the *Berea* case, Indiana had not passed legislation forbidding the instruction of black and white children together.

8. Four other cases had been appealed to the Supreme Court over the same issues presented in *Meyer. Bartels v. Iowa, Bohning v. State of Ohio, Pohl v. State of Ohio,* and *Nebraska District of Evangelical Lutheran Synod of Missouri et al. v. McKelvie,* 262 U.S. 404 (1923) were all reversed based on the *Meyer* decision.

9. The so-called "dead languages" such as Latin, Hebrew, and Greek were exempt.

10. ". . . Any parent, guardian or other person in the State of Oregon, having control or charge or custody of a child under the age of sixteen years and of the age of eight years or over at the commencement of a term of public school of the district in which said child resides, who shall fail or neglect to send such child to a public school for the period of time a public school shall be held during the current year in said district, shall be guilty of a misdemeanor and each day's failure to send such a child to a public school shall constitute a separate offense . . ." (Section 5259, *Oregon Laws,* as footnoted in *Pierce v. Society of Sisters,* 268 U.S. 510 at 530 (1925)).

Also see *Butler v. State,* 194 S.W. 166 (Tex. Crim. App. 1917), noting that the Texas legislature passed a bill requiring all children to attend public schools.

11. "*Pierce* stands as a charter of the rights of parents . . ." (*Wisconsin v. Yoder,* 406 U.S. 205, 237 (1972)).

12. Another important point affirmed by the Court was that parents and

children had legal standing as third parties in cases brought to trial by private schools. Regulations affecting private schools also had an immediate and direct impact on the rights of their patrons.

13. As early 1891 a suit was brought against the state of Ohio contesting the right of the state to require parochial schools to furnish enrollment reports and notify the truant officer of unexcused students. The principal of the school argued that such legislation interfered with the parental authority over the child and the right to direct the child's upbringing and education. The state supreme court upheld the rulings of the trial and circuit court, sustaining the state's right through *parens patriae* to look after the welfare of the child (*Quigley v. State,* 5 Ohio CC 638 (1891), *aff'd,* 27 WL Bull 332 (1892).

14. Although the right of the state to regulate private schools was *not* an issue in the *Pierce* case and was *not* addressed by the Court, the Supreme Court opinion in *Wisconsin v. Yoder,* 406 U.S. 205 (1972) curiously uses the *Pierce* decision as precedent to justify the right of the state to regulate private education. See *Yoder,* 406 U.S. at 213, 233, 236, 239.

15. See *Packer Collegiate Institute v. University of New York,* 81 S.E. 2d 80 (N.Y. 1948); *Santa Fe Community School v. New Mexico State Board of Education,* 518 P.2d 272 (N.M. 1974); *State v. Whisner,* 351 N.E. 2d 750 (Ohio 1976); *State ex rel. Nagle v. Olin,* 415 N.E. 2d 279 (Ohio 1980); *Bangor Baptist Church v. State of Maine,* Dept. of Education, 576 F.Supp. 1299 (D. Me. 1983); and *Strosnider v. Strosnider,* 686 P.2d 981 (N.M. 1984) for similar cases dealing with excessive regulations. For related cases declining to strike down regulations as overly broad, see *State v. Williams,* 117 S.E. 2d 444 (N.C. 1960); *Attorney General v. Bailey,* 436 N.E.2d 139, *cert. denied sub nom.* Bailey v. Bellotti, 459 U.S. 970 (1982); *Bangor Baptist Church v. State of Maine,* 549 F.Supp. 1208 (D. Me. 1982); and *Braintree Baptist Temple v. Holbrook Public Schools,* 616 F.Supp. 81 (D. Mass. 1984).

16. "Congress shall make no law respecting an establishment of religion, or prohibiting the free exercise thereof; or abridging the freedom of speech, or of the press; or the right of the people peaceably to assemble, and to petition the Government for a redress of grievances" (*United States Constitution*).

17. See *State v. Garber,* 419 P.2d 896, *cert. denied,* 389 U.S. 51 (1967) for similar denial by the state of Kansas to approve an alternative educational program for an Amish family. For related cases but not involving the Amish, see *Rice v. Commonwealth,* 49 S.E.2d 342 (Va. 1948); *Commonwealth v. Renfrew,* 126 N.E.2d 109 (Mass. 1955); *State v. Superior Court,* 346 P.2d 999, *cert. denied,* 363 U.S. 814 (Wash. 1960); and *Meyerkorth v. State,* 115 N.W. 2d 585, *appeal dismissed,* 372 U.S. 705 (1963).

18. In *Prince v. Massachusetts,* 321 U.S. 158 (1944), a case also involving Free Exercise claims and parental rights, the Court ruled in favor of the state instead of the parent. *Prince,* however, was considered by the Court as factually distinct from *Yoder* in that it dealt with child labor laws, which protected children from obvious physical or mental harm (*Yoder,* 406 U.S. at 229, 230).

19. When *Yoder* is not used as a controlling precedent, the outcome has been just the opposite. See *New Life Baptist Church Academy v. East Longmeadow,* 666 F.Supp. 293 (D. Mass. 1987). Compare *Kentucky State Board of Education v. Rudasill,*

589 S.W.2d 877, *cert. denied*, 446 U.S. 938 (1979), where the state constitution offered greater First Amendment protection than the federal constitution.

20. In *Wisconsin v. Yoder*, 406 U.S. at 211, the Court noted that "the high school tends to emphasize intellectual and scientific accomplishments, self-distinction, competitiveness, worldly success, and social life with other students. Amish society emphasizes informal learning-through-doing; a life of 'goodness,' rather than a life of intellect; wisdom, rather than competition; and separation from, rather than integration with, contemporary worldly society."

21. Chief Justice Burger discounts some "'progressive' or more enlightened process for rearing children" and the concurring opinion of J. White, Brennan and Stewart censure "idiosyncratic views of what knowledge a child needs to be a productive and happy member of society" (406 U.S. at 235, 239). These statements become even more curious and confusing when juxtaposed with the majority opinion extolling the "idiosyncratic separateness" of the Amish that "exemplifies the diversity we profess to admire and encourage" (406 U.S. at 226).

22. Some of these issues are: Title IX sex discrimination—*Ohio Civil Rights Commission v. Dayton Christian Schools, Inc.*, 477 U.S. 619 (1986); applicability of federal unemployment tax—*St. Martin Evangelical Lutheran Church v. South Dakota*, 451 U.S. 772 (1981); jurisdiction of the National Labor Relations Board—*National Labor Relations Board v. Catholic Bishop of Chicago*, 440 U.S. 490 (1979); racial discrimination in admission—*Runyon v. McCrary*, 427 U.S. 160 (1975).

23. For example, public funds may be used to buy textbooks for children attending private schools but these monies cannot be used to purchase maps. The rationale behind this distinction is far from clear. Furthermore, what about atlases, which are books of maps?

24. See also *Board of Education v. Allen*, 392 U.S. 236, 245–247 (1968); *Lemon v. Kurtzman*, 403 U.S. 602, 645, 655 (1971); *Committee for Public Education v. Regan*, 444 U.S. 646, 653, 654 (1980); *Ohio Civil Rights Commission v. Dayton Christian Schools, Inc.*, 477 U.S. 619, 628 (1986).

25. The same can be said of public schools. There is no constitutional mandate that education has to be provided through a system of state-sponsored and -operated schools or that there is a constitutional requirement for compulsory education laws. There are a variety of ways in which the compelling interest of the state in the education of its citizens could be accomplished. The present arrangement of public school systems with accommodations for private schools is but one of several educational configurations open to a state.

26. See also *Board of Education v. Allen*, 392 U.S. 236, 245 (1968); *Lemon v. Kurtzman*, 403 U.S. 602, 629, 645, 655, 663 (1971); *Norwood v. Harrison*, 413 U.S. 455, 461, 462 (1973); *Runyon v. McCrary*, 427 U.S. 160, 178, 179 (1975); *Grand Rapids School District v. Ball*, 473 U.S. 373, 397, 398 (1985).

27. See also *Griswold v. Connecticut*, 381 U.S. 479, 482 (1965); *Ginsberg v. New York*, 390 U.S. 629, 649 (1968), J. Stewart, concurring opinion; *Lemon v. Kurtzman*, 403 U.S. 602, 651 (1971), J. Brennan, concurring opinion; *Board of Education v. Pico*, 457 U.S. 853, 861, 866 (1982).

28. *Epperson v. Arkansas*, 393 U.S. 97, 107 (1968); *Mercer v. Michigan State*

Board of Education, 379 F.Supp. 580, 585, *aff'd,* 419 U.S. 1081 (1974); *Parham v. J. R.,* 442 U.S. 584, 602, 603 (1979); *Bellotti v. Baird,* 443 U.S. 622, 637, 638 (1979); *Board of Education v. Pico,* 457 U.S. 853, 861 (1982).

29. See also *Lemon v. Kurtzman,* 403 U.S. 602, 651, 655, 656 (1971), J. Brennan, concurring opinion; *Wolman v. Essex,* 342 F.Supp. 399, 411, *aff'd,* 409 U.S. 808 (1972).

30. *West Virginia Board of Education v. Barnette,* 319 U.S. 624, 640–642 (1943); *Tinker v. Des Moines School District,* 393 U.S. 503, 511 (1969); *Board of Education v. Pico,* 457 U.S. 853, 877 (1982).

31. *Lemon v. Kurtzman,* 403 U.S. 602 (1971), J. Douglas, concurring opinion.

32. See also *Norwood v. Harrison,* 413 U.S. 455, 461 (1973).

33. *Prince v. Massachusetts,* 321 U.S. 158, 166 (1944); *Ginsberg v. New York,* 390 U.S. 629, 639 (1968); *Lemon v. Kurtzman,* 403 U.S. 602, 663 (1971), J. White, concurring and dissenting in part; *Norwood v. Harrison,* 413 U.S. 455, 461 (1973); *Paul v. Davis,* 424 U.S. 693, 713 (1976); *Moore v. East Cleveland,* 431 U.S. 494, 499 (1977); *Parham v. J. R.,* 442 U.S. 584, 602 (1979); *Lehr v. Robertson,* 463 U.S. 248, 257 (1982); *Roberts v. United States Jaycees,* 468 U.S. 609, 618, 619 (1984); *Grand Rapids School District v. Ball,* 473 U.S. 373, 397, 398 (1985).

34. *Epperson v. Arkansas,* 393 U.S. 97, 105 (1968); *Board of Education v. Pico,* 457 U.S. 853, 866 (1982). See also concurring opinion by J. Stewart in *Ginsberg v. New York,* 390 U.S. 629, 649 (1968). *Epperson* and *Ginsberg* suggest that this right would be considered a fundamental right and thus would fall under the protection of the First Amendment.

35. "In a long series of cases this Court has held that where fundamental personal liberties are involved, they may not be abridged by the States simply on a showing that a regulatory statute has some rational relationship to the effectuation of a proper state purpose. 'Where there is a significant encroachment upon personal liberty, the State may prevail only upon showing a subordinating interest which is compelling,' *Bates v. Little Rock,* 361 U.S. 516, 524. The law must be shown 'necessary, and not merely rationally related, to the accomplishment of a permissible state policy.' *McLaughlin v. Florida,* 379 U.S. 184, 196. See *Schneider v. Irvington,* 308 U.S. 147, 161" (*Griswold v. Connecticut,* 381 U.S. 479, 497 (1965), J. Goldberg with Chief Justice and J. Brennan in a concurring opinion).

36. "Statutes regulating sensitive areas of liberty do, under the cases of this Court, require 'strict scrutiny,' *Skinner v. Oklahoma,* 316 U.S. 535, 541, and 'must be viewed in the light of less drastic means for achieving the same basic purpose.' *Shelton v. Tucker,* 364 U.S. 479, 488" (*Griswold v. Connecticut,* 381 U.S. 479, 503–504 (1965), J. White, concurring opinion).

" 'Precision of regulation must be the touchstone in an area so closely touching our most precious freedoms.' *NAACP v. Button,* 371 U.S. 415, 438" (*Griswold v. Connecticut,* 381 U.S. 479, 498 (1965), J. Goldberg with Chief Justice and J. Brennan in a concurring opinion).

"Only where state action impinges on the exercise of fundamental constitutional rights or liberties must it be found to have chosen the least restrictive alternative. Cf. *Dunn v. Blumstein,* 405 U.S., at 343; *Shelton v. Tucker,* 364 U.S. 479, 488 (1960)" (*San Antonio Independent School District v. Rodriguez,* 411 U.S. 1, 51 (1973)).

37. The application of the "hybrid" doctrine has been met with mixed results in the lower courts. A zoning ordinance that excluded churches and other nonprofit entities from building in area zoned for commercial and industrial purposes was declared unconstitutional when a local church brought suit with a free exercise claim conjoined with an equal protection claim (*Cornerstone Bible Church v. City of Hastings*, 948 F. 2d 464 (8th Cir. 1991). On the other hand, when a Quaker organization challenged a provision in the Immigration Reform and Control Act requiring employers to verify the legal immigration status of employees, the court declined to agree. At the heart of the Quaker case was the use of a "hybrid" claim consisting of free exercise and the right to employ. The court declared that the "right to hire" was not a fundamental right and not part of the examples used by the Supreme Court in the *Smith* decision (*American Friends Service Committee v. Thornburgh*, 941 F.2d 808 (9th Cir. 1991). Also see Fry (1993) for further discussion.)

38. While this statement is almost universally accepted, it is unclear and a matter of much debate whether a particular and specific statute or regulation also serves a "compelling" interest. The unproven assumption seems to be that since the objective of education is a compelling and substantial interest of the state, the *means* utilized by the state automatically takes on a compelling nature. In doing so they become nearly impregnable from constitutional assault.

39. Obviously, defining the precise nature of these competencies, as well as determining the point at which one is considered "competent," is problematic. The Court suggests in *San Antonio Independent School District v. Rodgriguez*, 411 U.S. 1, 36 (1973) that the level of competency that the state can legally require is a minimum rather than a maximum level, when it states that "we have never presumed to possess either the ability or the authority to guarantee to the citizenry the most *effective* speech or the most *informed* electoral choice." Compare this, however, with J. Powell's opinion in *Wolman v. Walter*, 433 U.S. 229, 262 (1977) that the state has a "legitimate interest in facilitating education of the highest quality for all children within its boundaries, whatever school their parents have chosen for them." The vital distinction between these two statements is that "facilitation" is of a very different character than "compulsory" or "guarantee."

40. *Wolman v. Walter*, 433 U.S. 229, 240 (1977); *Committee for Public Education v. Regan*, 444 U.S. 646, 653 (1980). See *Wolman v. Essex*, 342 F. Supp. 399, 411, *aff'd*, 409 U.S. 808 (1972) and *Lemon v. Kurtzman*, 403 U.S. 602, 663 (1971), where J. White, concurring and dissenting in part, and J. Douglas, concurring opinion, approves of "minimum standards." J. Brennan, in a concurring opinion, speaks approvingly of "minimum level of competency in certain skills" and "minimum levels of educational achievement" at 651 and 655. See also J. Marshall, concurring and dissenting in part, in *Wolman v. Walter*, 433 U.S. 229, 261 (1977).

41. J. Brennan refers to the "acquisition of certain knowledge" as a legitimate concern for the state in *Lemon v. Kurtzman*, 403 U.S. 602, 651 (1971), concurring opinion.

42. In a concurring opinion in *Lemon v. Kurtzman*, 403 U.S. 602, 655 (1971), J. Brennan listed "reading, writing, arithmetic . . . history, geography, science, literature, and law" as essential subjects that could be required of private schools.

43. J. Douglas, in a concurring opinion in *Lemon v. Kurtzman,* 403 U.S. 602, 631 (1971), also lists "accreditation of the school for diplomas, the number of hours of work and credits allowed" as legitimate minimum standards that the state could impose on private schools.

44. J. Douglas, in a concurring opinion in *Lemon v. Kurtzman,* 403 U.S. 602, 631 (1971), speaks of "competent teachers."

45. For a case contesting the manner in which fire and safety codes are applied to private schools, see *City of Sumner v. First Baptist Church,* 639 P. 2d 1358 (Wash. 1982).

46. *Griswold v. Connecticut,* 381 U.S. 479, 482 (1965); *Tinker v. Des Moines School District,* 393 U.S. 503, 506 (1969); *Board of Education v. Pico,* 457 U.S. 853, 861 (1982).

J. Brennan expanded this prohibition on state action to encompass "policing the content of courses, the specific textbooks used, . . . the words of the teacher . . . prescrib[ing] what shall *not* be taught, or what methods of instruction shall be used, or what opinions the teacher may offer in the course of teaching . . . [nor] prescribing the precise forum in which such skills and knowledge are learned" (*Lemon v. Kurtzman,* 403 U.S. 602, 651, 656 (1971)).

47. This same attitude was reflected very early on in a state court ruling on private education. "The great object of these provisions of the statutes has been that all children be educated, not that they shall be educated in any particular way" (*Commonwealth v. Roberts,* 34 N.E. 402, 403 (Mass. 1893)). See also *State v. Peterman,* 70 N.E. 550 (Ind. 1904).

48. In *Board of Education v. Allen,* 392 U.S. at 245–246, the Court held that the state could regulate the "quality and nature" of the curriculum, prescribe "subjects of instruction," and insist that teachers receive "specified training." Yet in *Lemon v. Kurtzman,* 403 U.S. at 651, 656, J. Brennan in a concurring opinion listed "policing of the content of courses, the specific textbooks used . . . the precise forum in which such skills and knowledge are learned . . . the words of the teacher . . . methods of instruction . . . opinions the teacher may offer in the course of teaching" as outside the power of the state to regulate.

49. For cases disputing the meaning of "equivalent," see *State v. Counort,* 124 P. 910 (Wash. 1912); *State v. Hoyt,* 146 A. 170 (N.H. 1929); *State v. Hershberger,* 144 N.E.2d 693 (1955); *State v. Massa,* 231 A. 2d 252 (N.J. 1967); *State v. LaBarge,* 357 A.2d 121 (Vt. 1976); *State v. Moorhead,* 308 N.W.2d 60 (Iowa 1981); *Bangor Baptist Church v. State of Maine,* 549 F.Supp. 1208 (D. Me. 1982); *Sheridan Road Baptist Church v. Department of Education,* 348 N.W.2d 263 (Mich. App. 1984); *Ellis v. O'Hara,* 612 F.Supp. 379 (D.C. Mo. 1985); *Fellowship Baptist Church v. Benton,* 620 F.Supp. 308, 815 F.2d 485 (8th Cir. 1987); and *State v. Newstrom,* 371 N.W.2d 525 (Minn. 1985).

50. Teacher qualifications have been a major point of litigation. *Wright v. State,* 209 P. 179 (Okla. 1922); *People v. Turner,* 263 P.2d 685, *appeal dismissed,* 347 U.S. 972 (1954); *Meyerkorth v. State,* 115 N.W.2d 585, *appeal dismissed,* 373 U.S. 705 (1963); *Kentucky State Board of Education v. Rudasill,* 589 S.W.2d 877, *cert. denied,* 446 U.S. 938 (1979); *State v. Shaver,* 294 N.W.2d 883 (N.D. 1980); *State v. Faith Baptist Church,* 301 N.W.2d 571, *appeal dismissed sub nom. Faith Baptist Church v.*

Douglas, 454 U.S. 803 (1981); *Jernigan v. State,* 412 S.2d 1242 (Ala. Crim. App. 1982); *State v. Rivinius,* 328 N.W.2d 220, *cert. denied,* 460 U.S. 1070 (1983); *Sheridan Road Baptist Church v. Department of Education,* 348 N.W.2d 263 (Mich. App. 1984); *Fellowship Baptist Church v. Benton,* 620 F.Supp. 308, 815 F.2d 485 (8th Cir. 1987); *State v. Patzer,* 382 N.W.2d 631, *cert. denied sub nom. Patzer v. North Dakota,* 479 U.S. 825 (1986); and *Sheridan Road Baptist Church v. Department of Education,* 396 N.W.2d 373 (Mich. 1986).

51. In discussions of abstract legal principles and judicial decisions, it is important that the human element not be forgotten and buried in legal briefs and court dicta. Behind all of these court cases are individuals and families who feel that their way of life and beliefs are being severely compromised if not threatened with destruction by state action. For them these cases are not stimulating exercises in legal gymnastics and the finer points of American jurisprudence, but desperate, final efforts made at great personal expense to alleviate what they perceive as an overly oppressive hand of the state.

NOTES TO CHAPTER 4

1. The pertinent part in the Declaration of Independence reads as follows: "We hold these truths to be self-evident, that all men are created equal, that they are endowed by their Creator with certain unalienable Rights, that among these are Life, Liberty, and the pursuit of Happiness."

In *Meachum v. Fano,* 427 U.S. 215, 230 (1976), J. Stevens, in a dissenting opinion, "thought it self-evident that all men were endowed by their Creator with liberty as one of the cardinal unalienable rights. It is that basic freedom which the Due Process Clause protects, rather than the particular rights or privileges conferred by specific laws or regulations."

H. L. A. Hart (1979) considers a natural right as "one which all men have if they are capable of choice; they have it *qua* men and not only if they are members of some society or stand in special relation to each other. . . . This right is not created or conferred by men's voluntary action" (p. 15).

2. James Q. Wilson (1981) observes that the "two most powerful and enduring ideas in American political culture" have been the "high value [attached] to the rationalization and moralization of society" and the theory of natural rights (pp. 34–35).

3. "One foundation for personal sovereignty . . . is a deep skepticism about whether there is any objectively correct view of the good for persons or the good life, objective in the sense that it is not ultimately based for each person on his or her own basic aims and values. This skepticism is one important support for a political liberalism that declines to found political institutions on any particular conception of the good life. Instead, it recognizes that different persons have reasonable but conflicting accounts of the good life and so seeks to secure conditions in which persons are free to define and pursue their own conception of it, constrained only by the rights of others to do so as well" (Brock, 1988, p. 561).

4. "We the People of the United States, in Order to form a more perfect

Union, establish Justice, insure domestic Tranquility, provide for the common defence, promote the general Welfare, and secure the Blessings of Liberty to ourselves and our Posterity, do ordain and establish this Constitution for the United States of America."

5. "Constitutional interpretation has consistently recognized that the parents' claim to authority in their own household to direct the rearing of their children is basic in the structure of our society" (*Ginsberg v. New York*, 390 U.S. 629, 639 (1968)). "Our jurisprudence historically has reflected Western civilization concepts of the family as a unit with broad parental authority over minor children. Our cases have consistently followed that course; our constitutional system long ago rejected any notion that a child is 'the mere creature of the state' and, on the contrary, asserted that parents generally 'have the right, coupled with the high duty, to recognize and prepare [their children] for additional obligations.' (*Pierce v. Society of Sisters*, 268 U.S. 510, 535 (1925)" (*Parham v. J. R.*, 442 U.S. 584, 602 (1979)).

6. "But the family itself is not beyond regulation in the public interest. . . . And neither rights of religion nor rights of parenthood are beyond limitation. Acting to guard the general interest in youth's well-being, the state as *parens patriae* may restrict the parent's control" (*Prince v. Massachusetts*, 321 U.S. 158, 166 (1944)).

7. Child abuse laws in many states allow the social service arm of the state to remove children from parents upon notification of *alleged* abuse only. This removal is only temporary unless it is ascertained that the parents are guilty of abusing the child.

8. A good example is the 1780 constitution for Massachusetts. "Wisdom and knowledge, as well as virtue, diffused generally among the body of people, being necessary for the preservation of their rights and liberties . . . it shall be the duty of the legislatures and magistrates, in all future periods of this commonwealth, to cherish the interest of literature and the sciences" (quoted in McLaughlin, 1946, p. 10).

9. " 'Religion, morality, and knowledge being necessary to good government and the happiness of mankind, schools and the means of education shall be forever encouraged' " (McLaughlin, 1946, p. 9).

10. This "right" to an education has not been declared a fundamental right under the federal constitution (*San Antonio Independent School District v. Rodriguez*, 411 U.S. 1 (1973)).

11. "There may be a difference in institution and government, but the purpose and end of both public and private education must be the same—the education of children of school age" (*State v. Counort*, 124 P. 910, 912 (Wash. 1912)).

12. John Elson (1969) identified "five predominant policies behind nonpublic school regulation: (1) to reinforce school attendance requirements, (2) to prevent the teaching of socially dangerous ideas, (3) to promote cultural unity, (4) to provide criteria for choosing quality nonpublic schooling, and (5) to protect the public from dangerous business, health, and building practices" (p. 104).

13. Carper and Devins (1985) have identified 12 areas of state regulations that have been contested in the courts: fire, health, and safety codes; curriculum;

selection of textbooks; instructional time; teacher certification; zoning ordinances; consumer protection; attendance reports; testing; state licensing and approval; interacting with the community; and guidance requirements (p. 104).

14. Two examples illustrate this problem. The many "national" reports on the condition of American education seem to agree only on one thing: There are serious problems with American education. There is little agreement on what our educational goals should be or how they should be achieved (Raspberry, 1986).

A recent study looking at decisions involving charges of incompetence on the part of public school teachers found only two states (Alaska and Tennessee) that had actually defined incompetence in their statutes (Gross, 1988).

15. William B. Ball (1969) confesses, "I do not understand—nor do most citizens—what sort of 'goals' public education has in mind, or how many different goals public education departments may have decided are to be 'the' goals, or by what popular processes, or according to what and whose philosophic presumptions the goals were ordained" (p. 194).

A good part of this problem—either ambiguous goals or the absence of goals—in education can be traced to an intellectual ideology built upon the objective pursuit of knowledge, and the myth of neutral, value-free problems and decisions. "Yet until teachers are willing to make value-judgments," states Alton Chase (1985), "they cannot define their mission. Saying what ought to be taught requires saying what knowledge is desirable. Designing a curriculum, limiting and directing knowledge, requires making moral judgments" (p. 40). The dilemma this presents to public policy decisions is how the imposition of one set of preferences or values through the legal machinery of the state is justified over the selection of another set of preferences. Public policy begins to take on uncomfortable dimensions of being arbitrary and prejudiced.

16. John I. Goodlad (1985) states that there are significant problems facing a universal, secondary education. American education is plagued with "ambiguous attitudes" of not being sure if what it has done is good or bad, nor has it "clearly articulat[ed] the means to achieve it. . . . And so we sidestep the questions that must be answered if our hopes are to be truly realized. We brush aside such questions as, What are the learnings—both knowledge and ways of knowing—that should constitute the common core? . . . Defining what constitutes this education becomes imperative" (pp. 269–270).

17. The lack of clear educational goals and an "objective nexus" between them and educational policy is a major complaint raised by James Gross's study (1988) of teacher competency cases in New York state.

18. Implicit in this statement is the assertion of natural rights—moral rights existing independent of the law. Many of these natural rights have been incorporated into our legal system and are also legal rights. It is beyond the scope of this study to enter into a detailed defense of natural rights and a critique of its major competitor, legal positivism—that which is right and moral is what the law declares it to be.

19. What these terms might mean in an educational sense is addressed in greater detail in Chapter 5.

20. A step in that direction was taken in one case by an attorney represent-

ing a group of private schools. He requested that the state "explain the *statutory basis for regulations* requiring private schools" to comply with certain prerequisites before approval was granted (*Bangor Baptist Church v. State of Maine, Department of Education,* 576 F.Supp. 1299, 1307 (D. Me. 1983)).

21. "Certainly there is nothing in the present records to indicate that they [private schools] have failed to discharge their obligations to patrons, students or the State" (*Pierce v. Society of Sisters,* 268 U.S. at 534). Christopher Klicka ("Iowa Parents" 1987), executive director of the Home School Legal Defense Association, stated that of the 150 cases he has handled, " 'we have not found one where the children were not being educated.' " (p. A10). "There is no claim," a federal court declared, "that non-public denominational schools in Ohio fail to provide quality education, generally equivalent to that provided in the public schools; nor does the Court so find. To the contrary, parochial schools provide a long recognized and valuable secular function in our society" (*Wolman v. Essex,* 342 F.Supp. 399, 405, *aff'd,* 409 U.S. 808 (1972)). "Underlying these cases, and underlying also the legislative judgments that have preceded the court decisions, has been a recognition that private education has played and is playing a significant and valuable role in raising the national levels of knowledge, competence, and experience. . . . The continued willingness to rely on the private school systems, including parochial systems, strongly suggests that a wide segment of informed opinion, legislative and otherwise, has found that these schools do an acceptable job of providing secular education to their students" (*Board of Education v. Allen,* 392 U.S. 236, 247–248 (1968); also quoted in *Lemon v. Kurtzman,* 403 U.S. 602, 655 (1971), J. Brennan concurring, and in *Committee for Public Education v. Nyquist,* 413 U.S. 756, 795 (1973)). "This case, of course, is not one in which any harm to physical or mental health of the child or to the public safety, peace, order, or welfare has been demonstrated or may be properly inferred. The record is to the contrary" (*Wisconsin v. Yoder,* 406 U.S. 205, 230 (1972)).

22. It is curious that in many of the court cases where evidence is presented showing satisfactory academic progress under private auspices, the state, and often the court, seems singularly *disinterested* with that showing. Part of the explanation for the lack of judicial interest is due to the statutory language, which is heavily oriented toward the means and process of education rather than the actual results or outcome (*Commonwealth v. Roberts,* 34 N.E. 402 (Mass. 1893); *State v. Peterman,* 70 N.E. 550 (Ind. 1904); *Wright v. State,* 209 P. 179 (Okla. 1922); *Rice v. Commonwealth,* 49 S.E.2d 342 (Va. 1948); *Commonwealth v. Renfrew,* 126 N.E.2d 109 (Mass. 1955); *State v. Superior Court,* 346 P.2d 999, *cert. denied,* 363 U.S. 814 (1960); *State v. Massa,* 231 A.2d 252 (N.J. 1967); *State v. Whisner,* 351 N.E.2d 750 (Ohio 1976); *In re Foster,* 330 N.Y.S.2d 8 (N.Y. 1972); *Wisconsin v. Yoder,* 406 U.S. 205, 222–223 (1972); *City of Akron v. Lane,* 416 N.E.2d 642 (Ohio App. 1979); *State ex rel. Nagle v. Olin,* 415 N.E.2d 279 (Ohio 1980); *State v. Shaver,* 294 N.W.2d 883 (N.D. 1980); *Delconte v. State,* 308 S.E.2d 898 (N.C. App. 1983), 329 S.E.2d 636 (N.C. 1985); *Mazanec v. North Judson–San Pierre School Corp.,* 614 F.Supp. 1152 (D.C. Ind. 1985); *State v. Newstrom,* 371 N.W.2d 525 (Minn. 1985)). Also see U.S. Congress, Senate, Committee on the Judiciary, "Appendix F—Student Test Scores," *Issues in Religious Liberty,* 1985, pp. 102–103.

23. In *Johnson v. Charles City Community School Board,* 368 N.W.2d 74, 87 (1985), the court stated that the "appellants have established strong and sincere religious beliefs which form the basis for educational goals, objectives and philosophies which substantially differ from those of public education."

24. "Scratch the surface of the public-school criticism of Christian fundamentalist schools in Kentucky and you find not a concern for critical thought and open minds but a fear that unacceptable values are being inculcated. . . .

". . . educators have linked the defense of their financial resources and their professional status to an ideology that strikes at the core beliefs of cultural dissenters.

". . . But the vast majority of issues over which the bitter battles of school and family are fought concern irreconcilable world views" (Arons, 1986, pp. 155, 179, 194, 210).

25. "State officials who act as if they know what areas of knowledge are essential for everyone must possess insights as yet undiscovered by leading scholars, must be unaware of their own ignorance, or must be guilty of colossal pretension, for there is little agreement or certitude among thinkers who have pondered these dilemmas most deeply. . . .

"Furthermore, state officials are probably the last group we should trust to decide how much commonality is essential. . . . It is in the interest of these officials to discourage the dissension and diversity that may jeopardize their positions, subject them to challenge, and make public institutions more difficult to run smoothly. . . .

"What we are most likely to end up with, then, is a type of regulatory system so prevalent in education today—a system that promotes the status and security of the educational profession, but has little demonstrable relationship to instructional quality" (Erickson, 1973, pp. 2/8, 2/30, 5/38–39).

26. "Teacher unions in Illinois as well as throughout the country have sought successfully to determine who teaches, what is taught, how much is spent, who shall be taught and how, and in fact whether teaching will occur at all. These essentially private organizations have been able to insinuate themselves into the political and administrative processes of government with the intention of operating the school system to their exclusive benefit as teachers and unionists" (Parrish, 1981, pp. 236–237).

27. That state and local officials are at times biased, prejudiced, and arrogant in their decision making is a matter of record. The following are examples. The school board used its power in an "arbitrary" way in denying withdrawal of a pupil from school with documented evidence of poor health (*State v. Jackson,* 53 A. 1021 (N.H. 1902)). The court condemned the state's very narrow definition of what constitutes a private school as "radically wrong" and said that the purpose of educational law is to ensure that children are educated, "not that they shall be educated in any particular way" (*State v. Peterman,* 70 N.E. 550 (Ind. 1904)). School officials were warned not to "too jealously assert or attempt to defend their supposed prerogatives" in responding to reasonable requests by parents (*State ex rel. Kelley v. Ferguson,* 144 N.W.1039 (Neb. 1914)). Education officials were reprimanded by the court for "exercising control over the courses of study" in private

schools without legislative authority (*State v. Will,* 160 P. 1025 (Kan. 1916); *Packer Collegiate Institute v. University of New York,* 81 N.E.2d 80 (N.Y. 1948); *State v. Williams,* 117 S.E.2d 444 (N.C. 1960)). School officials were cautioned against "overreaching" their authority" by "alien[ating]" children from their parents (*Hardwick v. Board of School Trustees,* 205 P. 49 (Colo. App. 1921)). A statute forbidding instruction in foreign languages was "unreasonable" and arbitrary (*Meyer v. Nebraska,* 262 U.S. 390 (1923)). Parents were indicted for offering an alternative education for their children. The court declared that "ostensibly this was an action to punish a parent for neglecting the education of his child; in reality, the record indicates that this prosecution grew out of religious differences and disputes arising out of the management of school affairs, involving a bond issue, the location of a consolidated school building, and methods of instruction and discipline (*Wright v. State,* 209 P. 179 (Okla. 1922)).

Local officials were castigated by the court for an unusual lack of understanding for the parental efforts to secure a safe educational environment for their children. "The actions of the Superintendent and the Local Board cannot be thought of other than as inflexible, short-sighted, bureaucratic and an unnecessary flexing of muscles to show these parents who was 'boss'" (*In re Foster,* 330 N.Y.S.2d 8 (N.Y. 1972)). The court instructed local officials when faced with First Amendment claims "not [to] be uncompromising and rigid" in enforcing "hypertechnical" safety and fire code regulations (*City of Sumner v. First Baptist Church,* 639 P.2d 1358 (Wash. 1982)). A federal court censured local officials for padlocking a church being used as an unapproved private school and bodily removing worshippers who were inside (*McCurry v. Tesch,* 738 F.2d 271 (8th Cir. 1984)). A district court openly acknowledged that "there may be problems when the responsibility of determining equivalent education is placed on local school boards even when it is more closely defined for two reasons. First, each local board may still have a different interpretation. Second, local school boards have an inherent conflict of interest since each student in a private school is potentially a source of additional state aid" (*Fellowship Baptist Church v. Benton,* 620 F. Supp. 308, 318 (D. Iowa 1985), 815 F.2d 485 (8th Cir. 1987)). Also see *Sheridan Road Baptist Church v. Department of Education,* 348 N.W. 2d 263 (Mich. App. 1984).

28. The requirement that private school teachers must possess a teaching certificate from the state before attendance at a private school is recognized as compliance with compulsory education laws has been a major source of contention between private schools and the state. The credibility of the state's assertion that certificated teachers are essential to the educational process is severely weakened by the many exemptions given teachers in public schools in the form of emergency certificates, assigning teachers to teach courses outside their field, and allowing alternative ways to certify. Graham Donn, the executive director for the Council for Basic Education, considers the "misassignment of teachers as a national scandal that is out of control." Albert Shanker, president of the American Federation of Teachers, estimates that 200,000 teachers are misassigned. In 1983 3.4% (88,260) of all public school teachers were not certificated. In 1981–82 20% of all the certificates given in Texas, 16% in Ohio, 13% in California, 12% in Florida, and 10% in Colorado and New Jersey were emergency or substandard

certificates (Roth, 1986, pp. 725–726). In 1984 Los Angeles filled many of its 1,800 teacher vacancies with teachers given "emergency credentials" where one possessing only a college degree could teach (Doyle & Hartle, 1985, p. 49). Also see Peirce (1985). Yet not a single public school was closed by any state. Private schools, however, were being taken to court in several states and closed if their teachers did not meet the certification requirement.

29. The intent of this section is to touch on several major issues with broad appeal and application. More technical legal issues such as overbreadth, vagueness, and *ultra vires* are more relevant to a particular and specific piece of state legislation and will not be dealt with except to acknowledge their presence and importance.

30. This fact was openly conceded by the United States Supreme Court, which acknowledged "only a handful" of cases that were successful in voiding legislation under the rational means test (*Cleburne v. Cleburne Living Center, Inc.,* 473 U.S. 432, 459, n. 4 (1985), J. Marshall, concurring and dissenting in part, joined by J. Brennan and J. Blackmun).

31. The question arises: Can two courses of action, diametrically opposed yet chosen under similar conditions, both be considered rational decisions? There are states that have chosen not only to *not* regulate private schools but also to expressly forbid their regulation, while other states have opted to extensively regulate private schools. Both legislative acts are presumptively rational but can they be in actuality? If this cannot be a logically consistent position, and is therefore irrational, then which decision was the rational one?

32. The state "must show that its regulation is necessary to serve a compelling state interest and that it is narrowly drawn to achieve that end" (*Widmar v. Vincent,* 454 U.S. 263, 270 (1981)). See also *Carey v. Brown,* 447 U.S. 455 (1980) and *Healy v. Jones,* 408 U.S. 169 (1972).

33. With the relatively recent development of an "intermediate" standard of review, there are technically three standards by which legislation may be examined for constitutionality. This middle standard of review is still undergoing conceptual and legal development and will be addressed in more detail in Chapter 5.

34. "The Constitution does not explicitly mention any right of privacy. In a line of decisions, however, going back perhaps as far as *Union Pacific R. Co. V. Botsford,* 1412 U.S. 250, 251 (1891), the Court has recognized that a right of personal privacy, or a guarantee of certain areas or zones of privacy, does exist under the Constitution. In varying contexts, the Court or individual Justices have, indeed, found at least the roots of that right in the First Amendment, *Stanley v. Georgia,* 394 U.S. 557, 564 (1969); in the Fourth and Fifth Amendments, *Terry v. Ohio,* 392 U.S. 1, 8–9 (1968), *Katz v. United States,* 389 U.S. 347, 350 (1967), *Boyd v. United States,* 116 U.S. 616 (1886), see *Olmstead v. United States,* 277 U.S. 438, 478 (1928) (Brandeis, J., dissenting); in the penumbras of the Bill of Rights, *Griswold v. Connecticut,* 381 U.S., at 484–485; in the Ninth Amendment, *id.,* at 486 (Goldberg, J., concurring); or in the concept of liberty guaranteed by the first section of the Fourteenth Amendment, see *Meyer v. Nebraska,* 262 U.S. 390, 399 (1923). These decisions make it clear that only personal rights that can be deemed 'fundamental' or 'implicit in the concept of ordered liberty,' *Palko v. Connecticut,* 302 U.S. 319,

325 (1937), are included in this guarantee of personal privacy. They also make it clear that the right has some extension to activities relating to marriage . . . procreation . . . contraception . . . family relationships . . . and child rearing and education [cites *Pierce* and *Meyer*]" (*Roe v. Wade,* 410 U.S. 113, 152, 153 (1973)).

35. For additional court decisions placing parental right over their children's education as a privacy right, see the following: "The entire fabric of the Constitution and the purposes that clearly underlie its specific guarantees demonstrate that the rights to marital privacy and to marry and raise a family are of similar order and magnitude as the fundamental rights specifically protected" (*Griswold v. Connecticut,* 381 U.S. 479, 495 (1965), J. Goldman concurring); and "The *Meyer–Pierce–Yoder* 'parental' right and the privacy right, while dealt with separately in this opinion, may be no more than verbal variations of a single constitutional right. See *Roe v. Wade,* 410 U.S. 113, 152–153 (citing *Meyer v. Nebraska* and *Pierce v. Society of Sisters* for the proposition that this Court has recognized a constitutional right of privacy)" (*Runyon v. McCrary,* 427 U.S. 160, 178, n. 15 (1975)).

36. "*Pierce v. Society of Sisters,* 268 U.S. 510 (1925), lends no support to the contention that parents may replace state educational requirements with their own idiosyncratic views of what knowledge a child needs to be a productive and happy member of society . . . the Court simply held that while a State may posit such standards, it may not pre-empt the educational process by requiring children to attend public schools" (*Wisconsin v. Yoder,* 406 U.S. 205, 239 (1972)). "Appellees fail to recognize the limited scope of *Pierce* when they urge the right of parents to send their children to private schools under that holding is at stake in this case" (*Norwood v. Harrison,* 413 U.S. 455, 461 (1973)). "Few familial decisions are as immune from governmental interference as parents' choice of a school for their children, so long as the school chosen otherwise meets the educational standards imposed by the state" (*Cook v. Hudson,* 429 U.S. 165 (1976)).

"Of course these officials will disagree with many of the claims that a minority makes. That makes it all the more important that they take their decisions gravely. They must show that they understand what rights are, and they must not cheat on the full implications of the doctrine . . . [to] take rights seriously" (Dworkin, 1979, p. 110).

37. "But freedom to differ is not limited to things that do not matter much. That would be a mere shadow of freedom. The test of its substance is the right to differ as to things that touch the heart of the existing order" (*West Virginia Board of Education v. Barnette,* 319 U.S. 624, 642 (1943)).

38. The Court in *Farrington* concluded that the Hawaii Foreign Language law and accompanying regulations would "deny both owners and patrons reasonable choice in discretion in respect to teachers, curriculum and textbooks . . . [and] would deprive parents of fair opportunity to procure for their children instruction which they think important and we cannot say is harmful" (273 U.S. 284, 298 (1927)).

39. See the very persuasive argument by Stephen Arons (1976) that *Pierce* should be read as a First Amendment case.

40. Free exercise rights as well as privacy rights almost invariably connect with associational rights—the right to meet with others in pursuit of a common

goal, the right to have "certain kinds of highly personal relationships [given] a substantial measure of sanctuary from unjustified interference by the state. [*Pierce* and *Meyer* cited]" (*Roberts v. United States Jaycees,* 468 U.S. 609, 618–619 (1984)).

41. See Proverbs 22:6, Deuteronomy 6:6–7, Ephesians 6:4. From these texts many parents perceive a biblical mandate to educate their children in a church school imbued with a Christian ethos. For a very interesting ethnographic study of a fundamentalist Christian school, see Peshkin (1986). This biblical interpretation is shared not only by many Protestants but also by the Catholic tradition (*Jernigan v. State,* 412 So. 2d 1242 (Ala. Crim. App. 1982)).

42. The pastor of an unapproved fundamentalist Baptist church school explained his position this way: "'We don't want approval, because we feel it's a matter of state control. Jesus said in Matthew, Chapter 16, 'I will build my church, and the gates of hell will not prevail against.' We believe the head of the Church is Jesus Christ, and if I let the State become the head of the Church, then I will be removing the Lord from His position, and this Church is definitely built on the Lord, Jesus Christ'" (*State v. Shaver,* 294 N.W.2d 883, 887 (N.D. 1980)). See similar rationales expressed in *State v. Faith Baptist Church,* 301 N.W.2d 571, 574 (Neb. 1981); *Bangor Baptist Church v. State of Maine, Department of Education,* 576 F.Supp. 1299 (D. Me. 1983); *Braintree Baptist Temple v. Holbrook Public Schools,* 616 F.Supp. 81 (D. Mass. 1984); *Johnson v. Charles City Community School Board,* 368 N.W. 2d 74, 76–77, *cert. denied sub nom. Pruessner v. Benton,* 474 U.S. 1033 (1985); *Fellowship Baptist Church v. Benton,* 620 F.Supp. 308, 815 F.2d 485 (8th Cir. 1987); and *New Life Baptist Church Academy v. Town of East Longmeadow,* 885 F.2d 940 (1st Cir. 1989), *cert. denied,* 110 S. Ct. 1782 (1990). Also see equivalent rationales expressed in different but related circumstances (*North Valley Baptist Church v. McMahon,* 696 F.Supp. 518 (E.D. Cal. 1988); *Blount v. Department of Educational & Cultural Services,* 551 A.2d 1377 (Me. 1988)).

43. For example, see *State v. Shaver,* 294 N.W.2d 883 (N.D. 1980); *State v. Faith Baptist Church,* 301 N.W.2d 571 (Neb. 1981); *Bangor Baptist Church v. State of Maine,* 549 F.Supp. 1208 (D. Me. 1982); *State v. Rivinius,* 328 N.W.2d 220, *cert. denied,* 460 U.S. 1070 (1983); *Sheridan Road Baptist Church v. Department of Education,* 348 N.W.2d 263 (Mich. App. 1984); *Fellowship Baptist Church v. Benton* 620 F.Supp. 308, 815 F.2d 485 (8th Cir. 1987); *Johnson v. Charles City Community School Board,* 368 N.W. 2d 74, *cert. denied sub nom. Pruessner v. Benton,* 474 U.S. 1033 (1985); *State v. Patzer,* 382 N.W. 2d 631, *cert. denied* 479 U.S. 825 (1986); *Sheridan Road Baptist Church v. Department of Education,* 396 N.W. 2d 373 (Mich. 1986).

44. In a blistering dissent, J. Riley criticizes the majority opinion for "reach[ing] their decision in this case, not by finding that enforcing the certification requirement is essential to the state's interest in education, but by dismissing plaintiffs' religious beliefs and practices as unimportant and characterizing the burdening of plaintiffs' free exercise of those beliefs as 'minimal.' Their insensitivity in this regard does not comport with this Court's constitutionally mandated responsibility to safeguard the individual freedoms guaranteed by the First and Fourteenth Amendments, and to enforce the limitations upon governmental authority commensurate therewith" (*Sheridan Road Baptist Church v. Department of Education,* 396 N.W. 2d 373, 427 (Mich. 1986)).

45. This pattern of intolerance by the state for views diverging from public orthodoxy does seem to repeat itself over and over again in American history with such diverse examples as Roger Williams, Catholics, Mormons, Jews, Quakers, Jehovah's Witnesses, Amish, and the many cultural and ethnic groups such as blacks, Irish, eastern Europeans, Chinese, and Japanese. For an insightful look at religious pluralism in American history, see Moore (1986).

As the Court reminded us in the flag salute case, "those who begin coercive elimination of dissent soon find themselves exterminating dissenters" (*West Virginia Board of Education v. Barnette*, 319 U.S. 624, 641 (1943)).

46. Laurence Tribe (1985), in testimony before the U.S. Senate Committee on the Judiciary, concluded, "I think the ultimate issue is disregard, disregard for fundamental constitutional and religious precepts. . . .

"What one hears in all of these cases is an attempt to compartmentalize. The people of Nebraska are told by State officials this is not a religious issue, it is an educational issue. . . .

"It seems to me, Mr. Chairman, that we can very well pigeonhole religious freedom to death, if every time religion becomes relevant in one or another sphere of our social life, it is possible for men of zeal, without understanding, simply to dismiss the relevance of religion, as though religion had a place only at the top of some very remote spiritual tower, and were not relevant to the ordinary concerns of life" (p. 183).

47. Delegates to the Kentucky constitutional convention in 1890 revealed perceptive insight in recognizing the fundamental issues of conscience involved in education. They also exercised uncanny foresight in amending section five of the Kentucky Bill of Rights by extending the right of religious freedom to its logical conclusion in education. The added phrase, "nor shall any man be compelled to send his child to any school to which he may be conscientiously opposed," makes explicit what is implicit in freedom of religion clauses found in other federal and state constitutions. It takes rights of free exercise and conscience seriously and in so doing practically resolves any disputes over regulations and private schools (*Kentucky State Board v. Rudasill*, 589 S.W.2d 877 (Ky. 1979). Also see Schwartz (1979).

48. *Wolman v. Walter*, 433 U.S. 229, 240–241 (1977) warns of the "supervision that gives rise to excessive entanglement." In *Lemon v. Kurtzman*, the Court declared unconstitutional a program that required the state to examine the schools' records to ferret out the proportion of expenditures used for secular and religious activities. "This kind of state inspection and supervision and evaluation of the religious content of a religious organization is fraught with the sort of entanglement that the Constitution forbids. It is a relationship pregnant with dangers of excessive direction of church schools and hence of churches . . . we cannot ignore here the danger that pervasive modern governmental power will ultimately intrude on religion and conflict with the Religion Clauses (403 U.S. 602, 620 (1971)). See additional comments in the same decision at 627, 634–635, 637.

49. The "Court has tended to treat private elementary and secondary schools as similar to public schools insofar as they are properly subject to the power of the state and federal regulatory agencies but to emphasize their separa-

tion when considering policies of direct or indirect general or categorical aid" (Vitullo-Martin, 1978, p. 131).

50. It would appear, however, that record-keeping requirements by the state serve a compelling state interest and would supersede any claims of First Amendment violations. See *Planned Parenthood of Missouri v. Danforth*, 428 U.S. 52, 80–81 (1976); *Tony and Susan Alamo Foundation v. Secretary of Labor*, 471 U.S. 290, 305 (1985); *Wallace v. Jaffree*, 472 U.S. 38, 110 (1985).

51. If the rational means test is the standard of review used by the court, then this point becomes moot in a practical sense.

52. Diane Ravitch (1985) argues that "to avoid unwise and dangerous politicization, government agencies should strive to distinguish between their proper role as protectors of fundamental constitutional rights and inappropriate intrusion into complex issues of curriculum and pedagogy.

"This kind of institutional restraint would be strongly abetted if judges and policymakers exercised caution and skepticism in their use of social science testimony. Before making social research the basis for constitutional edicts, judges and policymakers should understand that social science findings are usually divergent, limited, tentative, and partial" (p. 273).

53. Typical of the degree of unfairness and irrationality in what the courts often require of private schools and the state is reflected in an article by Baker (1978–1979). Baker insists that private religious schools show the "actual burdens" on their religious freedoms, while the state need only show a "logical connection" between regulations and state goals. Baker is forced into a lower standard of proof for the state by confessing that to "prove that these regulations ensure quality education . . . is impossible." Yet, what he does not explain is how such different standards of evidence are justified.

54. This study did not find a single instance where regulations for private schools had been assessed and evaluated.

55. The concurring condemnation of "idiosyncratic views" about education by J. White, Brennan, and Stewart in the *Yoder* case appears to be contradicted by this research finding. They appear to be denouncing that quality which most often leads to learning and academic achievement.

56. When the typical SES factors such as "income, education, and/or occupation of household heads" were used, White discovered these factors accounted for 5% ($r = .22$) of the variance in academic achievement at the individual level and 53% ($r = .73$) when the unit of analysis was aggregated. The classic study in this area is Coleman, Campbell, Hobson, McPartland, Mood, Weinfeld & York (1966), *Equality of Educational Opportunity*.

Coleman, Hoffer, and Kilgore (1982) report that "various studies indicate that variation in school characteristics can account for only 10 to 25 percent of the variance in student achievement. Even this fraction of the variance is in part accounted for by the differences in average family backgrounds in different schools. In contrast, measured differences in family background among students ordinarily account for 20 percent or more of the total variance; this constitutes something like a lower bound to the total effect of all measured and unmeasured background characteristics. The total between-family variance is usually found to be greater than .5" (p. xxvi, n .2).

57. "Educational malpractice" is defined as the "failure to adequately educate a student and includes the improper or inadequate instruction, testing, placement or counseling of a child" (Dye, 1987–1988, p. 499). Also see Loscalzo (1985) for additional discussion.

58. This is in spite of various approaches—constitutional, statutory, and professional—to prove that such a legal duty exists.

59. For example, in the realm of evaluating teacher competence, see Gross (1988).

60. For superior results in a statewide achievement test in reading, mathematics, and writing, see *Student Achievement in New York State, 1983–84* (New York State, 1984a, pp. 7–8).

61. The study also revealed that these students tended to come from homes with higher incomes and that private schools were more religiously segregated than public schools. With Supreme Court rulings on aid to private schools and religion in public schools, these results are not surprising at all.

To be sure, Coleman, Hoffer, and Kilgore's study has generated an intense debate over whether the superiority in achievement is due to the private school or to other factors, such as selection bias, that tip the results in favor of the private schools. See, for example, Alexander and Pallas (1985); Goldberger and Cain (1982); and Willms (1985). For our purposes these criticisms are simply irrelevant. The pertinent question for this study is whether students attending private schools are receiving an adequate education, not why or how. The answer to this question is an unequivocal yes.

62. U.S. Secretary of Education William Bennett considered the Chicago public schools as the "worst in the nation" having undergone an "educational meltdown" ("Chicago Schools Called Worst," 1987, p. 6A).

NOTES TO CHAPTER 5

1. For one thing, the mere existence of private schools challenges the idea of the need for a state system of education. It also poses a substantial threat to those in public education whose power, influence, and financial well-being are derived from their special claims to expertise and having the "one best system." See Chapter 2.

Nationalism is a powerful ideology characteristic of any nation-state.

2. C. B. Macpherson (1973) observes that "it is the mark of a civilized society that private violence be forbidden, and that violence, the power to compel by physical force or constraint, be a monopoly of government. It is because this kind of power must be a monopoly of the government that we are rightly concerned with controls on the government" (p. 68).

3. "Too often the choices about how to deal with a public problem are presented as either to regulate the activity or to retain virtually unlimited private

discretion—as if these were necessarily the only possible alternatives. Yet it is entirely conceivable that there are other techniques that would yield 'better' results. Policymakers must assess the relative merits and drawbacks of various alternatives according to the particular situation" (Stone, 1982, p. 12).

4. Prominent theorists include John Neville Figgis, Harold J. Laski, G. D. H. Cole, Bertrand Russell, and Robert A. Dahl.

5. Darryl Baskin (1971) frames the three principles of pluralism as "(1) social diversity and balance, (2) separation of powers, and (3) subsystem autonomy" (p. 2).

6. "Pluralistic theories on the whole do not deny that there are vast areas of state administration which are approved by all (*consensus omnium*) but consider it neither desirable nor possible that in a free country there should be a uniform common will that absorbs the diversified intentions of the various groups" (Ehrlich, 1982, p. xi).

Pluralism seems to strive for the Aristotelian mean that lies between excesses on either end of the spectrum.

7. "The rejection of state sovereignty was an essential preliminary to the formation of a political philosophy of pluralism. If the state is morally sovereign, then groups and individuals can never have rights against the state. A notion of political sovereignty will undermine the sociological idea of group personality, and the whole possibility of a plural society is called into question by state omnipotence. A narrow construction of legal sovereignty removes from the sphere of law the system of common law which is the basis of most of the guarantees of group life" (Nichols, 1975, p. 53).

8. Archibald Cox (1987) suggests three reasons why society should exercise respect for minority viewpoints: one, it shows respect for individual dignity; second, we may be the next victims of intolerance if we permit others to be marginalized; and third, no one has a corner on truth. A multiplicity of viewpoints and perspectives increases the probability of finding new truths.

9. Erickson (1973) contends that the "possibility must be entertained, contradictory as it may seem, that our society will make more progress towards rationality by encouraging community loyalties than by attempting to destroy them. . . . Perhaps the most rational interchange of ideas will occur when communities are secure from attacks on their unique values and when individuals are free from doubts about who they are" (p. 2/28).

"Autonomous organizations are highly desirable in a democracy for at least two reasons. First, they supply 'mutual controls,' or restraints, on the universal tendency towards hierarchy and domination in social life. Second, the rights required for democracy make organizational pluralism simultaneously possible and necessary, and hence both inevitable and desirable. . . . Organizational pluralism is the concomitant, both as a cause and effect, of the liberalization and democratization of 'hegemonic' (i.e. illiberal and undemocratic) regimes" (Krouse, 1983, p. 168).

10. This would also be true for the state itself in that it could "be monopolized by its own agents in accordance with the iron law of oligarchy" (Walzer, 1983, p. 15).

11. Also see where the Court notes that "private schools may serve as a benchmark for public schools" (*Muller v. Allen,* 463 U.S. 388, 395 (1983)). The Court also does "not doubt—indeed we fully recognize—the validity of the State's interest in promoting pluralism and diversity among its public and nonpublic schools" (*Committee for Public Education v. Nyquist,* 413 U.S. 756, 773 (1973)). The President's Panel on Nonpublic Schools in April 1970 stated that " 'no government can be indifferent to the collapse of such schools' " (Fantini, 1973, p. 230).

12. "Public schooling . . . was justified by the inability of the private sector to serve a constituency in need. It was the classic justification for public intervention in a private market: market failure—an old story in health, education and welfare.

"Today, however, the tables are turned. The schools that stand accused of failure are those under public control. . . . In this case it is important to remember the classic remedy for market failure: find alternate providers.

"The problem—and its solution—are structurally the same when the failure is in the public sector" (Doyle & Hartle, 1985, p. 65).

13. The bias that can arise in an educational setting comes not just in overt and purposeful forms but also as bias unrecognized as such. A way of seeing is also a way of not seeing. In addition, Donald Erickson (1973) reminds us that one's fellow classmates also bring their own sense of right and wrong to the educational setting. Peer influence and the "student subculture" can have incredible impact on the neutrality of the educational experience. This poses a great difficulty for conscientious public school officials because it is an indoctrinating influence that is difficult to control (p. 2/20–21).

14. This is *not* to say that private schools are neutral institutions. To the contrary, they obviously have their own viewpoints. The neutralizing influence comes about as various groups "balance each other off" in our pluralistic society (Erickson, 1973, p. 2/15).

15. The frequent reference in public discourse to things that are "religious" versus those which are supposedly "secular" or nonreligious is not very useful and often distorts the real issues of conscience. A more thoughtful examination of the alleged dichotomy between the religious and secular reveals more of a distinction without a real difference. For more on the problem of defining "religion" for public policy purposes, see Syle (1983).

16. The Supreme Court has stated that "the ability independently to define one's identity . . . is central to any concept of liberty" (*Roberts v. United States Jaycees,* 468 U.S. 609, 619 (1984)).

17. Also see Arons and Lawrence (1980). For some related comments on individual autonomy and the necessity of noncoercive influences on civic development, see Erickson (1973, pp. 2/15, 2/35).

18. Brendan F. Brown (1970), pointing to the same danger, stated that "a monopoly of education by the State offers great temptation to the dictatorial minded to exalt unduly the importance of the state in the life of the individual or to induce those taught to embrace a single ideology" (p. 533). A federal appeals court further stated that "the undesirability of cultural homogenization would lead us to oppose efforts by the state to assume a greater role in children's devel-

opment, even if we were confident that the state were capable of doing so effectively and intelligently. In short, our collective wish to preserve and promote the enlivening variety of our social and political life prompts us to be wary of any tampering with our highly decentralized, substantially unregulated, parent-dominated childrearing system" (*Franz v. United States,* 707 F. 2d 582, 598 (1983)).

19. Robert Dahl (1982) acknowledges that the "problem of democratic pluralism is serious . . . precisely because independent organizations are highly desirable and at the same time their independence allows them to do harm" (p. 31).

20. This is not to say that private schools have only a pecuniary interest in the child. Most private schools are nonprofit organizations sponsored by religious organizations. But reality often makes the bottom line an economic one.

21. Strike (1982b) would add two additional ones: "promotion of justice" and "promoting common forms of understanding" (p. 159). These are important concepts but they could probably be subsumed under the two announced by the Supreme Court.

22. Even among the groups in education there is a considerable amount of infighting and disagreement over the content and process of an adequate education. For example, in the basic area of curriculum a controversy has raged within the public schools for the past hundred years between those advocating a strong liberal arts approach as opposed to those favoring a more practical, vocational orientation. And there is the debate between the traditionalists who concentrate on the *content* of teaching versus those members of the progressive movement in education who focus on the *process* of teaching. In private education one need only look at the bewildering array of private options such as "free schools," military academies, single-sex schools, religious schools with all their diversity, and the elite "independent" schools. And finally, there are hundreds of educational reports of late, offering different suggestions about what constitutes a good education and the best way of providing it.

23. If the child were capable of making rational decisions on his or her own, he or she would obviously be in the best position to know and insure that his or her interests were protected. Immaturity and ignorance often prevent him or her from knowing and acting in his or her best interests. The rights of children against their parents is another issue that stalks us in the background. It is an important concern in its own right but is tangential to the present issue of the rights of parents and their proxies such as private schools as compared with the interests of the state. See *Wisconsin v. Yoder,* 406 U.S. at 230–232, 243–246, for an introduction of the issue of children's rights in education against the competing rights of their parents. Compare Hafen (1976). Since the state has recognized the primacy of parents with regard to the upbringing and care of their children, this is the issue that must be addressed first. Also see Gutman (1987) for expanded discussion on limits of state, family, and individuals as sole authorities.

24. Again, the one caveat is child abuse. Government social services in many states may remove the child from the home solely on the basis of *alleged* abuse. This removal, however, is only temporary if the allegations are proven unfounded.

25. "The law's concept of family . . . has recognized that natural bonds of

affection lead parents to act in the best interests of their children" (*Parham v. J.R.*, 442 U.S. 584, 602 (1979)).

26. "Both centralized decision making and legislated curriculum presume that there is 'one best way' to help young people learn. Both presume, too, that those farthest removed from the place where the action of teaching and learning take place can make better decisions about what should be taught and how improvement can be fostered than those who are closest to the action. Such presumptions are at the very least naive and they may actually be dangerous" (Frymier, 1986, p. 646). Also see West (1965, p. 9).

27. "A parent's right to the preservation of his relationship with his child derives from the fact that the parent's achievement of a rich and rewarding life is likely to depend significantly on his ability to participate in the rearing of his offspring. A child's corresponding right to protection from interference in the relationship derives from the psychic importance to him of being raised by a loving, responsive, reliable adult" (*Franz v. United States*, 707 F.2d 582, 599 (1983)). Strike (1982b) observes that parents "may project their hopes and aspirations onto their children. They may experience the child's injuries, the child's successes, the child's failures as their own," which gives parents "a stake in their children" (p. 158).

28. In another case the Supreme Court observed that "we have noted that certain kinds of personal bonds [e.g., parent–child] have played a critical role in the culture and traditions of the Nation by cultivating and transmitting shared ideals and beliefs" (*Roberts v. United States Jaycees*, 468 U.S. at 618–619).

29. Several diverse examples illustrate this point. There is the *Yoder* case with the distinctive religious and community life of the Amish. In the early 1970s the Santa Fe Community School with its nonreligious but distinctive "countercultural" emphasis was organized by a small group of parents and teachers (*Santa Fe Community School v. New Mexico State Board of Education*, 518 P.2d 272 (N.M. 1974)). The Christian schools in Kentucky during the late 1970s opposed state regulations requiring state-approved teachers and textbooks as determined by the state board of education (*Kentucky State Board of Education v. Rudasill*, 589 S.W.2d 877, *cert. denied*, 446 U.S. 938 (1979)). They felt such teaching and curricular requirements intruded too much on their efforts to infuse a particular religious outlook in a child's educational experience. And there is the case of Peter and Susan Perchemlides as related by Stephen Arons (1986). They objected to the "conformity, anti-intellectualism, passivity, alienation, classism, and hierarchy" that their children were being exposed to in the local public school. Only after a lengthy confrontation and litigation with local public school officials were they able to secure permission to teach their personal political, cultural, and sociological values in the context of their own educational philosophy.

30. At least nine states and the District of Columbia have some sort of "equivalency" curriculum and/instructional requirement for private schools. Connecticut requires "equivalent instruction in studies taught in public schools." In some states, such as Indiana and Iowa, the term "equivalency" is never really defined. In other states, the term is given an ambiguous definition. Maine stipulates that the commissioner of education will determine whether the instruction is equivalent. Maryland calls for "regular, thorough instruction . . . usually taught

in the public schools to children of the same age." New York's regulation is similar to that of Maryland. Massachusetts requires "instruction in all the studies required by law [be equal] in thoroughness and efficiency, and in the progress made therein, [of] that in the public schools of the same town." Nevada requires that instruction be "of the kind and amount approved by the state board of education." New Jersey stipulates that instruction should be "equivalent to that provided in the public schools." The District of Columbia requires "instruction . . . deemed equivalent" (Connecticut. *General Statutes* Sec. 10–184 (1985); Indiana. *Code Annotated* Title 20, Sec. 8.1–3-17 (Supp. 1985); Iowa. *Code Annotated* Title 12, Sec. 299.1 (Supp. 1985); Maine. *Revised Statutes Annotated* Title 20–A, Sec. 5001–A (Supp. 1985); Maryland. *Annotated Code* Chapter 22, Sec. 7–301 (Supp. 1985); Massachusetts. *Annotated Laws* Title XII, Sec. 76–1 (1985); Nevada. *Revised Statutes* Title 34, Sec. 392.070 (1983); New Jersey. *Statutes Annotated* Sec. 18A:38–25 (1968) and *Administrative Code* Title 6, Sec. 34–1.4 (1980); New York. *Education Law* Sec. 3204 (McKinney, 1981); District of Columbia. *Code Annotated* Title 31, Sec. 31–401 (1981)).

Of key importance is how "equivalency" is defined and with what precision the definition is applied to private schools. It is quite possible that "equivalency" could be construed to mean a mirror image of the public school program, with the same courses, textbooks, teaching methods, administrative policies, and so on. There is even the issue of the social milieu of the school. See *State v. Massa*, 231 A.2d 252 (N.J. 1967) where the superior court ruled that "equivalency" had reference only to academic areas but not to social dimensions of the educational experience. Also see Bristow (1977).

31. The limiting of parental choice also raises the important issue of public financing of private schools. While this is a secondary issue to the subject of this study, the economic resources available to parents play a significant role in their ability to exercise parental liberty. See Deborah Cohen's cogent study (1985) and Stephen Arons (1986, pp. 211–221).

32. This would hold true for state schools, although to a lesser degree.

33. This all-inclusive reach of regulations is, paradoxically, both its virtue and its vice.

34. It is of interest to note that the Don't Know category was not selected by any private school parent as a reason for preferring private education.

If the Religion/Spirituality category is dropped for private schools, the third category becomes Smallness, Individual Attention (5.6%).

The results remain basically the same, except for a reordering of rank, even when one looks at the first three reasons given for selecting either private or public schools. Private school parents selected Discipline (48.5%), Academic Quality/Emphasis (39.6%), and Religion/Spirituality (35.1%) or, if that category is dropped, Smallness, Individual Attention (19.8%). For public school parents, the selections were Proximity, Convenience (29.9%), Cheapness (19.3%), and Don't Know (17%).

35. See Diehl (1983) for opposing viewpoint. This is not to say that many public school parents do not investigate the quality of the state schools. One of

the prime considerations in purchasing a home is the quality of the local public school serving that residential neighborhood.

Coleman and Hoffer (1987) continue to find private school students coming from homes that are more stable and have a higher SES, "higher expectations for ... educational achievement," and greater parental involvement than those of public school students (pp. 34, 54).

36. Alan Peshkin (1986) reported in his study of a Christian fundamentalist school that both students and parents had to agree to abide by certain conditions as a prerequisite to enrollment.

For a good look at the criteria for admission decisions in elite private schools, see the interesting study by Cookson and Persell (1985).

37. Also see Furtwengler (1985, p. 265) and Grant (1982).

Private schools are described by Erickson (1982) more as a "*Gemeinschaft*— close-knit community in which people perform because of mutual commitment to special goals and to each other." In contrast, public schools seem more reflective of a "*Gesellschaft*—the complex 'society' where relationships among people are segmented and specialized, where goals are divergent, and where people make their various contributions calculatively, in exchange for special incentives" (p. 414). Also see Fech (1985).

38. Also see Chubb (1988). In his ethnographic study of a Christian fundamentalist private school, Alan Peshkin (1986) noted that the school was a "good school in conventional terms," and also exhibited many of the qualitative features of an effective school (p. 283).

An additional dimension suggested by Coleman and Hoffer (1987) in explaining the continued variance in achievement between public, Catholic, and other private schools is the presence of a "functional" community. Much of the success found in Catholic schools may be due to the existence of a Catholic community that enables a social subgroup to function somewhat independently of the rest of society.

39. Some scholars suggest that the state exercises far greater control over private schools through indirect means such as tax codes and requirements for tax-exempt status than through the direct supervision of the educational program. This is an important contribution to the overall perspective of state regulation of private schools. See Capps and Esbeck (1985) and Vitullo-Martin (1982).

40. Racial discrimination in admission policies would deny to another minority group the right to direct the education and upbringing of their children based on irrelevant and harmful criteria. "It must be seen that racial minorities," states Arons (1986), "are among those who have most systematically been denied the educational liberty, which, it is argued here, is the birthright of all" (p. 214). The question of admissions criteria does not become any clearer, though, when religious beliefs are raised as justification for nonadmission of racial groups (black or white) or of single-sex schools or schools requiring that one be of a particular religious persuasion.

41. For some examples of what has already been done in some states, see Nevada. *Revised Statutes Annotated* Sec. 394.241 (1985); New Jersey. *Administrative*

Code Title 6, Sec. 34–1.5 (1980); Vermont. *Statutes Annotated* Title 16, Sec. 165a (Supp. 1985).

42. A logical extension of this point would be to require the same amount of information to be disclosed by public schools as well.

43. The Court appears to have defined "basic education" as comprising the basic literacy skills of reading, writing, and arithmetic in *Wisconsin v. Yoder,* 406 U.S. at 213, 225–226.

44. "Illiteracy is an enduring disability. The inability to read and write will handicap the individual deprived of a basic education each and every day of his life" and will cause an "inestimable toll [and] deprivation on the social, economic, intellectual, and psychological well-being of the individual, and . . . individual achievement" (*Plyler v. Doe,* 457 U.S. 202, 222 (1982)).

45. See Chapter 3, "Regulation and the Supreme Court" and Chapter 4, "Rights, Liberties and State Action."

46. Erickson (1986) reported that the fundamentalist Christian school in Peshkin's study was unduly harassed "by public authorities through capricious application of health and safety codes" (p. 92). Also see Furst (1985).

47. Admittedly the exact nature and boundaries of this intermediate standard and the other two are far from clear. Archibald Cox (1987) critically observes that "in the middle ground confusion reigns. The original doctrinal purity of the 'strict scrutiny–compelling public purpose' and 'minimum rationality' tests has yielded to three formulations. All three have surrendered even the pretense of precision. . . .

"The net effect in the middle ground has been ten or twelve years of highly particularistic decisions resulting from shifting alliances among the Justices" (p. 321).

48. The categories of "race, national origin, or alien status" are considered as suspect classifications and require the strict scrutiny test (Tribe, 1978, p. 1060).

49. "History teaches us that there have been but few infringements of personal liberty by the state which have not been justified, as they are here, in the name of righteousness and the public good, and few which have not been directed, as they are now, at politically helpless minorities" (*Minersville School District v. Gobitis,* 310 U.S. 586, 604 (1940), J. Stone, dissenting opinion).

50. "All assertions as to the specific nature of a general, collective, public or national interest are, unless they are merely vacuous, themselves likely to become matters of public controversy . . . [because] it inherently involves debatable philosophical assumptions, together with judgments of fact and value" (Dahl, 1986, p. 256).

51. Some even question the notion of the need for a common core of educational experience, at least in the sense of common values. David Nichols (1975) suggests that the "idea that a state can exist only when the people share a common set of values is mistaken. Even in a relatively homogeneous state like the United Kingdom, values differ quite radically from one section of the population to another." What a society needs is "a majority of the people . . . shar[ing] a belief in the importance of civil peace, combined with a willingness to allow their

fellow citizens to live life as they choose to live it. They must also recognize some machinery which is the normal channel for resolving disputes" (pp. 122–123).

52. For example, the school in *God's Choice* that Peshkin studied was located in a state with no regulations specifying curricular topics. Its curriculum offering was, therefore, voluntary and included such courses as English, science, band, math, religious education, physical education, geography, choir, U.S. history, world history, journalism, physical science, algebra, functional math, biology, speech, driver education, industrial arts, drafting, typing, health, drama, office practice, Spanish, physics, government, and economics (1986).

It should be noted, however, the this particular private religious school, in contrast to many other private schools, was financially well off and could afford to offer a substantial curriculum. This illustrates a dilemma facing many private schools that is beyond their control. State policy may require that a substantial curriculum be offered at a private school, but the financial resources to pay for such programs are limited by current public funding policies for education. The private school gets simultaneously pushed in one direction and pulled in another by the state.

53. It is interesting to note the different treatment accorded those in the public school sector. If a child fails in a public school, are the parents charged with neglect? If uncertified teachers teach in public schools, are these schools closed?

54. Donald Erickson (1973) states that the "best safeguard against harmful governmental interference in nonpublic school affairs is . . . not reliance on either substantive or procedural legal rights, but on a constructive and cooperative approach towards the settlement of differences" (p. 4/50).

55. Also see the Court's rejection of the state as a Platonic guardian of the child by removing the parents from any parental role. This would result in "doing violence to both the letter and spirit of the Constitution" (*Meyer v. Nebraska*, 262 U.S. at 402).

NOTE TO CHAPTER 6

1. This study suggests some interesting and profound implications for regulations governing public education. Is there a need for massive deregulation in the public sector? Are decentralization efforts such as site-based management an important move in improving public education in America or simply analogous to rearranging the deck chairs on the Titanic? Is the radical restructuring of public education as proposed by Chubb and Moe (1990) the ultimate logical conclusion of the issues raised in this study?

REFERENCES

Abramowitz, S., & Stackhouse, E. A. (1980). *The private high school today.* Washington, DC: U.S. Department of Education.

Alexander, K. L., & Pallas, A. M. (1985, April). School sector and cognitive performance: When is a little a little? *Sociology of Education, 58,* 115–128.

Anyon, J. (1977, August). Ideology and United States history textbooks. *Harvard Educational Review, 49,* 361–386.

Aristotle. (1958). *The politics of Aristotle* (E. Barker, Ed. & Trans.). New York: Oxford University Press.

Arons, S. (1976, February). The separation of school and state: *Pierce* reconsidered. *Harvard Educational Review, 46,* 76–104.

Arons, S. (1986). *Compelling belief—The culture of American schooling.* Amherst: University of Massachusetts Press.

Arons, S., & Lawrence, C., III. (1980, Fall). The manipulation of consciousness: A first amendment critique of schooling. *Harvard Civil Rights–Civil Liberties Law Review, 15,* 309–361.

Atkinson, C., & Maleska, E. T. (1965). *The Story of education* (2nd ed.). Philadelphia: Chilton.

Axtell, J. (1974). *The school upon a hill.* New Haven, CT: Yale University Press.

Bailyn, B. (1960). *Education in the forming of American society.* New York: W. W. Norton.

Bailyn, B. (1963). Education as a discipline. In J. Walton & J. L. Kuethe (Eds.), *The discipline of education* (pp. 125–139). Madison: University of Wisconsin Press.

Bainton, D. M. (1983). State regulation of private religious schools and the state's interest in education. *Arizona Law Review, 25,* 123–149.

Baker, M. D. (1978–1979). Comments–Regulation of fundamentalist Christian schools: Free exercise of religion v. the state's interest in quality education. *Kentucky Law Journal, 67,* 415–429.

Ball, W. B. (1969). A Roman Catholic viewpoint. In D. A. Erickson (Ed.), *Public controls for nonpublic schools* (pp. 187–197). Chicago: University of Chicago Press.

Baskin, D. (1971). *American pluralist democracy: A critique.* New York: Van Nostrand Reinhold.

Baskin, S. J. (1974, June). State intrusion into family affairs: Justifications and limitations. *Stanford Law Review, 26,* 1383–1409.

Beach, F. R., & Will, R. F. (1958). *The state and nonpublic schools with particular reference to responsibility of the State Department of Education.* Washington, DC: U.S. Department of Health, Education and Welfare.

Becker, C. L. (1953). *Freedom and responsibility in the American way of life.* New York: Alfred A. Knopf.

Bellah, R. N., & Hammond, P. E. (1980). *Varieties of civil religion.* San Francisco: Harper & Row.

Belleau, W. E. (1931, September 26). State regulation of private schools. *School and Society, 34,* 436–440.

Berger, P. L., & Neuhaus, R. J. (1977). *To empower people: The role of mediating structure in public policy.* Washington, DC: American Enterprise Institute.

Besag, F. P., & Nelson, J. L. (1984). *The foundations of education: Stasis and change.* New York: Random House.

Binder, T. J. (1982). *Douglas v. Faith Baptist Church* under constitutional scrutiny. *Nebraska Law Review, 61,* 74–97.

Bird, W. R. (1979, Summer). Freedom from establishment and unneutrality in public school instruction and religious school regulation. *Harvard Journal of Law and Public Policy, 2,* 125–205.

Black, H. C. (1979). *Black's law dictionary.* St. Paul, MN: West Publishing.

Blaunstein, P. L. (1986, January). Public and nonpublic schools: Finding ways to work together. *Phi Delta Kappan, 67,* 368–372.

Bristow, C. H. (1977). Notes—Private schools in Vermont: The 'equivalency exception' to compulsory school attendance. *Vermont Law Review, 2,* 205–216.

Brock, D. W. (1988, April). Paternalism and autonomy. *Ethics, 98,* 550–565.

Brown, B. F. (1970). The law of church and state in the area of education. In J. H. Hazard & W. J. Wagner (Eds.), *Legal thought in the United States of America under contemporary pressures* (pp. 551–562). Brussels, Belgium: Establissements Emilie Bruylant.

Brown, S. E., & Cannon, K. (1993). Educational Malpractice actions: A remedy for what ails our schools? *Education Law Reporter, 78,* 643–657.

Brown, S. W. (1912). *The secularization of American education.* New York: Teachers College, Columbia University.

Burgess, C. (1976, May). The goddess, the school book, and compulsion. *Harvard Educational Review, 46,* 199–216.

Butts, R. F., & Cremin, L. A. (1953). *A history of education in the American culture.* New York: Henry Holt.

Capps, K., & Esbeck, C. H. (1985, October). The use of government funding and taxing power to regulate religious schools. *Journal of Law and Education, 4,* 553–574.

Carey, E. B. (1949). *The state and non-public schools: A critical analysis of past and present trends in the relationship of New York State to its private and religious schools at the elementary and secondary level.* Unpublished doctoral dissertation, New York University, New York.

Carper, J. C. (1982). The Whisner decision: A case study in state regulation of Christian Day Schools. *Journal of Church and State, 24,* 281–302.

Carper, J. C., & Devins, N. E. (1985, Winter). Rendering unto Caesar: State regulation of Christian Day Schools. *Journal of Thought, 20,* 99–113.

Carper, J. C., & Hunt, T. C. (Eds.). (1984). *Religious schooling in America.* Birmingham, AL: Religious Education Press.

Century Digest (Vol. 43). (1903). In *American digest system*. St. Paul, MN: West Publishing.

Chapman, J. W. (1969). Voluntary association and the political theory of pluralism. In J. R. Pennock & J. W. Chapman (Eds.), *Voluntary associations* (pp. 87–118). New York: Atherton Press.

Chase, A. (1985, August). Is intelligence evil? *BYU Today*, pp. 29–41.

Chicago schools called worst. (1987, November 7). *Ithaca Journal*, p. 6A.

Chubb, J. E. (1988, Winter). Why the current wave of school reform will fail. *The Public Interest, 90*, 28–49.

Chubb, J. E., & Moe, T. M. (1985, August 28–September 1). *Politics, markets and the organization of schools*. New Orleans, LA: American Political Science Association. (ERIC Document Reproduction Service No. ED 263 674)

Chubb, J. E., & Moe, T. M. (1990). *Politics, markets, and America's schools*. Washington, DC: The Brookings Institution.

Cibulka, J. G., O'Brien, T. J., & Zewe, S. J. (1982). *Inner-city private elementary schools: A study*. Milwaukee, WI: Marquette University Press.

Cohen, D. R. (1985). *Public funding of nonpublic schools and the constitution: Moral imperatives and legal strategies*. Unpublished doctoral dissertation, Cornell University, Ithaca, NY.

Cohen, S. S. (1974). *A history of colonial education, 1607–1776*. New York: Wiley.

Cohen, S. (1974). *Education of the United States: A documentary history* (Vol. 1). New York: Random House.

Coleman, J. S. (1982, Winter). Summer learning and school achievement. *The Public Interest, 66*, 140–144.

Coleman, J. S., Campbell, E. Q., Hobson, C. J., McPartland, J., Mood, A. M., Weinfeld, F. D., and York, R. L. (1966). *Equality of Educational opportunity*. Washington, DC: National Center for Educational Statistics, U.S. Government Printing Office.

Coleman, J. S., & Hoffer, T. (1987). *Public and private high schools: The impact of community*. New York: Basic Books.

Coleman, J. S., Hoffer, T., & Kilgore, S. (1982). *High school achievement—Public, Catholic, and private schools compared*. New York: Basic Books.

Collins, R. (1976, May). Review of *Schooling in capitalist America: Educational reform and the contradictions of economic life* by Samuel Bowles & Herbert Gintis. *Harvard Educational Review, 46*, 247–251.

Cookson, P. W., Jr., & Persell, C. H. (1985). *Preparing for power—America's elite boarding schools*. New York: Basic Books.

Coons, J. E. (1984, Spring). The voucher alternative. *Journal of Social, Political and Economic Studies, 9*, 94–107.

Coons, J. E., & Sugarman, S. D. (1972). *Education by choice*. Berkeley: University of California Press.

Cox, A. (1987). *The court and the constitution*. Boston: Houghton Mifflin.

Cremin, L. (1951). *The American common school*. New York: Teachers College, Columbia University.

Cremin, L. (1964). *The transformation of the school*. New York: Random House.

Cremin, L. (1970). *American education: The colonial experience 1607–1783.* New York: Harper & Row.

Cremin, L. (1980). *American education: The national experience.* New York: Harper & Row.

Cubberley, E. (1919). *Public education in the United States: A study and interpretation of American educational history.* Boston: Houghton Mifflin.

Cubberley, E. (1934). *Public education in the United States: A study and interpretation of American educational history.* Boston: Houghton Mifflin.

Curti, M. (1974). *The social ideas of American educators.* Totowa, NJ: Littlefield & Adams.

Dahl, R. A. (1982). *Dilemmas of pluralist democracy.* New Haven, CT: Yale University Press.

Dahl, R. A. (1986). *Democracy, liberty and equality.* Vojens, Denmark: Norwegian University Press.

Damsen, P. (1986, February). How not to fix the schools. *Harpers,* pp. 39–51.

Davidson, T. (1900). *A history of education.* New York: Charles Scribner's Sons.

Decennial education (1906) (Vol. 17). (1910). In *American digest system.* St. Paul, MN: West Publishing.

Denver, D. J. (1953). *The legal status of Catholic schools under the constitutional and statutory law of Hawaii.* Unpublished master's thesis, Catholic University of America, Washington, DC.

Devins, N. (1983, Summer). State regulation of Christian schools. *Journal of Legislation, 10,* 351–381.

Diehl, B. (1983, Winter). The right to regulate nonpublic education. *Urban Lawyer, 15,* 97–111.

Dixon, J. L. (1944). *The courts and the private schools in the middle atlantic states.* Unpublished doctoral dissertation, Rutgers University, New Brunswick, NJ.

Doyle, D. P., & Hartle, T. W. (1985). *Excellence in education: The states take charge.* Washington, DC: American Enterprise Institute for Public Policy Research.

Drake, J. A. (1980, October). Attempted state control of the religious school: The free exercise of religion? *Ohio Northern Law Review, 7,* 954–974.

Dubay, T. (1959). *Philosophy of the state as educator.* Milwaukee: Bruce Publishing.

Dworkin, R. (1979). Taking rights seriously. In D. Lyons (Ed.), *Rights* (pp. 92–110). Belmont, CA: Wadsworth Publishing.

Dye, D. D. (1987–1988). Educational malpractice: A cause of action that failed to pass the test. *West Virginia Law Review, 90,* 499–512.

Ehrlich, S. (1982). *Pluralism on and off course.* Elmsford, NY: Pergamon Press.

Eighth decennial digest (Vol. 36). (1978). In *American digest system.* St. Paul, MN: West Publishing.

Elson, J. (1969). State regulation of nonpublic schools: The legal framework. In D. A. Erickson (Ed.), *Public controls for nonpublic schools* (pp. 103–134). Chicago: University of Chicago Press.

Elson, J. (1973). *Legal dimensions of the state regulation of nonpublic schools.* In D. A. Erickson (Ed.), *Super-parent: An analysis of state educational controls* (pp. 4/1–4/68). Chicago: Illinois Advisory Committee on Nonpublic Schools. (ERIC Document Reproduction Service No. ED 096 770)

Elson, R. M. (1964). *Guardians of tradition: American schoolbooks of the nineteenth century.* Lincoln: University of Nebraska Press.

Ely, J. H. (1980). *Democracy and distrust.* Cambridge, MA: Harvard University Press.

Emerson, T. (1966). *Toward a general theory of the first amendment.* New York: Random House.

Encarnation, D. J. (1983). Public finance and regulation of nonpublic education: Retrospect and prospect. In T. James & H. M. Levin (Eds.), *Public dollars for private schools* (pp. 175–193). Philadelphia: Temple University Press.

Ensign, F. C. (1921). *Compulsory school attendance and child labor.* Iowa City, IA: Athens Press.

Erickson, D. A. (1969a). Introduction: Beech Grove isn't far from Andover. In D. A. Erickson (Ed.), *Public controls for nonpublic schools* (pp. 1–6). Chicago: University of Chicago Press.

Erickson, D. A. (1969b). Showdown at an Amish schoolhouse: A description and analysis of the Iowa controversy. In D. A. Erickson (Ed.), *Public controls for nonpublic schools* (pp. 15–59). Chicago: University of Chicago Press.

Erickson, D. A. (1973). *Super-parent: An analysis of state educational controls.* Chicago: Illinois Advisory Committee on Nonpublic Schools. (ERIC Document Reproduction Service No. ED 096 770)

Erickson, D. A. (1982). Disturbing evidence about the 'one best system.' In R. B. Everhart (Ed.), *The public school monopoly: A critical analysis of education and the state in American society* (pp. 393–422). Cambridge, MA: Ballinger Publishing.

Erickson, D. A. (1984). Bad fences make bad neighbors: A look at state regulation of private schools. In J. C. Carper & T. C. Hunt (Eds.), *Religious schooling in America* (pp. 227–244). Birmingham, AL: Religious Education Press.

Erickson, D. A. (1986). Choice and private schools: Dynamics of supply and demand. In D. C. Levy (Ed.), *Private education—Studies in choice and public policy* (pp. 82–109). New York: Oxford University Press.

Evenson, J. E., II. (1980, June). Comments—State regulation of private religious schools in North Carolina—A model approach. *Wake Forest Law Review, 16,* 405–437.

Fantini, M. D. (1973). *Public schools of choice.* New York: Simon & Schuster.

Fech, E. B. (1985, March 31–April 4). *Belief patterns of Catholic elementary school principals and teachers.* Chicago, IL: American Educational Research Association. (ERIC Document Reproduction Service No. ED 262 481)

Fifth decennial digest (Vol. 39). (1949). In *American digest system.* St. Paul, MN: West Publishing.

Finn, C. E., Jr. (1982, May). Public support for private education, part 1. *American Education, 18*(4), 4–9.

Fletcher, C. L., Jr. (1979, Fall). Secular control of nonpublic schools. *West Virginia Law Review, 82,* 111–127.

Fourth decennial digest (Vol. 28). (1938). In *American digest system.* St. Paul, MN: West Publishing.

Fowerbaugh, R. (1955). *Requirements and aids of the forty-eight states relative to nonpublic elementary schools.* Unpublished master's thesis, Catholic University of America, Washington, DC.

Friedman, L. M. (1985). On regulation and legal process. In R. D. Noll (Ed.), *Regulatory policy and the social sciences* (pp. 111–135). Berkeley: University of California Press.

Fry, B. (1993). Breeding constitutional doctrine: The provenance and progency of the "hybrid situation" in current free exercise of jurisprudence. *Texas Law Review, 71,* 833–863.

Frymier, J. (1986, May). Legislating centralization. *Phi Delta Kappan, 67,* 646–648.

Furst, L. G. (1985, March 31–April 4). *Indirect government control of non-public schools: A review of court decisions.* Chicago, IL: American Educational Research Association. (ERIC Document Reproduction Service No. ED 262 482)

Furtwengler, W. J. (1985, December). Implementing strategies for a school effectiveness program. *Phi Delta Kappan, 67,* 262–265.

Gardner, H. (1954). *Catholic elementary and secondary education under Kansas state law.* Unpublished master's thesis, Catholic University of America, Washington, DC.

Gaustad, E. S. (1984). Church, state, and education in historical perspective. In J. E. Wood, Jr. (Ed.), *Religion, the state and education* (pp. 11–23). Waco, TX: Baylor University Press.

Glazer, N. (1975, Fall). Toward an imperial judiciary? *The Public Interest, 41,* 104–123.

Goldberger, A. S., & Cain, G. G. (1982, April). The causal analysis of cognitive outcomes in the Coleman, Hoffer and Kilgore report. *Sociology of Education, 55,* 103–122.

Goodlad, J. I. (1985, December). The great American schooling experiment. *Phi Delta Kappan, 67,* 266–271.

Gordon, R. M. (1984, October). Freedom of expression and values inculcation in the public school curriculum. *Journal of Law and Education, 13,* 523–579.

Grant, G. (1982, January/February). The character of education and the education of character. *American Education, 18,* 37–46.

Gross, J. A. (1988). *Teachers on trial: Values, standards and equity in judging conduct and competence.* Ithaca, NY: ILR Press, Cornell University.

Gunther, G. (1980). *Cases and materials on constitutional law.* Mineola, NY: Foundation Press.

Gutman, A. (1987). *Democratic education.* Princeton, NJ: Princeton University Press.

Hafen, B. C. (1976). Children's liberation and the new egalitarianism: Some reservations about abandoning youth to their rights. *Brigham Young University Law Review, 3,* 605–658.

Hafen, B. C. (1984, Spring). The family, private education, and the public schools. *Journal of Social, Political and Economic Studies, 9*(1), 17–37.

Haggard, T. (1983). Government regulation of the employment relationship. In T. R. Machan & M. B. Johnson (Eds.), *Rights and regulation: Ethical, political and economic issues* (pp. 13–41). Cambridge, MA: Ballinger Publishing.

Haley, K. H. D. (1972). *The Dutch in the seventeenth century.* London: Thames & Hudson.

Hanushek, E. A. (1981). Throwing money at schools. *Journal of Policy Analysis and Management, 1,* 19–41.

Hanushek, E. A. (1986, September). The economics of schooling: Production and efficiency in public schools. *Journal of Economic Literature, 24,* 1141–1177.

Harnischfeger, A., & Wily, D. E. (1976). Achievement test score decline: Do we need to worry? St. Louis: CREMEL.

Hart, H. L. A. (1979). Are there any natural rights? In D. Lyons (Ed.), *Rights* (pp. 14–25). Belmont, CA: Wadsworth Publishing.

Herbert, A. (1978). *The right and wrong of compulsion by the state and other essays* (E. Mack, Ed.). Indianapolis, IN: Liberty Fund.

Herman, H. Y. (1980). Comments—The history and utility of the Supreme Court's present definition of religion. *Loyola Law Review, 26,* 87–113.

Herrick, D. J. (1972). Comments—Religious freedom and compulsory education: The plight of the Amish. *South Dakota Law Review, 17,* 251–263.

Heyns, B. (1978). *Summer learning and the effects of schooling.* New York: Academic Press.

Higgins, M. J. (1981–1982). State v. Faith Baptist Church: State regulation of religious education. *Creighton Law Review, 15,* 183–195.

Higham, J. (1974, June). Hanging together: Divergent unities in American history. *The Journal of American History, 61,* 5–28.

Hiner, N. R. (1973, Spring). The cry of Sodom enquired into: Educational analysis in seventeenth-century New England. *History of Education Quarterly, 13,* 3–22.

Hirsch, E. D., Jr., Kett, J. F., & Trefil, J. (1988). *The dictionary of cultural literacy.* Boston: Houghton Mifflin.

Hirsch, H. N. (1992). *A theory of liberty—the constitution and minorities.* New York: Routledge.

Hirschman, A. O. (1970). *Exit, voice and loyalty: Responses to decline in firms, organizations and states.* Cambridge, MA: Harvard University Press.

Hirschoff, M. U. (1977, July). Parents and the public school curriculum: Is there a right to have one's child excused from objectionable instruction? *Southern California Law Review, 50,* 871–959.

Hirschoff, M. U. (1986). Public policy towards private schools: A focus on parental choice. In D. C. Levy (Ed.), *Private education. Studies in choice and public policy* (pp. 33–56). New York: Oxford University Press.

Hurst, J. W. (1956). *Law and the conditions of freedom in the nineteenth-century United States.* Madison: University of Wisconsin Press.

Iowa parents symbols of defiance on schools. (1987, March 25). *New York Times, 136,* p. A10.

Jackson, R. (1977). *Plural societies and new states.* Berkeley: Institute of International Studies, University of California.

James, T., & Levin, H. (Eds.). (1983). *Public dollars for private schools.* Philadelphia: Temple University Press.

Jamieson, L. S. (1991, July). Educational malpractice: A lesson in professional accountability. *Boston College Law Review, 32*(4), 899–965.

Jellison, H. M. (1975). *State and federal laws relating to nonpublic schools.* Silver Springs, MD & Washington, DC: Office of Education, Department of Health, Education and Welfare.

Jernegan, M. W. (1915, May). The beginning of public education in New England. *The School Review, 23,* 319–330.

Jernegan, M. W. (1919a, January). Compulsory education in the American colonies, part II. *The School Review, 27,* 24–43.

Jernegan, M. W. (1919b, May). The educational development of the southern colonies. *The School Review, 27,* 360–376.

Johnson, D. (1987). *Private schools and state schools: Two systems or one?* Philadelphia: Open University Press.

Johnson, G. R. (1986). *Fundamentalist Christians v. Nebraska: The conflict over regulation of private schools.* Unpublished doctoral dissertation, University of Kansas, Lawrence.

Jones, T. A. (1983). *Private schools and national policy: A comparative study of Australia and the U.S.A.* Hamilton, New Zealand: Australian Comparative and International Education Society. (ERIC Document Reproduction Service No. ED 265 266)

Jorgenson, L. P. (1968). The birth of a tradition. In R. Foy (Ed.), *The world of education—Selected readings* (pp. 261–275). New York: Macmillan.

Jorgenson, L. P. (1987). *The state and the non-public school, 1825–1925.* Columbia: University of Missouri Press.

Kaestle, C. F. (1972, Winter). Common schools before the 'common school revival': New York schooling in the 1790's. *History of Education Quarterly, 12,* 465–500.

Kaestle, C. F. (1983). *Pillars of the republic: Common schools and American society, 1780–1860.* New York: Hill & Wang.

Karier, C. (1986). *The individual, society and education* (2nd ed.). Urbana & Chicago: University of Illinois Press.

Karlin, N. (1983). Substantive due process: A doctrine for regulatory control. In T. R. Machan & M. B. Johnson (Eds.), *Rights and regulation: Ethical, political and economic issues* (pp. 43–70). Cambridge: MA: Ballinger Publishing.

Katz, M. B. (1968). *The irony of early school reform.* Cambridge, MA: Harvard University Press.

Katz, M. B. (1975). *Class, bureaucracy, and schools.* New York: Praeger.

Katz, M. S. (1974). *The concepts of compulsory education and compulsory schooling: A philosophical inquiry.* Unpublished doctoral dissertation, Stanford University, Palo Alto, CA.

Keane, J. (n.d.). Response to Mr. Mead. *Denominational Schools—A Discussion at the National Educational Association Meeting in Nashville, Tenn. July 1889* (pp. 39–44). Topeka, Kansas: Kansas Publishing House.

Kelso, W. A. (1978). *American democratic theory: Pluralism and its critics.* Westport, CT: Greenwood Press.

Kelly, K. D. (1991, Summer). Abandoning the compelling interest test in free exercise cases: Employment Division, Department of Human Resources v. Smith. *Catholic University Law Review, 40*(4), 929–965.

Kephart, C. I. (1933). *State control and regulation of private and parochial schools of primary and secondary grades.* Unpublished doctoral dissertation, The American University, Washington, DC.

Kilpatrick, J. J. (1979, November 18). Kentucky court decision hailed. *The Farmington Daily Times,* p. 4a.

Kinder, P. A. (1982). *The regulation and accreditation of non-public schools in the United*

States. Unpublished doctoral dissertation, University of Missouri–Columbia, Columbia.

King, P. (1974). *The ideology of order: A comparative analysis of Jean Bodin and Thomas Hobbes.* New York: Harper & Row.

Kirst, M. W. (1978). State role in regulating local schools. *Proceedings of the Academy of Political Science, 33,* 45–56.

Koos, L. V. (1931). *Private and public secondary education—A comparative study.* Chicago: University of Chicago Press.

Kotin, L. A., & Aikman, W. F. (1980). *Legal foundations of compulsory school attendance.* Port Washington, NY: Kennikat Press.

Kraushaar, O. F. (1972). *American nonpublic schools—Patterns of diversity.* Baltimore: John Hopkins University Press.

Krouse, R. (1983, Fall). Some (further) dilemmas of pluralist democracy. *Yale Law and Policy Review, 2,* 167–178.

Kurland, P. B. (1973). The Supreme Court, compulsory education and the first amendment religion clauses. *West Virginia Law Review, 75,* 213–245.

Kurland, P. B. (1978). The irrelevance of the Constitution: The religion clauses of the first amendment and the Supreme Court. *Villanova Law Review, 24,* 3–27.

Landes, W. M., & Solomon, L. C. (1972, March). Compulsory schooling legislation: An economic analysis of law and social change in the nineteenth century. *The Journal of Economic History, 32,* 54–91.

Leahy, J. E. (1991). *The first amendment 1791–1991.* Jefferson, NC: McFarland.

Lerner, B. (1982, Fall). American education: How are we doing? *The Public Interest, 69,* 59–82.

Levin, H. M. (1983). Educational choice and the pains of democracy. In T. James & H. Levin (Eds.), *Public dollars for private schools* (pp. 17–38). Philadelphia: Temple University Press.

Levin, H. M. (1987). Education as a public and private good. *Journal of Policy Analysis and Management, 6,* 628–641.

Levine, E. M. (1983, Winter). Why middle class students aren't learning. *The Journal of Social, Political and Economic Studies, 8,* 411–425.

Levy, D. C. (Ed.). (1986). *Private education—Studies in choice and public policy.* New York: Oxford University Press.

Link, A. S., Link, W. A., & Catton, W. B. (1986). *American epoch—A history of the United States since 1900* (Vol. 2). In *An era of economic and social change, reform, and world wars 1900–1945.* New York: Alfred A. Knopf.

Lischka, C. N. (1924, October). *Private schools and state laws* (Education Bulletin, no. 4). Washington, DC: National Catholic Welfare Conference, Bureau of Education.

Locke, J. (1979). *Second treatise of government and letter concerning toleration* (C. L. Sherman, Ed.). New York: Irvington Publishers.

Loscalzo, T. E. (1985, October). Liability for malpractice in education. *Journal of Law and Education, 14,* 595–607.

Lyons, D. (Ed.). (1979). *Rights.* Belmont, CA: Wadsworth Publishing.

Lyons, R. O. (1983). *Compulsory school attendance laws and their application to students in Christian schools.* Unpublished doctoral dissertation, Northern Arizona University, Flagstaff.

Machan, T. R. (1983). The petty tyranny of government regulations. In T. R. Machan & M. B. Johnson (Eds.), *Rights and regulation: Ethical, political and economic issues* (pp. 259–288). Cambridge, MA: Ballinger Publishing.

Macpherson, C. B. (1973). Liberal democracy as a double system of power. In D. Baskin (Ed.), *Pluralism and protest: Notes and readings on the theory and practice of American politics* (pp. 68–84). Cupertino, CA: James E. Freel & Associates.

Magers, T. A. (1983). *Problems associated with unaccredited private schools and home instruction programs and solutions to the problems as perceived by state education officials.* Unpublished doctoral dissertation, Ball State University, Muncie, IN.

Mapel, J. J. (1891). The repeal of the compulsory education laws in Wisconsin and Illinois. *Educational Review, 1,* 52–57.

McCarthy, M. M., & Deignan, P. T. (1982). *What legally constitutes an adequate public education.* Bloomington, IN: Phi Delta Kappa Educational Foundation.

McCarthy, R. M., Skillen, J. W., & Harper, W. A. (1982). *Disestablishment a second time—Genuine pluralism for American schools.* Grand Rapids, MI: Christian University Press.

McConnell, G. (1969). The public values of the private association. In J. R. Pennock & J. W. Chapman (Eds.), *Voluntary associations* (pp. 147–160). New York: Atherton Press.

McConnell, G. (1970). *Private power and American democracy.* New York: Random House.

McConnell, M. W. (1990). Free exercise revisionism and the Smith decision. *University of Chicago Review, 57,* 1109.

McCoy, D. S. (1983). Note—State regulation of private church schools: An examination of Vermont's Act 151. *Vermont Law Review, 8,* 75–118.

McGrew, E. B., Jr. (1971). *The private school: A study of an American phenomenon.* Unpublished doctoral dissertation, University of Minnesota, Minneapolis.

McLaughlin, R. (1946). *A history of state legislation affecting private elementary and secondary schools in the United States, 1870–1945.* Washington, DC: The Catholic University of America Press.

McMillan, R. C. (1984). *Religion in the public schools.* Macon, GA: Mercer University Press.

Mehl, B. (1963). Education in American history. In G. Kneller (Ed.), *Foundations of education* (pp. 1–44). New York: Wiley.

Meiklejohn, A. (1961). The first amendment is an absolute. *Supreme Court Review* (pp. 245–266).

Meyer, A. E. (1957). *An educational history of the American people.* New York: McGraw-Hill.

Meyer, D. (1976). *The democratic enlightenment.* New York: G. P. Putnam's Sons.

Middlekauff, R. (1963). *Ancients and axioms: Secondary education in eighteenth-century New England.* New Haven, CT: Yale University Press.

Mill, J. S. (1980). *On liberty* (C. V. Shields, Ed.). Indianapolis: Bobbs-Merrill Educational Publishing.

Miller, G. F. (1969). *The academy system of the state of New York.* New York: Arno Press & The New York Times.

Monroe, P. (1905). *Textbook on educational history.* New York: Macmillan.

Moore, R. L. (1986). *Religious outsiders and the making of Americans.* New York: Oxford University Press.

Moskowitz, J. S. (1978). The making of the moral child: Legal implications of values education. *Pepperdine Law Review, 6,* 105–137.

Murnane, R. (1981). Interpreting the evidence on school effectiveness. *Teachers College Record, 83*(11), 19–35.

Murnane, R. (1983). The uncertain consequences of tuition tax credits: An analysis of student achievement and economic incentives. In T. James & H. Levin (Eds.), *Public dollars for private schools* (pp. 210–222). Philadelphia: Temple University Press.

Murnane, R. (1986a). Comparisons of private and public schools: The critical role of regulations. In D. C. Levy (Ed.), *Private education—Studies in choice and public policy* (pp. 138–152). New York: Oxford University Press.

Murnane, R. (1986b). Comparisons of private and public schools: What can we learn? In D. C. Levy (Ed.), *Private education—Studies in choice and public policy* (pp. 153–169). New York: Oxford University Press.

Nader, L., & Nader, C. (1985). A wide angle on regulation: An anthropological perspective. In R. G. Noll (Ed.), *Regulatory policy and the social sciences* (pp. 141–160). Berkeley: University of California Press.

Nasaw, D. (1979). *Schooled to order—A social history of public schooling in the United States.* New York: Oxford University Press.

National Center for Educational Statistics. (1991). *Private schools in the United States: A statistical profile, with comparisons to public schools.* Washington, DC: U.S. Government Printing Office.

National Commission on Excellence in Education. (1983). *A nation at risk.* Washington, DC: U.S. Department of Education.

Neely, R. (1981). *How courts govern America.* New Haven, CT: Yale University Press.

New York State. (1984). *Annual educational summary, 1983–84.* Albany: New York State Education Department.

Nichols, D. (1974). *Three varieties of pluralism.* London: Macmillan Press.

Nichols, D. (1975). *The pluralist state.* London: Macmillan Press.

Ninth decennial digest, part 1 (Vol. 28). (1983). In *American digest system.* St. Paul, MN: West Publishing.

Ninth decennial digest, part 2 (Vol. 35). (1988). In *American digest system.* St. Paul, MN: West Publishing.

Olson, M. (1971). *The logic of collective action.* Cambridge, MA: Harvard University Press.

Oregon School Cases. (1925). Baltimore, MD: Belvedere Press.

Parrish, J. B. (1981, Fall). Unionization and education: Lessons from the Illinois schoolroom. *The Journal of Social, Political and Economic Studies, 6,* 236–237.

Peirce, N. (1985, May 1). Shakeups & shapeups for teachers. *Ithaca Journal,* p. 8.

Pelletier, R. J. (1950). *Educational legislation affecting elementary and secondary schools in the state of Michigan.* Unpublished master's thesis, Catholic University of America, Washington, DC.

Personal-liberty—May the state control private schools? (1890). Toledo, OH: no publisher.

Peshkin, A. (1986). *God's choice—The total world of a fundamentalist Christian school.* Chicago: University of Chicago Press.

Pickard, M. G. (1955). *The history and present status of legal relationships between the state of Mississippi and private elementary and secondary schools.* Unpublished master's thesis, Catholic University of America, Washington DC.

Pierce, D. R. (1982, Summer). Comment—Satisfying the state interest in education with private schools. *Tennessee Law Review, 49,* 955–978.

Powers, R. H. (1984). *The dilemma of education in a democracy.* Chicago: Regnery Gateway.

Randall, E. V. (1989). *Pluralism and Public Policy: State Regulation of Private Schools.* Unpublished doctoral dissertation, Cornell University, Ithaca, NY.

Raspberry, W. (1986, March 13). The school's purpose: Still a puzzle. *Ithaca Journal,* p. 10.

Ravitch, D. (1974). *The great school wars.* New York: Basic Books.

Ravitch, D. (1985). *The schools we deserve.* New York: Basic Books.

Rawls, J. (1979). Constitutional liberty and the concept of justice. In D. Lyons (Ed.), *Rights* (pp. 26–45). Belmont, CA: Wadsworth Publishing.

Rebell, M. A., & Block, A. R. (1982). *Educational policy making and the courts.* Chicago: University of Chicago Press.

Rebescher, K. M. (1991, June). The illusory enforcement of first amendment freedom: *Employment Division, Department of Human Resources v. Smith* and the abandonment of the compelling government interest test. *North Carolina Law Review, 69*(5), 1332–1356.

Reeder, W. G. (1923). State control of private and parochial schools. *School and Society, 17,* 426–429.

Rice, C. E. (1978). Conscientious objection to public education: The grievance and the remedies. *Brigham Young University Law Review, 4,* 847–888.

Romans, C. S. (1981). *State regulation of private religious schools: 'Compelling state interest' and the first amendment.* Unpublished doctoral dissertation, Kent State University, Kent, OH.

Rose, S. D. (1985). *Christian schools in secular society.* Unpublished doctoral dissertation, Cornell University, Ithaca, NY.

Rosen, A. (1978, June). Sectarian school asserts its religious beliefs: Have the courts narrowed the constitutional right to free exercise of religion? *University of Miami Law Review, 32,* 709–720.

Roth, R. A. (1986, June). Emergency certificates, miasassignments of teachers, and other 'dirty little secrets.' *Phi Delta Kappan, 67,* 725–726.

Rushdoony, R. J. (1978). The state as an establishment of religion. In D. P. Kommers & M. J. Wahoske (Eds.), *Freedom and education: Pierce v. Society of Sisters reconsidered* (pp. 37–46). South Bend, IN: Center for Civil Rights, University of Notre Dame Law School.

Rutter, M., Maughan, B., Mortimore, P., Ouston, J. and Smith, A. (1979). *Fifteen thousand hours: Secondary schools and their effects on children.* Cambridge, MA: Harvard University Press.

Saltsman, R. (1977). *State v. Whisner:* State minimum educational standards and non-public religious schools. *Ohio Northern University Law Review, 4,* 710–719.

Sanders, W. J. (1969). Regulation of nonpublic schools as seen by a state commissioner. In D. A. Erickson (Ed.), *Public controls for nonpublic schools* (pp. 177–186). Chicago: University of Chicago Press.

Scanlan, J. W. (1940). *The state and the nonstate school including consideration of the support of the nonstate school.* Unpublished doctoral dissertation, Northwestern University, Evanston, IL.

Schaller, L. E. (1979, November 7). Public versus private schools: A divisive issue for the 1980's. *The Christian Century, XCVI,* 1086–1090.

Schultz, S. K. (1973). *The culture factory—Boston public schools, 1789–1860.* New York: Oxford University Press.

Schwartz, B. H. (1979, Winter). Parental rights: Educational alternatives and curriculum control. *Washington and Lee Law Review, 36,* 277–297.

Second decennial edition (Vol. 20). (1922). In *American digest system (1916).* St. Paul, MN: West Publishing.

Seeley, D. S. (1985). *Education through partnership.* Washington, DC: American Enterprise Institute for Public Policy Research.

Seventh decennial digest (Vol. 27). (1968). In *American digest system.* St. Paul, MN: West Publishing.

Seybolt, R. F. (1935). *The private school of colonial Boston.* Cambridge, MA: Harvard University Press.

Shanker, A. (1987). Comment. *Journal of Policy Analysis and Management, 6,* 644.

Shea, J. P. (1948). *The extent of state control over Catholic elementary and secondary education in Pennsylvania.* Unpublished master's thesis, Catholic University of America, Washington, DC.

Sixth decennial digest (Vol. 26). (1958). In *American digest system.* St. Paul, MN: West Publishing.

Smith, C. B. (1984, August). Compulsory education: Weak justifications in the aftermath of *Wisconsin v. Yoder. North Carolina Law Review, 62,* 1167–1172.

Smith, T. L. (1966–1967). Protestant schooling and American nationality, 1800–1850. *The Journal of American History, 53,* 679–795.

Smith, W. (1753). *A general idea of the College of Mirania.* New York: J. Parker and W. Weyman.

Smolin, D. M. (1986). Comment—State regulation of private education: Ohio law in the shadow of the United States Supreme Court decisions. *University of Cincinnati Law Review, 54,* 1003–1033.

Snyder, H. B. (1948). *The development and status of the public controls of private elementary and secondary schools of California.* Unpublished doctoral dissertation, University of Southern California, Los Angeles.

Spring, J. (1986). *The American schools 1642–1985.* New York: Longman.

Spring, J. (1990). *The American schools 1642–1990* (2nd ed.). New York: Longman.

Stolee, M. J. (1963). *Legal control by the states over the areas of instruction in private elementary and secondary schools.* Unpublished doctoral dissertation, University of Minnesota, Minneapolis.

Stone, A. (1982). *Regulation and its alternatives.* Washington, DC: Congressional Quarterly Press.

Strike, K. A. (1982a). *Educational policy and the just society.* Urbana: University of Illinois Press.

Strike, K. A. (1982b). *Liberty and learning.* New York: St. Martin's Press.

Strike, K. A., & Soltis, J. F. (1985). *The ethics of teaching.* New York: Teachers College Press.

Swiger, E. P. (1983). Recent developments in school law. *The Urban Lawyer, 15,* 909–917.

Syle, T. L. (1983, Summer). Rendering unto Caesar: Defining 'religion' for purposes of administering religion-based tax exemptions. *Harvard Journal of Law and Public Policy, 6,* 219–294.

Tavel, D. (Ed.). (1984). *Modern educational controversies.* Lanham, MD: University Press of America.

Third decennial edition (Vol. 24). (1926). In *American digest system.* St. Paul, MN: West Publishing.

Thomas, M. P., Jr. (1972). Child abuse and neglect part I: Historical overview, legal matrix, and social perspective. *North Carolina Law Review, 50,* 293–349.

Toner, J. F. (1984–1985). Rendering unto Caesar 'til it hurts: How far may the states constitutionally regulate private schools? *Journal of Christian Jurisprudence, 5,* 55–85.

Tribe, L. H. (1978). *American constitutional law.* Mineola, NY: Foundation Press.

Tribe, L. H. (1988). *American constitutional law.* Mineola, NY: Foundation Press.

Triesch, N. (1954). *Catholic elementary and secondary schools under Washington state law.* Unpublished master's thesis, Catholic University of America, Washington, DC.

Tyack, D. B. (1966a). Forming the national character. *Harvard Educational Review, 36,* 29–41.

Tyack, D. B. (1966b, Fall). The kingdom of God and the common school: Protestant ministers and the educational awakening in the west. *Harvard Educational Review, 36,* 447–467.

Tyack, D. B. (1967). *Turning points in American educational history.* New York: Wiley.

Tyack, D. B. (1974). *The one best system—A history of American urban education.* Cambridge: MA: Harvard University Press.

Tyack, D. B. (1976, August). Ways of seeing: An essay on the history of compulsory schooling. *Harvard Educational Review, 46,* 355–389.

Tyack, D. B. (1986). Toward a social history of law and public education. In D. L. Kirp (Ed.), *School days, rule days* (pp. 212–237). Philadelphia: Falmer Press.

Tyack, D., & Hansot, E. (1982). *Managers of virtue—Public school leadership in America, 1820–1920.* New York: Basic Books.

Tyack, D., & James, T. (1986, Spring). State government and American public education: Exploring the 'primeval forest.' *History of Education Quarterly, 26,* 39–69.

Tyack, D., James, T., & Benavot, A. (1987). *Law and the shaping of public education, 1785–1954.* Madison: University of Wisconsin Press.

U.S. Congress. (1984). *Quality of education, 1983—part 2.* Washington, DC: Senate, Committee on Labor and Human Resources, U.S. Government Printing Office.

U.S. Bureau of the Census. (1987). *Statistical abstract of the United States: 1988* (108th ed.). Washington, DC: U.S. Government Printing Office.

U.S. Congress. (1985). *Issues in religious liberty.* Washington, DC: Senate, Committee on the Judiciary, U.S. Government Printing Office.

Updegraff, H. (1907). *The origin of the moving school in Massachusetts.* Albany, NY: Brandow Printing.

van Geel, T. (1976). *Authority to control the school program.* Lexington, MA: D. C. Heath.

van Geel, T. (1987). *The courts and American education law.* Buffalo, NY: Prometheus Books.

Vitullo-Martin, T. W. (1978). Federal policies and private schools. *Proceedings of the Academy of Political Science, Government in the classroom: Dollars and power in education, 33*(2), 124–135.

Vitullo-Martin, T. W. (1982). The impact of taxation policy on public and private schools. In R. B. Everhart (Ed.), *The public school monopoly: A critical analysis of education and the state in American society* (pp. 423–469). Cambridge, MA: Ballinger Publishing.

Wald, M. (1975, April). State intervention on behalf of 'neglected' children: A search for realistic standards. *Stanford Law Review, 27,* 985–1040.

Walther, J. F. (1982). *State regulation of nonpublic schools.* Unpublished doctoral dissertation, University of Illinois at Urbana Champaign, Champaign.

Walzer, M. (1983). *Spheres of justice: A defense of pluralism and equality.* New York: Basic Books.

Wasserstrom, R. (1979). Rights, human rights and racial discrimination. In D. Lyons (Ed.), *Rights* (pp. 46–57). Belmont, CA: Wadsworth Publishing.

Welter, R. (1963). *Popular education and democratic thought in America.* New York: Columbia University Press.

West, C. W. (1980). Comments—The state and sectarian education: Regulation to deregulation. *Duke Law Review,* pp. 801–846.

West, E. G. (1965). *Education and the state* (p. 10). London: Institute of Economic Affairs.

West, E. G. (1983, Winter). Failing school systems in America and elsewhere. *Journal of Social, Political and Economic Studies, 8,* 395–410.

White, K. R. (1982). The relation between socioeconomic status and academic achievement. *Psychological Bulletin, 91,* 461–481.

Whitehead, J. W., & Conlan, J. (1978, Winter). The establishment of the religion of secular humanism and its first amendment implications. *Texas Tech Law Review, 10,* 1–66.

Whyte, W. F. (1927, June). The Bennett law campaign in Wisconsin. *Wisconsin Magazine of History, 10,* 363–390.

Wiebe, R. H. (1967). *The search for order—1877–1920.* New York: Hill & Wang.

Wildavsky, A. (1983). Foreword: If regulation is right, is it also safe? In T. R. Machan & M. B. Johnson (Eds.), *Rights and regulation: Ethical, political and economic issues* (pp. xv–xxv). Cambridge, MA: Ballinger Publishing.

Williams, W. E. (1978, Spring). Tuition tax credits: Other benefits. *Policy Review, 4*, 85–89.

Willms, J. D. (1983). Do private schools produce higher levels of academic achievement? New evidence for the tuition tax credit debate? In T. James & H. Levin (Eds.), *Public dollars for private schools* (pp. 223–231). Philadelphia: Temple University Press.

Willms, J. D. (1985, April). Catholic school effects on academic achievement: New evidence from the high school and beyond follow-up study. *Sociology of Education, 58*, 98–114.

Worthing, S. L. (1984, Winter). The state and the church school: The conflict over social policy. *Journal of Church and State, 26*, 91–104.

Wyman, R. (1968, Summer). Wisconsin ethnic groups and the election of 1890. *The Wisconsin Magazine of History, 51*, 269–293.

COURT CASES

Abington School District v. Schempp, 374 U.S. 203 (1963).

Akron v. Akron Center for Reproductive Health, 462 U.S. 416 (1983).

American Friends Service Committee v. Thornburgh, 941 F.2d 808 (9th Cir. 1991).

Attorney General v. Bailey, 436 N.E. 2d 139, *cert. denied sub nom.* Bailey v. Bellotti, 459 U.S. 970 (1982).

Bangor Baptist Church v. State of Maine, 549 F. Supp. 1208 (D. Me. 1982).

Bangor Baptist Church v. State of Maine, Department of Education, 576 F. Supp. 1299 (D. Me. 1983).

Bartels v. Iowa, 181 N.W. 508 (1921), 262 U.S. 404 (1923).

Bellotti v. Baird, 443 U.S. 622 (1979).

Berea College v. Commonwealth, Circuit Court, Madison County, 94 S.W. 623 (Ky. 1906).

Berea College v. Commonwealth of Kentucky, 211 U.S. 45 (1908).

Blount v. Department of Educational & Cultural Services, 551 A.2d 1377 (Me. 1988).

Board of Education v. Allen, 392 U.S. 236 (1968).

Board of Education v. Pico, 457 U.S. 853 (1982).

Bohning v. State of Ohio, 132 N.E. 20 (1921), 262 U.S. 404 (1923).

Braintree Baptist Temple v. Holbrook Public Schools, 616 F. Supp. 81 (D. Mass. 1984).

Brown v. Board of Education, 347 U.S. 483 (1954).

Butler v. State, 194 S.W. 166 (Tex. Crim. App. 1917).

Carey v. Brown, 447 U.W. 455 (1980).

City of Akron v. Lane, 416 N.E. 2d 642 (Ohio App. 1979).

City of Sumner v. First Baptist Church, 639 P. 2d 1358 (Wash. 1982).

Clark v. Jeter, 486 U.S. 456 (1988).

Cleburne v. Cleburne Living Center, Inc., 473 U.S. 432 (1985).

Committee for Public Education v. Nyquist, 413 U.S. 756 (1973).

Committee for Public Education v. Regan, 444 U.S. 646 (1980).

Commonwealth v. Renfrew, 126 N.E. 2d 109 (Mass. 1955).

Commonwealth v. Roberts, 34 N.E. 402 (Mass. 1893).

Cook v. Hudson, 429 U.S. 165 (1976).

Cornerstone Bible Church v. City of Hastings, 948 F.2d 464 (8th Cir. 1991).

Craig v. Boren, 429 U.S. 190 (1976).

Dartmouth College v. Woodward, 17 U.S. (4 Wheat.) 518 (1819).

Delconte v. State, 308 S.E. 2d 898 (N.C. App. 1983), 329 S.E. 2d 636 (N.C. 1985).

Doe v. Board of Education, 453 A. 2d 814 (1982).

Donahue v. Copiague Union Free School District, 391 N.E. 2d 1352 (1979).

Duncan v. Louisiana, 391 U.S. 145 (1968).

D.S.W. v. Fairbanks No. Star Bor. Sch. Dist., 628 P.2d 554 (1981).

Ellis v. O'Hara, 612 F. Supp. 379 (D.C. Mo. 1985).

Employment Division, Department of Human Resources v. Smith, 110 S.Ct. 1595 (1990).

Engel v. Vitale, 370 U.S. 421 (1962).

Epperson v. Arkansas, 393 U.S. 97 (1968).

Farrington v. Tokushige, 11 F. 2d 710, 273 U.S. 284 (1927).

FCC v. Pacifica Foundation, 438 U.S. 726 (1978).

Fellowship Baptist Church v. Benton, 620 F. Supp. 308 (D. Iowa 1985), 815 F. 2d 485 (8th Cir. 1987).

Fogg v. Board of Education, 82 A. 172 (N.H. 1912).

Franz v. United States, 707 F.2d 582 (1983).

Ginsberg v. New York, 390 U.S. 629 (1968).

Grand Rapids School District v. Ball, 473 U.S. 373 (1985).

Griswold v. Connecticut, 381 U.S. 479 (1965).

H. L. v. Matheson, 450 U.S. 398 (1981).

Hardwick v. Board of School Trustees, 205 P. 49 (Col. App. 1921).

Healy v. Jones, 408 U.S. 169 (1972).

Heffron v. International Society for Krishna Conscience, 452 U.S. 640 (1981).

Hill Military Academy v. Same, 296 F. 928 (D. Ore. 1924).

Hoffman v. Board of Education of City of New York, 400 N.E. 2d 317 (1979).

Hunter v. Board of Education of Montgomery County, 425 A. 2d 681 (1981).

In re Foster, 330 N.Y.S.2d 8 (N.Y. 1972).

Jernigan v. State, 412 So. 2d 1242 (Ala. Crim. App. 1982).

Johnson v. Charles City Community School Board, 368 N.W. 2d 74, *cert. denied sub nom.* Pruessner v. Benton, 474 U.S. 1033 (1985).

Kentucky State Board of Education v. Rudasill, 589 S.W. 2d 877, *cert. denied,* 446 U.S. 938 (Ky. 1979).

Lehr v. Robertson, 463 U.S. 248 (1982).

Lemon v. Kurtzman, 403 U.S. 602 (1971).

Lochner v. New York, 198 U.S. 45 (1905).

Mazanec v. North Judson–San Pierre School Corp., 614 F.Supp. 1152 (D.C. Ind. 1985).

McCurry v. Tesch, 738 F. 2d 271 (8th Cir. 1984).

McGowan v. Maryland, 366 U.S. 420 (1961).

Meachum v. Fano, 427 U.S. 215 (1976).

Mercer v. Michigan State Board of Education, 379 F. Supp. 580, *aff'd,* 419 U.S. 1081 (1974).

Meyer v. Nebraska, 187 N.W. 100, 262 U.S. 390 (1923).

Meyerkorth v. State, 115 N.W. 2d 585, *appeal dismissed,* 373 U.S. 705 (1963).

Minersville School District v. Gobitis, 310 U.S. 586 (1940).

Moore v. East Cleveland, 431 U.S. 494 (1977).

Muller v. Allen, 463 U.S. 388 (1983).

National Labor Relations Board v. Catholic Bishop of Chicago, 440 U.S. 490 (1979).

Nebraska District of Evangelical Lutheran Synod of Missouri et al. v. McKelvie, 175 N.W. 531 (1921), 262 U.S. 404 (1923).

New Life Baptist Church Academy v. East Longmeadow, 666 F. Supp. 293 (D. Mass. 1987).

New Life Baptist Church Academy v. Town of East Longmeadow, 885 F.2d 940 (1st Cir. 1989), *cert. denied,* 110 S.Ct. 1782 (1990).

Norwood v. Harrison, 413 U.S. 455 (Miss. 1973).

North Valley Baptist Church v. McMahon, 696 F.Supp. 518 (E.D. Cal. 1988).

Ohio Civil Rights Commission v. Dayton Christian Schools, Inc., 477 U.S. 619 (1986).

Packer Collegiate Institute v. University of New York, 81 N.E.2d 80 (N.Y. 1948).

Parham v. J. R., 442 U.S. 584 (1979).

Paul v. Davis, 424 U.S. 693 (1976).

People v. American Socialist Society, 202 App.Div. 640 (N.Y. 1922).

People v. Turner, 263 P.2d 685, *appeal dismissed,* 347 U.S. 972 (1954).

Peter W. v. San Francisco Unified School District, 60 Cal. App.3d 814, 131 Cal. Rptr. 854 (1975).

Pierce v. Society of Sisters, 268 U.S. 510 (1925).

Pierce et al. v. Hill Military Academy, 268 U.S. 510 (1925).

Planned Parenthood of Missouri v. Danforth, 428 U.S. 52 (1976).

Plyler v. Doe, 457 U.S. 202 (1982).

Poe v. Hamilton, 56 Ohio App.3d 137, 565 N.E.2d 887 (1990).

Pohl v. State of Ohio, 132 N.E. 20 (1921), 262 U.S. 404 (1923).

Polke v. Harper, 5 Ind. 241 (1854).

Prince v. Massachusetts, 321 U.S. 158 (1944).

Quigley v. State, 5 Ohio CC 638 (1891), *aff'd,* 27 WL Bull 332 (1892).

Rice v. Commonwealth, 49 S.E.2d 342 (Va. 1948).

Roberts v. United States Jaycees, 468 U.S. 609 (1984).

Roe v. Wade, 410 U.S. 113 (1973).

Runyon v. McCrary, 427 U.S. 160 (1975).

San Antonio Independent School District v. Rodriguez, 411 U.S. 1 (1973).

Santa Fe Community School v. New Mexico State Board of Education, 518 P.2d 272 (N.M. 1974).

Seone v. Ortho Pharmaceuticals, Inc., 660 F.2d 146 (1981).

Sherbert v. Verner, 374 U.S. 398 (1963).

Sheridan Road Baptist Church v. Department of Education, 348 N.W.2d 263 (Mich. App. 1984).

Sheridan Road Baptist Church v. Department of Education, 396 N.W.2d 373 (Mich. 1986).

Skinner v. Oklahoma, 316 U.S. 535 (1942).

Smith v. Donahue, 195 N.Y.S. 715, 202 A.D. 656 (1922).

Smith v. Organization of Foster Families, 431 U.S. 816 (1977).

Society of Sisters v. Pierre, 296 F. 928 (D. Ore. 1924).

St. Martin Evangelical Lutheran Church v. South Dakota, 451 U.S. 772 (1981).

Stanley v. Georgia, 394 U.S. 557 (1969).

State v. Bailey, 61 N.E. 730 (Ind. 1901).

State v. Counort, 124 P. 910 (Wash. 1912).

State v. Faith Baptist Church, 301 N.W.2d 571, *appeal dismissed sub nom. Faith Baptist Church v. Douglas,* 454 U.S. 803 (1981).

State v. Garber, 419 P. 2d 896, *cert. denied,* 389 U.S. 51 (1967).

State v. Hershberger, 144 N.E.2d 693 (1955).

State v. Hoyt, 146 A. 170 (N.H. 1929).

State v. Jackson, 53 A. 1021 (N.H. 1902).

State v. LaBarge, 357 A.2d 121 (Vt. 1976).

State v. Massa, 231 A.2d 252 (N.J. 1967).

State v. McDonough, 468 A.2d 977 (Me. 1983).

State v. Moorhead, 308 N.W.2d 60 (Iowa 1981).

State v. Newstrom, 371 N.W.2d 525 (Minn. 1985).

State v. Patzer, 382 N.W.2d 631, *cert. denied sub nom.* Patzer v. North Dakota, 479 U.S. 825 (N.D. 1986).

State v. Peterman, 70 N.E. 550 (Ind. 1904).

State v. Rivinius, 328 N.W.2d 220, *cert. denied,* 460 U.S. 1070 (N.D. 1983).

State v. Shaver, 294 N.W.2d 883 (N.D. 1980).

State v. Superior Court, 346 P.2d 999, *cert. denied,* 363 U.S. 814 (1960).

State v. Trucke, 410 N.W.2d 242 (Iowa 1987).

State v. Whisner, 351 N.E.2d 750 (Ohio 1976).

State v. Will, 160 P. 1025 (Kan. 1916).

State v. Williams, 117 S.E.2d 444 (N.C. 1960).

State v. Yoder, 182 N.W.2d 539 (Wis. 1971).

State ex rel. Douglas v. Faith Baptist Church, 301 N.W.2d 571, *appeal dismissed sub nom.* Faith Baptist Church v. Douglas, 454 U.S. 803 (1981).

State ex rel. Kelley v. Ferguson, 144 N.W. 1039 (Neb. 1914).

State ex rel. Nagle v. Olin, 415 N.E.2d 279 (Ohio 1980).

Strosnider v. Strosnider, 686 P.2d 981 (N.M. 1984).

Thomas v. Review Board, Indiana Employment Security Division, 450 U.S. 707 (1981).

Tinker v. Des Moines School District, 393 U.S. 503 (1969).

Tony and Susan Alamo Foundation v. Secretary of Labor, 471 U.S. 290 (1985).

United States v. Carolene Products Co., 304 U.S. 144 (1938).

United States v. Lee, 455 U.S. 252 (1982).

United States v. Orito, 413 U.S. 139 (1972).

United States v. Seeger, 380 U.S. 163 (1965).

Wallace v. Jaffree, 472 U.S. 38 (1985).

Welsh v. United States, 398 U.S. 333 (1970).

West Coast Hotel v. Parrish, 300 U.S. 379 (1937).

West Virginia Board of Education v. Barnette, 319 U.S. 624 (1943).

Whalen v. Roe, 429 U.S. 589 (1977).

Widmar v. Vincent, 454 U.S. 263 (1981).

Windsor Park Baptist Church v. Arkansas Activities Association, 658 F. Supp. 618 (8th Cir. 1981).

Wisconsin v. Yoder, 406 U.S. 205 (1972).

Wolman v. Essex, 342 F.Supp. 399, *aff'd,* 490 U.S. 808 (1972).

Wolman v. Walter, 433 U.S. 229 (1977).

Wright v. State, 209 P. 179 (Okla. 1922).

STATE STATUTES AND REGULATIONS

District of Columbia. *Code Annotated* Title 31, Sec. 31–401 (1981).

Connecticut. *General Statutes* § 10 (1958, 1985, & Supp. 1986).

Indiana. *Code Annotated* Title 20 (Burns 1975 & Supp. 1985).

Iowa. *Code Annotated* Title 12 (West 1949, 1972, & Supp. 1985).

Maine. *Revised Statutes Annotated* Title 20 (1983 & Supp. 1985).

Maryland. *Annotated Code* Chapter 22 (1985 & Supp. 1985).

Massachusetts. *Annotated Laws* Title XII (Law Co-op. 1985 & Supp. 1986).

Nebraska. *Revised Statutes* § 79 (1943, 1981 & Supp. 1984, 1986).

Nevada. *Revised Statutes* Title 34 (1983).

Nevada. *Revised Statutes Annotated* Sec. 394 (Mich. 1985).

New Jersey. *Administrative Code* Title 6 (1980).

New Jersey. *Statutes Annotated* § 18A (1968 & Supp. 1986).

New York. *Education law.* (McKinney 1981, 1985, & Supp. 1986).

Vermont. *Statutes Annotated* Title 16 (1974 & Supp. 1985).

INDEX

ABOUT THE AUTHOR

E. Vance Randall is an assistant professor in the Department of Educational Leadership at Brigham Young University. Before his faculty appointment at BYU, he worked seventeen years as a religious educator for The Church of Jesus Christ of Latter-day Saints. In 1989 he received his Ph.D. from Cornell University in educational administration with minor concentrations in philosophy of education and public policy. His research interests include the areas of social philosophy and policy analysis with particular emphases on the relationship of the state to education and the impact of educational policy on the family.